EXCHANGE SERVER 2013

STEP BY STEP

RAIHAN AL-BERUNI

DEDICATION

Dear Mom and Dad, thank you for your endless support and encouragement. You have always inspired me to do my best and have supported me in every decision I have made. I love you to pieces.

ISBN-10: 1481197290

ISBN-13: 978-1481197298

Who Should Buy This Book

This book is for Wintel Engineer, Exchange Server Administrator and Microsoft Messaging Architect looking to strengthen their knowledge of designing, deploying, administering and managing Exchange Server 2013. While the book can also be helpful for those who new to Microsoft Messaging Environment, a set of assumptions is made about the target reader:

- A basic understanding of Microsoft Messaging Software
- A basic understanding of Microsoft Networking Architecture such as DNS
- Experience in Active Directory Certificate Services administration
- Experience in Active Directory Domain Services administration
- Experience in Windows Server 2008 or Windows Server 2012 administration
- An understanding of Virtualization Technology
- An understanding of Computer Firewall such as Forefront TMG 2010
- An understanding of Storage Infrastructure such as SAN, iSCSI, HBA, Fabric

CHAPTERS

Forward

Chapter 1: Introduction to Exchange Server 2013

Chapter 2: Planning and Designing Exchange Server 2013 Deployment

Chapter 3: Installing and Configuring an Exchange 2013 Farm

Chapter 4: Advanced Configuration of Mail Flow and Message Delivery

Chapter 5: Administering Exchange Server 2013

Chapter 6: Configuring Unified Communication in Exchange 2013

Chapter 7: Configuring Load Balancer and SSL offloading for Exchange 2013

Chapter 8: Configuring Federated Exchange Server 2013

Chapter 9: Transitioning from Exchange 2007/2010 to Exchange 2013

Chapter 10: Supporting Exchange Server 2013

Index

FORWARD

Exchange Server 2013 Step by Step provides you a practical guide on how to install and configure Exchange Server 2013 in production. This book depicts deployment diagram of exchange infrastructure and publishing infrastructure. This book also illustrate how to administer a complete exchange farm. A practical approach has been taken while writing this book such as configuring client access protocol high availability using F5 load balancer and publishing Exchange 2013 using Forefront TMG 2010.

Based on final version of Exchange Server 2013, this book provides an in-depth knowledge for you to deploy and manage Microsoft Messaging Platform. In a nutshell this book covers:

- Planning and Designing of Exchange Server
- Installing and Configuring of Exchange Server
- Configuring High Availability of Mailbox Databases and Protocols
- Administering Exchange Server
- Securing and Protecting of Exchange Server 2013
- Transitioning from Exchange 2007/2010 to Exchange 2013
- Supporting Exchange Server 2013

TABLE OF CONTENTS

Chapter1. Introduction to Exchange Server 2013 19

1.1 Exchange Server 2013 Overview..19

1.2 What's New in Exchange Server 2013 19

1.3 What's New for Transport Rules...20

1.4 What's Discontinued in Exchange 2013 21

1.5 Release Notes for Exchange 2013..23

1.6 What's New for Unified Messaging in Exchange 2013 24

1.7 What's New for Outlook Web App in Exchange 2013 24

1.8 Licensing Exchange Server 2013 25

1.9 Hosted Exchange..25

1.10 Microsoft Exchange Online 25

Chapter2. Planning and Designing Exchange 2013 Deployment...........................27

2.1 Exchange 2013 System Requirements...28

2.2 Hybrid deployment Scenario 29

2.3 Supported Exchange Clients 31

2.4 Unsupported Installation 31

2.5 Exchange 2013 Prerequisites for Windows Server 2012 31

2.6 Exchange Server 2013 Storage Requirements...34

2.7 Preparing Active Directory Domain Services 35

2.8 Pre-installation Check List...36

2.9 Post Installation Check List 37

2.10 Integration with SharePoint and Lync...37

2.11 Virtualizing Exchange Server 2013..37

2.12 Designing Exchange Server 2013 38

2.12.1 Preparing Exchange Server 2013 Data Sheet..............................39

2.12.2 Role Based Access Control 40

2.12.3 Firewall Deployment Data Sheet 40

2.12.4 Sizing Exchange Server 2013 for Deployment 40

2.13 Exchange 2013 Solutions Overview 45

2.13.1 Exchange 2013 Client Access Configuration 45

2.13.2 Exchange and TMG 2010 Topology 46

2.13.3 Database Availability Group Topology 46

2.13.4 Exchange 2013 Network Topology 47

2.13.5 Exchange 2013 Mail Flow 48

2.13.6 NLB Multicast Mode – Static ARP Resolution for CAS servers 48

2.14 Designing Operating Systems 49

2.15 Setting up Mailbox and Address List 50

2.16 Configuring Exchange 2013 Protocol 50

2.17 Configure Exchange Organization and Server 51

2.18 Publishing Exchange for External Client 53

2.19 Configure Backup Agent and Schedule 56

2.20 Designing Security in Exchange Server 2013 57

2.21 Performance Management & monitoring 58

Chapter3. Installing and Configuring Exchange Server 2013 Farm 59

3.1 Installing Exchange Server 2013 59

3.2 Install Exchange 2013 Using Unattended Mode 61

3.3 Configure Basic Mail Flow in Exchange Server 2013 62

3.4 Adding additional accepted domains 63

3.5 Configure the default email address policy 63

3.6 Configure an SSL certificate 64

3.7 Configure Outlook Web Access for External Users 67

3.8 Verify an Exchange 2013 Installation 69

3.8.1 Configuring server certificates 69

3.8.2 Configuring virtual directories using Windows PowerShell 69

3.9 Configure Exchange Organization 70

3.10 Configure High Availability for Resilient Exchange Systems 70

   3.10.1 Network Requirements 71

   3.10.2 Preparing Base infrastructure 72

   3.10.3 TCP/IP Configuration 72

   3.10.4 Pre-Stage the Cluster Network Object for a DAG 73

   3.10.5 Database Availability Group Creation 74

   3.10.6 Mailbox Databases and Mailbox Database Copies 78

   3.10.7 Creating a Database Availability Group Network 81

   3.10.8 Test Database Availability Group and Database Copy 82

   3.10.9 Recover a Database availability Group member 82

   3.10.10 Configuring Root Path of Database and Volumes 82

   3.10.11 Removing Database Availability Group 85

3.11 Configure Mailbox Database and Database Properties 85

   3.11.1 Configure mailbox database properties 85

   3.11.2 Configure mailbox database properties using PowerShell 87

   3.11.3 Enable, Disable circular logging 87

   3.11.4 Configuring the activation policy for a mailbox database 88

   3.11.4 Suspend or resume a database for activation 88

   3.11.5 Configure the activation policy for a server 88

   3.11.6 Update a mailbox database 89

   3.11.7 Update a mailbox database using Windows PowerShell 89

   3.11.8 Manually moving a database 90

   3.11.9 Suspend a mailbox database 91

   3.11.10 Resume a mailbox database 91

   3.11.11 Move the active mailbox database 91

   3.11.12 Move/switchover the active mailbox database to different server 91

   3.11.13 Activating a lagged mailbox database to a specific point in time 92

3.11.14 Activating a lagged mailbox database by replaying log files...............93

3.11.16 Remove a mailbox database 94

3.11.17 Remove a mailbox database using PowerShell...................................94

3.11.18 Monitoring Database Availability Group and Exchange Server...........94

Chapter4. Advanced Configuration of Mail Flow and Message Delivery.............101

4.1 Configure Exchange Mail Routing Settings in Active Directory 101

4.2 Create a Send Connector for Email (Sent to the Internet)...........................102

4.3 Create a Send Connector to Route Outbound Email through a Smart Host 103

4.4 Create a Send Connector to Send Email to a Partner 104

4.5 Configuring Receive Connector Authentication 105

4.6 Create a Foreign Connector for a non-SMTP Fax Gateway 107

4.6.1 Create a Foreign connector to a non-SMTP gateway server 108

4.6.2 Configure the Drop directory for a Mailbox server 108

4.7 Delivery Agents and Delivery Agent Connectors 108

4.8 Configure an Accepted Domain within Exchange Organization 109

4.8.1 Configure an accepted domain as authoritative...................................109

4.8.2 Configure an Accepted Domain for an Independent Business Unit 109

4.8.3 Configure an Accepted Domain outside Exchange Organization 110

4.9 Configure Remote Domain Out of Office Replies 110

4.9.1 Configure out-of-office replies...110

4.9.2 Configure Remote Domain Automatic Replies 110

4.9.3 Configure Remote Domain Message Reporting 111

4.10 Enable Support for Legacy Transport Agents 111

4.11 Manage Transport Agents...112

4.12 Configure Anti-Spam Agent Logging 115

4.13 Configure Connectivity Logging 116

4.14 Configure Protocol Logging...117

4.15 Configure a Moderated Recipient..120

4.16 Configure Content Transfer Encoding 122

4.17 Message Encoding Options 123

4.18 DSN Message Identity 124

4.19 Viewing Mailflow Queue 126

4.20 Configure the Pickup Directory and the Replay Directory 129

    4.20.1 Configure the Pickup directory 129

    4.20.2 Configure the Replay directory 130

4.21 Publish Exchange Server 2013 using Forefront TMG 2010 130

    4.21.1 Configuring access for Outlook Web Access clients 131

    4.21.2 Configuring the idle session time-out period for OWA clients 133

    4.21.3 Configuring ActiveSync publishing 134

    4.21.4 Redirect OWA Traffic from HTTP to HTTPS using TMG 2010 135

4.22 Redirect OWA traffic from HTTP to HTTPS in CAS Servers 136

4.23 Configure Mail Apps for Outlook Client 137

Chapter5. Administering Exchange Server 2013 139

5.1 Configure Role Based Administration for Exchange Server 2013 139

5.2 Creating Recipients in Exchange Server 2013 140

    5.2.1 Creating a user mailbox 140

    5.2.2 Change user mailbox properties 141

    5.2.3 Change user mailbox properties 142

    5.2.4 Bulk edit user mailboxes 143

5.3 Configure Shared Mailbox 143

    5.3.1 Create a Shared mailbox 143

    5.3.2 Create a shared mailbox 144

    5.3.3 Convert a User Mailbox into a Shared Mailbox 144

5.4 Configure Public Folder in Exchange Server 144

    5.4.1 Create Public Folders 144

    5.4.2 Create a public folder hierarchy mailbox 145

5.4.3 Configure quota limits and retention settings for public folders 146

5.4.4 Create the primary public folder mailbox 146

5.4.5 Assign permissions to the public folder 146

5.4.6 Mail-enable or Mail-Disable the public folder 147

5.4.7 View Statistics for Public Folders and Public Folder Items 148

5.5 Remove Public Folders in Exchange 2013 148

5.6 Manage Site Mailbox Provisioning Policies in Exchange 2013 149

5.7 Create a Distribution Group Naming Policy 150

5.7.1 Create a Group Naming Policy 150

5.7.2 Manage Dynamic Distribution Groups 151

5.7.3 Change dynamic distribution group properties 152

5.8 Manage Mail Contacts 153

5.8.1 Create a mail contact 153

5.8.2 Manage Mail Users 153

5.9 Manage Room Mailboxes 154

5.10 Manage Equipment Mailboxes 155

5.11 Creating and Configuring Address List 156

5.12 Create a Global Address List 158

5.13 Deploying Address Book Policies 159

5.14 Configure Transport Rules 161

5.15 Create an Offline Address Book 162

5.16 Configure Mailbox Journaling 164

5.17 Client Protocol and Mobility Configuration 164

5.17.1 Outlook Anywhere 164

5.17.2 Exchange ActiveSync 164

5.17.3 Change a user's mobile device mailbox policy 165

5.17.4 Exchange 2013 Client Access Server Configuration 167

5.17.5 POP3 and IMAP Services 168

5.18 Office Web Apps Server Integration in Exchange 2013.............................170

5.19 Create an Outlook Web App Mailbox Policy.....................................172

Chapter6. Configuring Unified Communication in Exchange 2013......................175

6.1 UM listening ports...176

6.2 UM dial plans 177

6.3 Deploy Exchange 2013 UM 178

6.3.1 Deploy and configure telephony components 178

6.3.2 Installing the Mailbox and Client Access servers 179

6.3.3 Add the required UM language packs if necessary.......................179

6.3.4 Create and configure UM dial plans 179

6.3.5 View or configure UM dial plan settings.................................180

6.3.6 Change the audio codec on a Unified Messaging dial plan 182

6.3.7 Configure the number of sign-in failures 183

6.3.8 Configure the maximum call duration 184

6.3.9 Configure the maximum recording duration 184

6.3.10 Configure the recording idle time-out value 185

6.3.11 Configure the input failures before disconnect.........................185

6.3.12 Configure VoIP security on a UM dial plan 186

6.4 Create and configure your UM IP gateways 186

6.4.1 Create a UM IP gateway...187

6.4.2 Create and configure your UM hunt groups.............................187

6.4.3 Create and configure UM auto attendants...............................188

6.4.4 Add an extension or phone numbers for a UM auto attendant............189

6.4.5 Specify business hours for a UM auto attendant 189

6.4.6 Configure a speech-enabled auto attendant with a DTMF fallback 190

6.4.7 Configure UM auto attendant navigation menus.........................190

6.4.8 Enable non-business hours key mappings on a UM auto attendant.....192

6.4.9 Enable business hours key mappings on a UM auto attendant 193

6.4.10 Enable a UM auto attendant..193

6.4.11 Delete a UM auto attendant..194

6.4.12 Disable a UM auto attendant..194

6.5 Create and configure a UM mailbox policy................................195

6.6 Deploying Exchange UM and Lync Server overview.....................195

6.7 Installing a UM language pack...196

6.8 Configure Voice Mail for User..197

6.8.1 Enable a user for Unified Messaging and voice mail.............197

6.8.2 View or configure a UM-enabled user's properties..............198

6.8.3 Change the UM mailbox policy assigned to a UM-enabled user..........200

6.8.4 Disable Unified Messaging and voice mail for a user...........201

Chapter7. Configuring Load Balancer and SSL Offloading for Exchange 2013.....203

7.1 What is a F5 Load Balancer...204

7.2 What is F5 iApp?..204

7.3 Prerequisites of deploying a F5 Load Balancer.........................204

7.4 Deployment Scenarios...208

7.4.1 BIG-IP LTM with BIG-IP Edge Gateway................................208

7.4.2 BIG-IP LTM with TMG 2010..208

7.5 Configuring F5 Load Balancer for Exchange 2013 Client Access...................209

7.6 Configure SSL Offloading in Exchange 2013.............................212

Chapter8. Configuring Federated Exchange Server 2013........................213

8.1 Configure Trusted Root Certification Authorities for Federation Trusts......213

8.2 Deploying a Federated Trust...214

8.2.1 Create and configure a federation trust...........................214

8.2.2 Create an organization relationship................................216

8.2.3 Create a sharing policy..220

8.3 Manage a Federation Trust..223

Chapter9. Transitioning from Exchange 2007/2010 to Exchange 2013 227

9.1 Prerequisite of Transitioning Exchange Server 228

9.2 Take Precautions before Proceeding 228

9.3 Transition Sequencing...229

9.4 Transitioning steps from Exchange 2007/2010 to Exchange 2013...............230

9.5 Test Procedure 231

9.6 Migrate Mailboxes and Resources to Exchange Server 2013 231

9.7 Migrate Public Folders from Exchange 2010 SP3 to Exchange 2013 232

Chapter10. Supporting Exchange Server 2013 239

10.1 Performance Monitoring in Exchange Server 2013.......................................239

10.1.1 Exchange 2013 Workload Management Reference 239

10.1.2 Changing workload management policy settings 245

10.1.3 Create a custom workload management policy 246

10.1.4 Create a workload policy 246

10.1.5 Apply the custom workload management policy to a specific server .246

10.2 Manage Mailbox Databases in Exchange 2013..247

10.3 Working with Backup, Restore and Database Recovery...............................249

10.4 Recover an Exchange Server 2013 251

10.5 Recover a Databases...251

10.5.1 Create a Recovery Database 253

10.5.2 Restore Data Using a Recovery Database..254

10.6 AntiSpam and Antivirus Configuration 254

10.6.1 Enable Anti-Spam Functionality on a Mailbox Server....................254

10.6.2 Manage Sender Filtering 255

10.6.3 Manage Recipient Filtering 257

10.6.4 Manage Sender ID..258

10.6.5 Manage Content Filtering 259

10.6.6 Configure Anti-Spam Settings on Mailboxes 263

10.6.7 Manage Sender Reputation 264

10.6.8 Configure a Spam Quarantine Mailbox................................. 266

10.6.9 Configure Outlook to Show the Sender in the Quarantine Mailbox....266

10.7 Working with Windows PowerShell.. 270

10.8 Turn off Internet access to the EAC 271

10.9 Failover Scenario in Exchange DAG and CAS Array...................... 272

10.10 Manage MailTips for Organization Relationships 272

10.11 Manage On-Premises Moves 273

10.11.1 Move only a user's primary mailbox.................................. 273

10.11.2 Create a cross-forest move using a .csv batch file............. 273

10.11.3 Move only an archive mailbox 274

10.11.4 Move primary mailbox to separate databases 274

10.11.5 Move a user's primary mailbox and allow a large bad item limit......275

10.16 Exchange Remote Connectivity Analyzer................................. 275

CHAPTER 1

In This Chapter

- Exchange Server 2013 Overview
- What's New in Exchange Server 2013
- What's New for Transport Rules
- What's Discontinued in Exchange 2013
- Release Notes for Exchange 2013
- What's New for Unified Messaging in Exchange 2013
- What's New for Outlook Web App in Exchange 2013
- Licensing
- Hosted Exchange
- Exchange Online

Chapter1. Introduction to Exchange Server 2013

1.1 Exchange Server 2013 Overview

Exchange Server 2013 is a messaging platform that provides email, scheduling, collaboration, messaging-service to and from organization, partners and vendors. Exchange Server 2013 delivers a state of the art collaboration platform for small, medium and enterprise customer. Exchange 2013 is also available for Hoster or Cloud Service provider as Hosted Exchange. Microsoft offers Exchange online using Exchange 2013.

Key Features of Exchange Server 2013
- Exchange Administration Center
- Exchange architecture revisions
- A new managed store
- Modern public folders
- New PowerShell cmdlets
- Site Resilience

1.2 What's New in Exchange Server 2013

Exchange Management Console replaced by a Web-based Exchange Administrative Center (EAC)

Offline OWA support Emails are automatically synced when you connect next time.
Outlook Web App offers three different User Interface layouts optimized for desktop, slate, and phone browsers
Site Mailboxes Bring Exchange emails and SharePoint documents together.
Ability to customize Outlook and OWA by integrating Email Apps from the Office marketplace.
Support for up to 8 TB disks and multiple databases per disk via Database Availability Group (DAG) management
Built-in basic anti-malware protection with ability to configure and manage settings from inside EAC.
New Data Loss Prevention (DLP) capabilities for identifying and protecting sensitive data. DLP policies are based on regulatory standards.
In-Place eDiscovery can be run across Exchange, SharePoint, and Lync Server from a single interface
Combine Roles Microsoft made an architectural change in Exchange Server 2013 reducing roles to only Client Access Server role and Mailbox Server role.
The Mailbox server role handles all the traditional server components found in Exchange 2010: the Client Access protocols, Hub Transport service, Mailbox databases, and Unified Messaging that is the Mailbox server handles all activity for any given mailbox.
The Client Access server handles authentication, SIP redirection, and proxy services. The Client Access server doesn't render, store and queue anything. The Client Access server offers protocols like HTTP, POP3, IMAP, and SMTP. The Client Access Servers handles Outlook Web App.
FAST Search now integrated into Exchange 2013 which provides a more consistent indexing and searching experience
Inclusion of a Managed Store with is the name of the rewritten information store processes, which is now written in C#.
Replication Public folders are now stored in mailbox databases and can take advantage of Database Availability Groups for replication and high availability.

1.3 What's New for Transport Rules

Support for data loss prevention (DLP) features in Exchange 2013 prevents unintentional disclosure of sensitive data. Transport rules have been updated to support creating rules that accompany and enforce DLP policies.

Support for extended regular expression syntax in Exchange 2013 are based on the Microsoft.NET Framework regular expression (regex) functionality and now support extended regular expression syntax.

Transport rules agent invocation in Exchange 2013 for Transport rules is the Transport Rules Agent is invoked on onResolvedMessage. This change allowed you to add new actions such as TLS.

Detailed Transport rule information in message tracking logs is now included in message tracking logs. The information includes which rules were triggered for a specific message and the actions taken as a result of processing those rules.

New rule monitoring functionality is configured and measured the cost of running these rules both when you are creating the rule and also during regular operation. Exchange can detect and generate alerts for rules that are causing delays in mail delivery.

1.4 What's Discontinued in Exchange 2013

This section lists the Microsoft Exchange Server 2010 features that are no longer available in Exchange Server 2013.

Architecture features

Discontinued feature	New Features
Hub Transport server	Mailbox servers in Exchange 2013 handle HT role
Unified Messaging server	Mailbox Server in Exchange 2013 handle UM role

Management interfaces

Discontinued feature	New Features
Exchange Management Console	Exchange Administration Center is introduced in Exchange Server 2013. Exchange 2010 EMC is no longer available.

Client access Outlook 2003 and RPC/TCP access have been removed.

Outlook Web App In Exchange 2013, the following OWA functionality has been removed.

- Access to shared email folders

- Distribution list moderation
- S/MIME
- Spell check
- Reading pane at the bottom of the page
- Reply to embedded emails

Mail flow The ability to link a Send connector to a Receive connector has been removed.

Anti-spam and anti-malware

Discontinued feature	New Features
Anti-spam agent management in the EMC	In Exchange 2013, when you enable the anti-spam agents in the Transport service on a Mailbox server, you can't manage the agents in the Exchange Administration Center (EAC). Use PowerShell instead.
Connection Filtering agent on Hub Transport servers	In Exchange 2013, when you enable the anti-spam agents in the Transport service on a Mailbox server, the Attachment Filter agent and the Connection Filtering agent aren't available. The Connection Filtering agent provides IP Allow List and IP Block List capabilities.

Messaging policy and compliance

Managed Folders In Exchange 2013, managed folders aren't supported. You must use retention policies instead.

Port Managed Folder wizard In Exchange 2013, the Exchange Administration Center doesn't include this functionality. You have to use the New-RetentionPolicyTag PowerShell cmdlet.

Tools

In Exchange 2013 the following tools has been discontinued. You can still use Windows Server 2008 BPA and Perfmon to obtain performance related data.

- Exchange Best Practice Analyser
- Mail flow troubleshooter
- Performance monitor

- Performance troubleshooter
- Routing Log Viewer

Discontinued features from Exchange 2007 to Exchange 2013

The following lists of Exchange Server 2007 features are no longer available in Exchange 2013

- Exchange WebDAV
- Storage groups
- Extensible Storage Engine (ESE) streaming backup APIs
- User Datagram Protocol (UDP) notifications
- Cluster continuous replication (CCR)
- Local continuous replication (LCR)
- Standby continuous replication (SCR)
- Single cluster (SCC)
- Exchange 2007 cmdlets
- Clustered mailbox servers
- Client authentication using Integrated Windows authentication (NTLM) for POP3 and IMAP4 users
- Setup /recoverCMS, Move-Mailbox, Export-Mailbox and Import-Mailbox cmdlets
- Managed folders

1.5 Release Notes for Exchange 2013

The following are key extract from Microsoft Exchange 2013 release notes.

Coexistence with Exchange 2007 and Exchange 2010 Exchange 2013 can't be installed in the same Active Directory forest as Exchange 2007 or Exchange 2010. You have to use an Active Directory forest with no prior installations of Exchange 2007 or Exchange 2010. Coexistence scenario isn't supported until Microsoft release Service Pack 3 for Exchange 2007 and Exchange 2010.

Mailbox When you move a mailbox from a previous version of Exchange to Exchange 2013, the mailbox size may increase 30% to 40%.

Mail flow

- Client Access server doesn't support NTLM authentication
- TransportAgent cmdlets on Client Access Servers require local PowerShell

Compliance

- In Exchange 2013, the Transport Rules agent treats .png and .gif files as supported file types. AttachmentExtensionMatchesWords with the values "GIF,PNG". The command below is an example of how to create such a rule:

  Add-PSSnapin Microsoft.Exchange.Management.PowerShell.SnapIn

  New-TransportRule "Process GIF and PNG files" - AttachmentExtensionMatchesWords GIF,PNG - RejectMessageEnhancedStatusCode 5.7.1 -RejectMessageReasonText "This message contains unsupported attachment types."

- DLP policy creation could fail because of invalid characters
- Transport rules and DLP policies may not detect contents of subjects in attached messages
- Start and end dates are always interpreted as MM/DD/YYYY in legal discovery search

1.6 What's New for Unified Messaging in Exchange 2013

In Exchange 2013, all the Unified Messaging components are split between a Client Access server running the Microsoft Exchange Unified Messaging Call Router service and a Mailbox server running the Microsoft Exchange Unified Messaging service. Since architecture has been changed, Exchange 2013 Setup performs a single check for UCMA 4.0 and automates installation of UCMA 4.0. Read system requirements section in chapter 2 to learn more. In Exchange 2013 Client Access and Mailbox servers fully support IPv6 networks. Voice Mail Preview is enhanced and improved in Exchange 2013.

1.7 What's New for Outlook Web App in Exchange 2013

Outlook Web App is now integrated with Bing Maps, Suggested Appointments and Action Items. Users can link multiple entries for the same person and view the information in a single contact card. Users can now view multiple calendars in a merged view. Outlook Web App emphasizes a streamlined user interface that supports the use of touch, enhancing the mobile device experience with Exchange.

1.8 Licensing Exchange Server 2013

Like other Windows Server products, Exchange Server requires client access licenses, which are different from Windows CALs. Corporate license agreements, such as the Enterprise Agreement includes Exchange Server CALs.

User CALs are assigned to a user or employee not a mailbox. User CALs allow a user to access Exchange e-mail from any device. There are two types of Exchange CAL are available: Exchange CAL Standard and Exchange CAL Enterprise. The Enterprise CAL is an add-on license to the Standard CAL.

For Service Providers looking to host Microsoft Exchange and sell hosted exchange to client, there is an SPLA (Service Provider License Agreement) available whereby Microsoft receives a monthly service fee in the place of the traditional Client Access Licenses.

1.9 Hosted Exchange

Microsoft Exchange Server can also be purchased as a hosted service from a number of Cloud service providers. Though Exchange hosting has been around for more than 10 years, it is only recently that many providers have been marketing the service as "Hosted Exchange". Exchange hosting allows for Microsoft Exchange Server to be running in the Internet also called the Cloud and managed by a Hosted Exchange Server provider instead of on-premises Exchange Server.

1.10 Microsoft Exchange Online

Microsoft Exchange Online is an email, calendar and contacts solution delivered as a cloud service and hosted by Microsoft. It is essentially the same service and product like "Hosted Exchange" offered by Microsoft. Exchange Online provides end users with a familiar email experience across PCs, the Web and mobile devices. In house IT Administrators can manage their own mailbox, calendar and contact using web-based tools. Customers can also choose to combine both on-premises and online options in a hybrid deployment.

CHAPTER 2

In This Chapter

- Exchange Server 2013 systems requirements
- Supported Configuration of Exchange Server 2013
- Supported Operating Systems
- Preparing Active Directory Domain Services
- SharePoint and Lync Server Connectivity
- Practical Design Guide of Exchange Server
- Firewall designing guide
- Publishing Exchange Server to external client

Chapter2. Planning and Designing Exchange 2013 Deployment

It is utmost important that you evaluate, plan, design and deploy Exchange Server 2013. Evaluate your situation that may raise specific questions relevant to your organization's business needs and record correct answer of those questions. Also ask yourself the following questions and record correct answer of these questions.

What are your current messaging and collaboration systems in your organization?
What is current Active Directory Domain Functional level?
How many sites you have?
How many domain controllers you have in each sites?
Do you have Global Catalog in each site?
Would like to use IPv6 in new exchange environment?
How many mailboxes, contacts you would like to have in Exchange 2013 farm?
What sort of Firewall and DMZ you have?
Have you hosted MX record with ISP then how many?
Do you have a smart host in your organization including business continuity options?
Would you like to change current OWA URL to new URL?
What sort Microsoft licenses you have?
Would like to virtualize Exchange using Hyper-V or other means?

Only correct answer will lead you to a functional, resilient and robust messaging and collaboration platform. Record any other information that may relevant to the growth of your organization.

2.1 Exchange 2013 System Requirements

You have to be meticulous when comes to Exchange 2013 deployment. Before you begin deploying exchange server, learn key components and architecture of Exchange Server 2013.

Supported coexistence scenarios

Exchange version	Exchange organization coexistence
Exchange Server 2003	Unsupported
Exchange 2007	Supported but requires Exchange 2007 Service Pack 3 and update rollup
Exchange 2010	Supported but requires Exchange 2010 SP3 and update rollup
Mixed Exchange 2010 and Exchange 2007 organization	Supported but requires SP3 and update rollup in both Exchange 2007 Exchange 2010.

Minimum Hardware requirements for Exchange 2013

Component	Requirement
Processor	x64 Architecture
Memory	Depending on Exchange roles that are installed: Mailbox 8GB minimum Client Access 4GB minimum Mailbox and Client Access combined 8GB minimum
Paging file size	Check Maximum paging on the server where Exchange 2013 is installed. Do not add page file equivalent to 1.5 times of the RAM at the beginning when you build server.
Disk space	System Partition plus additional 30 GB free space on a separate drive where you install Exchange 500 MB of free disk space for each Unified Messaging (UM) language pack 20 GB of free disk space on the system drive Separate hard disks for mailbox, recovery and logs partitions.
File format	NTFS file systems on all partitions of the disks

Note that hardware requirements can dramatically change based on number of mailboxes, contacts, and sites. Don't stick to the minimum requirements. Evaluate hardware requirement based on practical needs and justification.

Supported operating systems for Exchange 2013

Component	Requirement
Mailbox Server Role Client Access server Role	Windows Server 2012 Windows Server 2008 R2 with SP
Management tools	Windows Server 2012 Windows Server 2008 R2 Windows 8 64-bit edition Windows 7 64-bit edition

Network and directory server requirements for Exchange 2013

Component	Requirement
Schema master ,Global Catalog, Domain controller	Windows Server 2012 Windows Server 2008 R2 SP1 Windows Server 2008 SP2 Windows Server 2003 with SP2
Active Directory forest Operational Level	Active Directory must be at Windows Server 2003 forest functionality level or higher.
IPv6 Support	You must install both IPv6 and IPv4. You can disable IPv4 when IPv6 is enabled but you cannot uninstall IPv4.

2.2 Hybrid deployment Scenario

The following prerequisites must be meet before considering Exchange 2013 hybrid deployment:

On-premises Exchange organization you can configure on-premises Hybrid Exchange Organization with Exchange 2007 or Exchange 2010 based organizations. However you must have at least one Exchange 2013 Client Access and one Exchange 2013 Mailbox Server installed in single server or multiple servers in on-premises organization to run the Hybrid Configuration wizard and support hybrid deployment functionality. Microsoft recommends combining the Exchange 2013 Client Access and Mailbox server roles on a single server when configuring hybrid deployments with Exchange 2007 and Exchange 2010 environments. You must install all latest service pack on existing exchange organisation.

Office 365 for enterprises you must have Office 365 version 15.0.000.0 or greater to configure a hybrid deployment with Exchange 2013.

Custom domains you can use custom domain to use in your hybrid deployment with Office 365. You can do this by using the Office 365 Administrative webmail, or configuring an Active Directory Federation Services (AD FS) in on-premises organization.

Active Directory synchronization you can deploy Office 365 Active Directory synchronization in your on-premises organization.

AutoDiscover DNS records Configure the Autodiscover public DNS records for your existing SMTP domains to point to an on-premises Exchange 2013 Client Access server.

Office 365 organization in the Exchange Administration Center (EAC) The Office 365 organization node is included by default in the on-premises EAC, but you must connect the EAC to your Office 365 organization using Office 365 tenant administrator credentials before running the Hybrid Configuration wizard. This also allows you to manage both the on-premises and Exchange Online organizations from a single management console.

Certificates Install and assign Exchange services to a valid commercial certificate signed by a trusted public certificate authority (CA) such as verisign, entrust, geotrust. The Internet Information Services (IIS) instance on the Client Access server configured in the hybrid deployment must have a valid digital certificate purchased from a trusted CA. Additionally, the EWS external URL and the Autodiscover endpoint specified in your public DNS must be listed in Subject Alternative Name (SAN) of the certificate installed on Client Access Server. The certificate installed on the Mailbox and Client Access servers used for mail transport in the hybrid deployment must have same certificate issued by same Certificate Authority with same Subject Alternative Name (SAN).

EdgeSync If you have deployed Edge Transport servers in your on-premises organization and want to configure the Edge Transport servers for hybrid secure mail transport, you must configure EdgeSync prior to running the Hybrid Configuration wizard.

Additional Tools and services

In addition to the required prerequisites described earlier, the following tools and services are beneficial when you are configuring hybrid deployments with the Hybrid Configuration wizard:

• Remote Connectivity Analyzer tool

- Single sign-on

2.3 Supported Exchange Clients

Exchange 2013 supports the following minimum versions of Microsoft Office Outlook and Entourage for Mac:

- Outlook 2013
- Outlook 2010 with latest SP and Cumulative Update
- Outlook 2007 with latest SP and Cumulative Update
- Entourage 2008 for Mac, Web Services Edition
- Outlook 2011 for Mac

2.4 Unsupported Installation

The following are the unsupported configuration at all time.

- Installing Exchange 2013 on a Domain Controller
- Installing Exchange 2013 on Itanium based hardware
- Renaming a server after installing an Exchange 2013 server role is not supported.

2.5 Exchange 2013 Prerequisites for Windows Server 2012

The following are the prerequisites when you deploy Mailbox Server and Client Access Server together.

AS-HTTP-Activation
Desktop-Experience
NET-Framework-45-Features
RPC-over-HTTP-proxy
RSAT-Clustering
RSAT-Clustering-CmdInterface
Web-Mgmt-Console
WAS-Process-Model
Web-Asp-Net45
Web-Basic-Auth
Web-Superplaneteers-Auth
Web-Digest-Auth
Web-Dir-Browsing
Web-Dyn-Compression

Web-Http-Errors
Web-Http-Logging
Web-Http-Redirect
Web-Http-Tracing
Web-ISAPI-Ext
Web-ISAPI-Filter
Web-Lgcy-Mgmt-Console
Web-Metabase
Web-Mgmt-Console
Web-Mgmt-Service
Web-Net-Ext45
Web-Request-Monitor
Web-Server
Web-Stat-Compression
Web-Static-Content
Web-Windows-Auth
Web-WMI
Windows-Identity-Foundation

Additional Application Requirements: Download and install the following prerequisites on Windows Server 2012.

Windows Media Foundation. Use Add Roles and features Wizard to install Media Foundation on Windows Serer 2012.

Microsoft Unified Communications Managed API 4.0, Core Runtime 64-bit
http://www.microsoft.com/en-us/download/details.aspx?id=34992

Microsoft Office 2010 Filter Pack 64 bit
http://www.microsoft.com/en-us/download/details.aspx?id=17062

Microsoft Office 2010 Filter Pack SP1 64 bit
http://www.microsoft.com/en-us/download/details.aspx?id=26604

Exchange 2013 setup automatically install features required by Exchange. Alternatively you can use the following PowerShell Command to install all the features at that same time. A reboot is required after installing features.

Install-WindowsFeature AS-HTTP-Activation, Desktop-Experience, NET-Framework-45-Features, RPC-over-HTTP-proxy, RSAT-Clustering, RSAT-Clustering-CmdInterface, Web-Mgmt-Console, WAS-Process-Model, Web-Asp-Net45, Web-

Basic-Auth, Web-Superplaneteers-Auth, Web-Digest-Auth, Web-Dir-Browsing, Web-Dyn-Compression, Web-Http-Errors, Web-Http-Logging, Web-Http-Redirect, Web-Http-Tracing, Web-ISAPI-Ext, Web-ISAPI-Filter, Web-Lgcy-Mgmt-Console, Web-Metabase, Web-Mgmt-Console, Web-Mgmt-Service, Web-Net-Ext45, Web-Request-Monitor, Web-Server, Web-Stat-Compression, Web-Static-Content, Web-Windows-Auth, Web-WMI, Windows-Identity-Foundation

The following are the prerequisites when you deploy Client Access Server on a separate server.

Desktop-Experience
NET-Framework
NET-HTTP-Activation
RPC-over-HTTP-proxy
RSAT-Clustering
RSAT-Web-Server
WAS-Process-Model
Web-Asp-Net
Web-Basic-Auth
Web-Superplaneteers-Auth
Web-Digest-Auth
Web-Dir-Browsing
Web-Dyn-Compression
Web-Http-Errors
Web-Http-Logging
Web-Http-Redirect
Web-Http-Tracing
Web-ISAPI-Ext
Web-ISAPI-Filter
Web-Lgcy-Mgmt-Console
Web-Metabase
Web-Mgmt-Console
Web-Mgmt-Service
Web-Net-Ext
Web-Request-Monitor
Web-Server
Web-Stat-Compression
Web-Static-Content
Web-Windows-Auth
Web-WMI

Exchange 2013 setup automatically install features required by Exchange. Alternatively you can use the following PowerShell Command to install all the features at that same time. A reboot is required after installing features.

Add-WindowsFeature Desktop-Experience, NET-Framework, NET-HTTP-Activation, RPC-over-HTTP-proxy, RSAT-Clustering, RSAT-Web-Server, WAS-Process-Model, Web-Asp-Net, Web-Basic-Auth, Web-Superplaneteers-Auth, Web-Digest-Auth, Web-Dir-Browsing, Web-Dyn-Compression, Web-Http-Errors, Web-Http-Logging, Web-Http-Redirect, Web-Http-Tracing, Web-ISAPI-Ext, Web-ISAPI-Filter, Web-Lgcy-Mgmt-Console, Web-Metabase, Web-Mgmt-Console, Web-Mgmt-Service, Web-Net-Ext, Web-Request-Monitor, Web-Server, Web-Stat-Compression, Web-Static-Content, Web-Windows-Auth, Web-WMI

Additional Application Requirements Download and install the following prerequisites on Windows Server 2012.

Windows Media Foundation. Use Add Roles and features Wizard to install Media Foundation on Windows Serer 2012.

Microsoft Unified Communications Managed API 4.0, Core Runtime 64-bit http://www.microsoft.com/en-us/download/details.aspx?id=34992

If you would like to install Exchange Server 2013 on Windows Server 2008 R2 SP1 you have to install the following Microsoft KBs in order to run Exchange 2013 installer.

- KB974405 (Windows Identity Foundation)
- KB2619234 (Enable the Association Cookie/GUID that is used by RPC over HTTP)
- KB2533623 (Insecure library loading could allow remote code execution)

Exchange 2013 management tools can be installed on a domain member running Windows 8 64-bit operating system.

2.6 Exchange Server 2013 Storage Requirements
You can have any of the following Storage architecture for Exchange 2013

- Direct-attached storage (DAS)
- Fibre Channel SAN, iSCSI (IP SAN)
- Solid-state drive (SSD)

Performance Factors in disk type choice: Do not use any disk below 10K rpm. 10k rpm disk will provide you an average performance. To get best I/O for Exchange Server 2013, use minimum 15K rpm disk or SSD disk. However capacity will be a concern for SSD disk. The following are the key factors when considering storage configuration and expected performance from exchange server.

- RAID1/10 disk in a dedicated LUN for OS, System or Pagefile volume
- RAID1/10 in a dedicated LUN for Exchange Database, Log files.
- RAID stripe size 256KB.
- 75 percent write cache and 25 percent read cache
- Support up to 16 terabytes storage
- Database size 200 gigabytes (GB) or less.
- Provision 120% of calculated maximum database size
- Disable circular logging
- Provision for minimum three days of log generation capacity
- Use Basic Disk
- Use GPT partitions
- NTFS 64KB allocation unit

2.7 Preparing Active Directory Domain Services

You have to prepare Active Directory Domain Services before you can install Exchange Server 2013. To prepare AD DS, verify the following in AD DS:

- AD DS site has domain controller from where you will prepare AD DS.
- Verify that you have writable Global Catalog (GC) Server in AD DS.
- Verify that there is no pending replication queue among AD DS Sites

To run this command, you must be a member of the Schema Admins group and the Enterprise Admins group. Log on to a Domain Controller (with Global Catalog configured) in the Forest where you want to install Exchange 2013. Insert or mount Exchange 2013 DVD on to Domain Controller. Open Elevated Command Prompt in Windows Server and run the following:

setup /PrepareSchema /IAcceptExchangeServerLicenseTerms

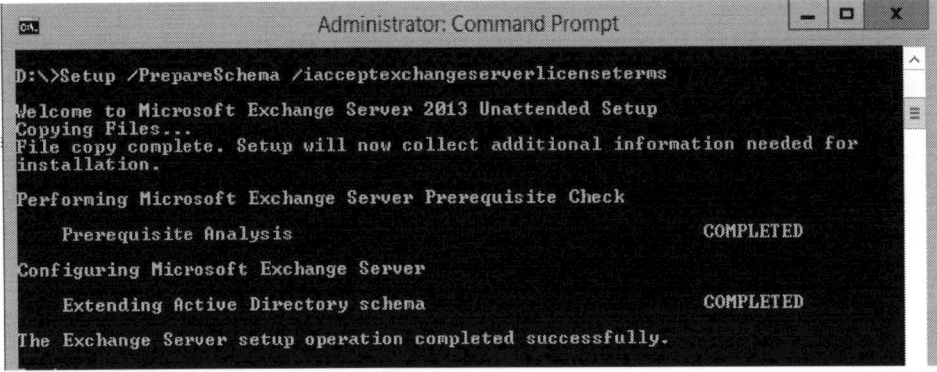

setup /PrepareAD /OrganizationName:<organization name>
/IAcceptExchangeServerLicenseTerms

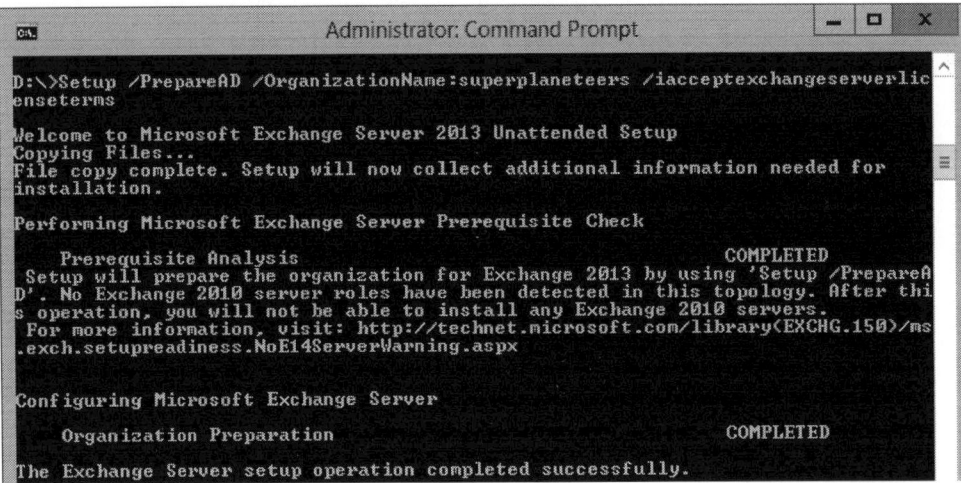

Note that if you run setup /PrepareAD you don't have to run setup
/PrepareDomain. You cannot run /PrepareSchema and /PrepareAD together.

2.8 Pre-installation Check List

1. Download Exchange Server 2013 software
2. Obtain License and CALS from Microsoft Volume Licensing Center
3. Read the release notes.
4. Verify system requirements.
5. Check Server is secured, up to date with correct patching level, Antivirus installed
6. Confirm prerequisite steps are done.
7. Install the Mailbox server role.

8. Install the Client Access server role.

2.9 Post Installation Check List

1. Configure Transport rules.
2. Configure email address policies.
3. Add digital certificates on the Client Access server.
4. Configure settings on virtual directories, including the offline address book, Exchange Web Services, Outlook Web App, and Exchange ActiveSync virtual directories.
5. Configure Database Availability Group and Database
6. Create Public Folder.
7. Configure Unified Messaging (Optional)
8. Create test mailbox, contacts and distribution group
9. Test Installation and Configuration
10. Test internal and external Mail flow
11. Test ActiveSync on Windows Mobile or other mobile devices.

2.10 Integration with SharePoint and Lync

One of the significant design consideration is when you deploy Lync Server 2013 with Exchange 2013 in an organization, you can configure Lync to archive instant messaging and on-line meeting content such as shared presentations or documents in the user's Exchange 2013 mailbox. Exchange 2013 allows SharePoint 2013 to search Exchange mailbox content using Federated search API. SharePoint 2013 provides an eDiscovery Center to allow authorized personnel to perform eDiscovery.

Unified contact store (UCS) is a feature that provides a consistent contact experience across Microsoft Office products. This feature enables users to store all contact information in their Exchange 2013 mailbox so that the same contact information is available globally across Lync, Exchange, Outlook and Outlook Web App.

In Exchange 2013, there are two configuration objects you must manage for OAuth authentication with partner applications: AuthConfig and Partner applications.

2.11 Virtualizing Exchange Server 2013

This is most likely scenario that an organisation would prefer to virtualize on-premises Exchange Server. Microsoft supports virtualizing Exchange Server 2013 in production environment using hardware virtualization technology. The hardware virtualization software is running one of the following:

- Windows Server 2008 R2 with Hyper-V technology
- Microsoft Hyper-V Server 2008 R2
- Windows Server 2012
- Microsoft Hyper-V Server 2012
- Any third-party hypervisor that has been validated by Microsoft

CPU Requirements: The virtual processors located in the guest virtual machine share a fixed number of logical processors in the physical system. Exchange supports a virtual processor-to-logical processor ratio no greater than 2:1, although Microsoft recommend a ratio of 1:1. For example a dual processor system using quad core processors contains a total of 2 Physical x 4core each=8 logical processors in the host system. On a system with this configuration, don't allocate more than a total of 16 virtual processors to all guest virtual machines combined.

Disk Allocation: The operating system for an Exchange guest machine must use a disk that has a size equal to at least 15 GB plus the size of the virtual memory that's allocated to the guest machine. For example, if the guest machine is allocated 16 GB of memory, the minimum disk space needed for the guest operating system disk is 31 GB. Exchange guest machine for storage of Exchange data must be block-level storage because Exchange 2013 doesn't support the use of network attached storage (NAS) volumes.

Memory: Allocate fixed memory in operating systems instead of dynamic memory. Allocating dynamic memory may result poor performance in Exchange 2013. As a result, using dynamic memory features for Exchange is not supported.

Live Migration: Exchange Server 2013 supports live migration using Hyper-v Manager installed in Windows Server 2008 R2 SP1 or windows Server 2012. In case of host failover and Exchange Server did not migrate properly you have to shut down the system and do a cold boot that is to start the virtual machine from power off state. Saved State of virtual machine is not supported in Exchange Server 2013.

2.12 Designing Exchange Server 2013

In this section, you will learn a practical design guide of Exchange Server. You can copy all the data provided in this section and amend as necessary to deploy

Exchange Server in production environment. You can add executive summary and objectives with this section (**2.12**) to adopt this document as design and as-build guide and utilize this document later on for Server Operations Manual (SOM). Before you begin designing an Exchange organization, you must create the data sheet that will be vital for successful deployment of messaging system. Once you have collected the following information, you are ready to create a design overview of Exchange Server and build guide.

Assumptions:

Hyper-V Server 2012 cluster is ready and configured in Highly Available Configuration. Additional storage (LUN) has been presented to Hyper-V Servers to roll out new virtual machines for Exchange Server 2013 project. We will be using VHD disks in all virtual machines.

As part of this design guide, we will consider the following infrastructure in lab environment. Domain Controller and Exchange servers will be installed on Windows Server 2012. TMG 2010 will be installed on Windows Server 2008 R2.

Service/Application	Roles and Features	Server Name
Active Directory Domain Services	Domain Controller Enterprise CA	DC
Forefront TMG 2010	Publishing and Firewall	TMGSRV
Exchange 2013 Mailbox	Mailbox Server	EXCHMBXSRV1 EXCHMBXSRV2
Exchange 2013 CAS	CAS Server	EXCHCASSRV1 EXCHCASSRV2
Outlook 2013 installed	Windows 8 Client	Client

Note that installing Certificate Authority in a Domain Controller is not a best practice for a production environment.

2.12.1 Preparing Exchange Server 2013 Data Sheet
The values inserted into the **Value Field** of the following data sheets are **DUMMY** data. Download and use Exchange sizing tools to find out correct data in production environment. In production environment you will have different value for each individual section based on your situation.

Item Description	Meet initial	Further

	requirement? Y/N	Investigation
Design and Assessment	Y	
Role Based Access Control	Y	
Systems Requirements	Y	
Server Roll Out	Y	
Forest Functional level	Y	
AD DS	Y	
MX Record	Y	
CNAME	Y	
TCP/IP	Y	
Firewall	Y	
Database configuration	Y	

2.12.2 Role Based Access Control

Exchange Management Role	Permission Level
Organization Administrator	Full
Exchange Administrator	Full
Migration Engineer	Full
Helpdesk	Create Mailbox, Read Property
Backup Administrator	Read Only

2.12.3 Firewall Deployment Data Sheet

Rule Order	Source	Destination	Port	Status
1	Anywhere	Exchange CAS	25	Allow
2	Anywhere	Exchange CAS	143	Allow
3	Anywhere	Exchange CAS	110	Allow
4	Anywhere	Exchange CAS	443	Allow

2.12.4 Sizing Exchange Server 2013 for Deployment

Exchange Environment Configuration	Value
Global Catalog Server Processor Architecture	64-bit
Server Multi-Role Configuration (Mailbox +CAS)	No
Server Role Virtualization	Yes

High Availability Deployment	Yes
Number of Mailbox Servers Hosting Active Mailboxes / DAG (Primary Data Center)	2
Number of CAS Servers (Primary Data Centre)	2
Number of Database Availability Groups	1

Site Resilience Configuration	Value
Site Resilient Deployment	Yes
Site Resilience User Distribution Model	Active/Passive
Site Resilience Recovery Point Objective (Hours)	24
Activation Block Secondary Data Center Mailbox Servers	No
Dedicated DR in Second Data Center	No

Mailbox Database Configuration	Value
Total Number of HA Database Instances within DAG	3
Total Number of Lagged Database Instances within DAG	0
Number of HA Database Instances Deployed in Secondary Data Center	0
No of Lagged DB in Second Data Center	0

Exchange Data Configuration	Value
Data Overhead Factor	20%
Mailbox Moves / Week Percentage	1%
Dedicated Maintenance / Restore LUN?	Yes
LUN Free Space Percentage	10%
Log Shipping Network Compression	Enabled
Log Shipping Compression Percentage	30%
Total Number of Tier-1 User Mailboxes / Environment	500
Projected Mailbox Number Growth Percentage	10%
Total Send/Receive Capability / Mailbox /	50 messages

Day	
Average Message Size (KB)	180
Mailbox Size Limit (MB)	1024
Personal Archive Mailbox Size Limit (MB)	0
Deleted Item Retention Window (Days)	14
Single Item Recovery	Enabled
Calendar Version Storage	Enabled
IOPS Multiplication Factor	1.00
Megacycles Multiplication Factor	1.00
Desktop Search Engines Enabled (for Online Mode in Clients)	Yes
Predict IOPS Value?	Yes
IOPS/Mailbox	-
DB read/Write Ratio	-

Mailbox Server Hardware Configuration	Value
Hardware Architecture	X64
Processors	2 Virtual CPU
Memory	12GB
System Partition	50GB
Apps Partition	50GB
Page File	-
Database Partition	500GB
Log Partition	500GB
Journal Data Partition	200GB
Journal Log Partition	500GB
Recovery Partition	300GB

CAS Server Hardware Configuration	Value
Hardware Architecture	X64
Processors	2 Virtual CPU
Memory	8GB
System Partition	50GB
Apps Partition	50GB
Page File	-

TCP/IP Configuration for Mailbox Server	IP Address & Subnet	Default Gateway & DNS
EXCHMBXSRV1 MAPI (Production) Network	10.10.10.5 255.255.255.0	DG: 10.10.10.254 DNS: 10.10.10.1
EXCHMBXSRV2 MAPI (Production) Network	10.10.10.6 255.255.255.0	DG: 10.10.10.254 DNS: 10.10.10.1
EXCHMBXSRV1 Replication (Heartbeat) Network	192.168.2.1 255.255.255.0	No Default Gateway No DNS
EXCHMBXSRV2 Replication (Heartbeat) Network	192.168.2.2 255.255.255.0	No Default Gateway No DNS

TCP/IP Configuration for CAS Server	IP Address & Subnet	Default Gateway & DNS
EXCHCASSRV1 MAPI (Production) Network	10.10.10.7 255.255.255.0	DG: 10.10.10.254 DNS: 10.10.10.1
EXCHCASSRV2 MAPI (Production) Network	10.10.10.8 255.255.255.0	DG: 10.10.10.254 DNS: 10.10.10.1
EXCHCASSRV1 Replication (Heartbeat) Network	192.168.2.3 255.255.255.0	No Default Gateway No DNS
EXCHCASSRV2 Replication (Heartbeat) Network	192.168.2.4 255.255.255.0	No Default Gateway No DNS

Database Configuration	Value
Executive-DB	E:\Data\Executive
Assistant-DB	E:\Data\Assistant
Manager-DB	G:\Data\Manager
General-DB	G:\Data\General
Journal1-DB	J:\Data\Journal1

Journal2-DB	J:\Data\Journal2
Recovery-DB	R:\Recovery
Logs	L:\Logs
SpamQ (Database will be used to quarantine Spam emails)	Q\SpamDB

DAG Configuration	Value
Prod-DAG	EXCHMBXSRV1 EXCHMBXSRV2
DR-DAG	-

Important! If you would like to achieve DR functionality in an Exchange Organization, you must configure at least 4 Exchange mailbox server. Two servers serve as an active mailbox server in DAG and another two servers serve as passive mailbox server in DAG. For example, you can have EXCHMBXSRV1A and EXCHMBXSRV1B in one DAG, EXCHMBXSRV2A and EXCHMBXSRV2B are in another DAG. All "A" nodes serve as active node and "B" node serve as passive node achieving DR functionality. For this book, we will configure only one DAG with two mailbox servers.

2.13 Exchange 2013 Solutions Overview

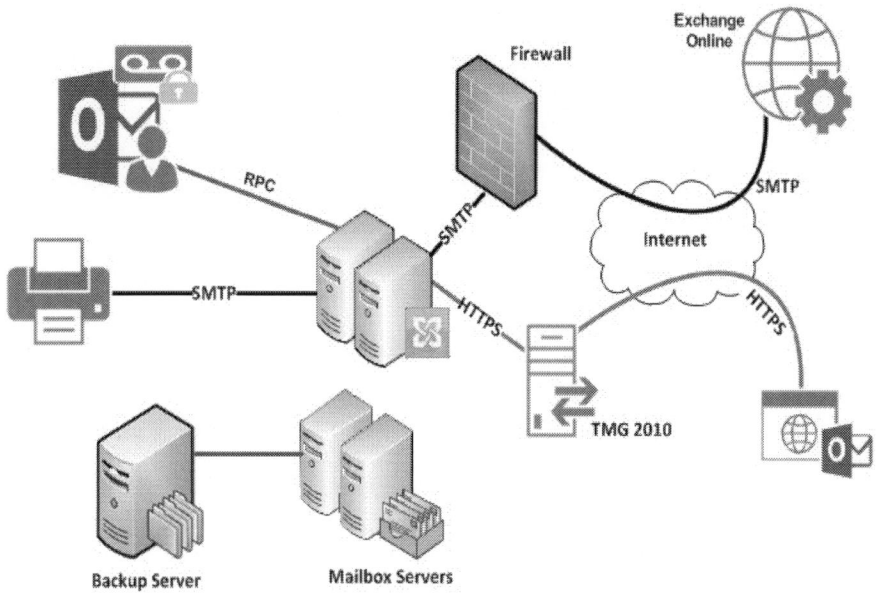

2.13.1 Exchange 2013 Client Access Configuration

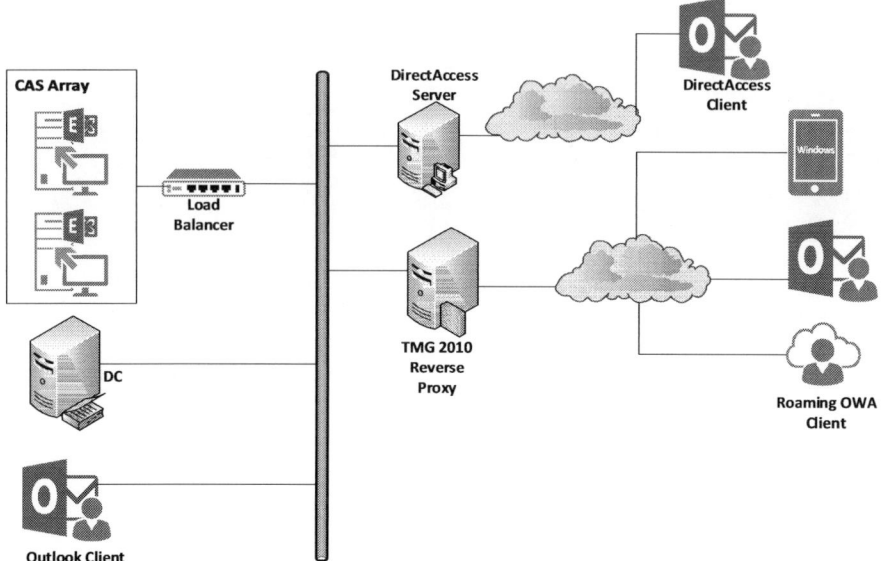

2.13.2 Exchange and TMG 2010 Topology

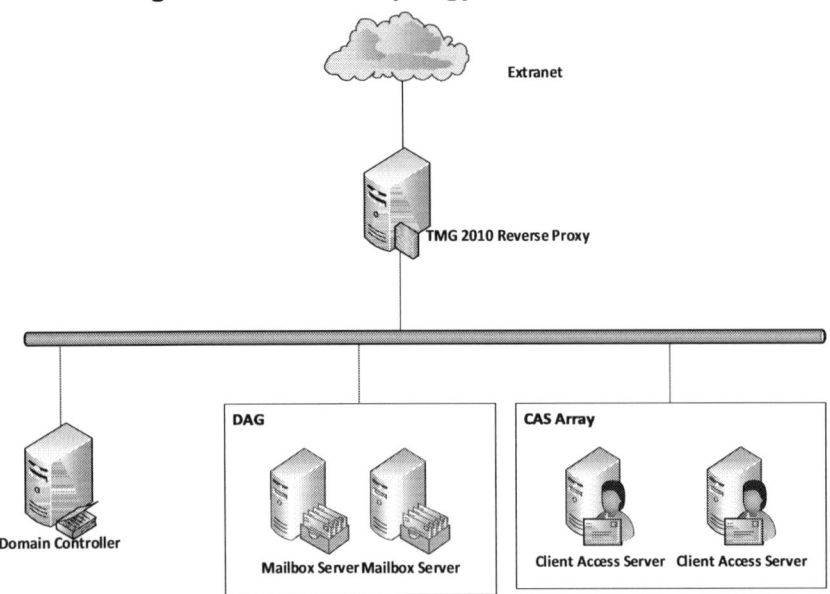

2.13.3 Database Availability Group Topology

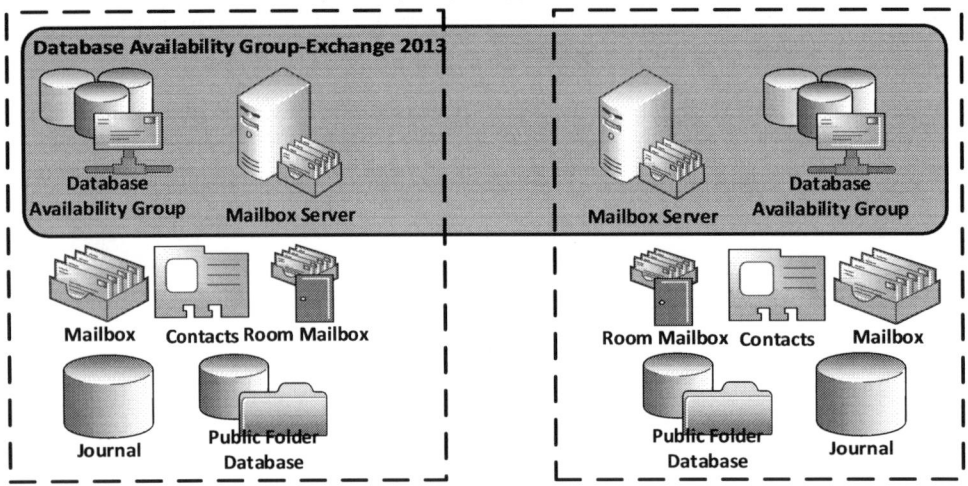

2.13.4 Exchange 2013 Network Topology

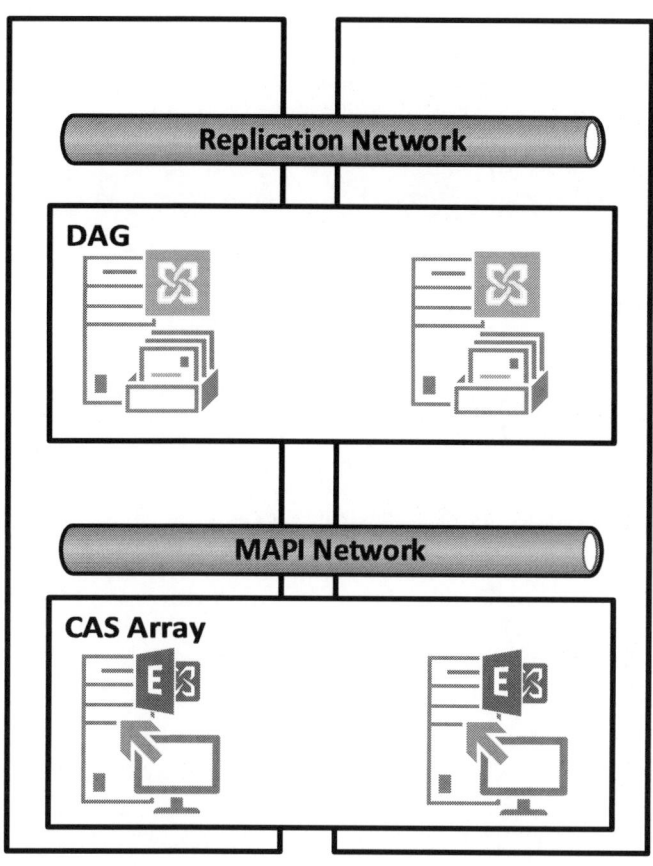

2.13.5 Exchange 2013 Mail Flow

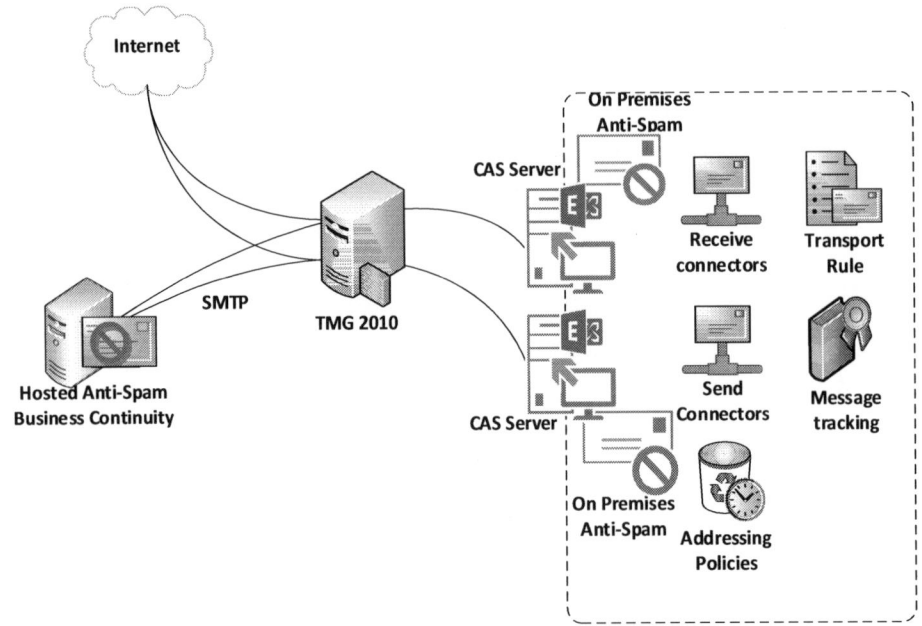

2.13.6 NLB Multicast Mode – Static ARP Resolution for CAS servers

If you decide to utilize Microsoft NLB instead of hardware load balancing then you have to follow this section and configure core switch to avoid traffic snooping. NLB in Windows Server operating systems run in Multicast mode, the unicast IP address with a multicast address must be statically assigned to the switch to ensure it is inserted into the arp cache of the switch or router its connected to. Perform the following commands from global configuration mode on the Core switch.

arp <IP Address> <Mac Address> ARPA
mac address-table static <Mac Address> vlan <vlan ID> interface TenGigabitEthernet <Port ID> disablesnooping
mac address-table static <Mac Address> vlan <vlan ID> interface TenGigabitEthernet <Port ID> disablesnooping
mac address-table static <Mac Address> vlan <vlan ID> interface TenGigabitEthernet <Port ID> disablesnooping
mac address-table static <Mac Address> vlan <vlan ID> interface TenGigabitEthernet <Port ID> disablesnooping
mac address-table static <Mac Address> vlan <vlan ID> interface port-channel <Channel ID>
mac address-table static <Mac Address> vlan <vlan ID>   interface port-channel <Channel ID>

Where <IP Address> is NLB Cluster Multicast IPv4 IP Address, <Mac Address> is mac address of NLB Cluster, <VLAN ID> is the vlan ID from where traffic of Multicast NLB Network passing through, <Port ID> is the Switch port where NLB Nodes are connected to.

2.14 Designing Operating Systems

Partition Type and backend storage RAID type in SAN

Partition	RAID Type	Size in GB	Description
SYSTEM	RAID1	50GB	C:\ SYSTEM
APPS	RAID1	50GB	E:\ APPS
Mailbox Data	RAID5	500GB	H:\Data,G:\Data
Mailbox Logs	RAID1	500GB	L:\ Logs
Journal Data	RAID5	300GB	J:\ Journal
Journal Logs	RAID1	500GB	K:\ Logs
Recovery	RAID5	300GB	R:\ Recovery

Operating Systems in which Exchange Server 2013 Farm will be installed

EXCHMBXSRV1	Windows Server 2012 Data Center
EXCHMBXSRV1	Windows Server 2012 Data Center
EXCHCASSRV1	Windows Server 2012 Data Center
EXCHCASSRV2	Windows Server 2012 Data Center
Backup Server	Windows Server 2012 Data Center
TMGSRV	Windows Server 2012 Data Center

DNS Record and Corresponding IP

CAS Roles, Mailbox Roles	Private IP point to FQDN
webmail.superplaneteers.com	Public IP point to FQDN (TMG External NIC)

Antivirus File Exclusion

File types	File locations
.edb, .chk, .log	H:\Data , J:\Journal, L:\Logs G:\Data, K:\Logs, R:\Recovery

Exchange Installation Location

Exchange 2013 will be installed on the APPS partition E:\Exchange Server 2013

2.15 Setting up Mailbox and Address List

Mailbox Settings & Quotas

Issue Warning:	1000000
Prohibit Send:	1100000
Prohibit Send\Receive:	1200000
Deleted Items Retention:	30
Deleted mailbox retention:	7
Public Folder:	PER-PUBLICFOLDER
Offline Address List:	Default Offline Address List
Archive Mailbox:	Journalmbx01 Journalmbx02

2.16 Configuring Exchange 2013 Protocol

ActiveSync and OWA Configuration

ActiveSync devices connecting from the internal wired and wireless VLAN will use the URL (https://webmail.superplaneteer.com/Microsoft_server_activesync). OWA will use the URL https://webmail.superplaneteers.com/owa and will point to the load balancer VIP for Exchange 2013 CAS Server. If you don't have network Load Balancer you can use Microsoft Network Load Balancing (NLB cluster VIP).

Both Exchange 2013 CAS servers require a trusted SSL certificate with both server names and subject alternative name as webmail.superplaneteers.com and

Autodiscover.superplaneteers.com. The same certificate will be added to TMG 2010 Edge Server.

Outlook Web Services

The following is the Outlook Web Service Settings. All authentications settings are set to basic.

Owa (Default Web Site) Internal URL:	https://webmail.superplaneteers.com/owa
External URL:	https://webmail.superplaneteers.com/owa
Ecp (Default Web Site) Internal URL:	https://webmail.superplaneteers.com/ecp
Microsoft-Server-ActiveSync Internal URL:	https://webmail.superplaneteers.com/Microsoft-Server-ActiveSync
External URL:	https://webmail.superplaneteers.com/Microsoft-Server-ActiveSync
OAB Internal URL:	https://webmail.superplaneteers.com/oab
External URL:	https://webmail.superplaneteers.com/oab

Protocol Settings:

POP3 and IMAP4 setting will be unchanged i.e. stay default.

2.17 Configure Exchange Organization and Server

Default remote domains policy

- Out of office notifications to remote domains will be allowed.
- Delivery reports will be allowed
- Non-delivery reports will be allowed.
- Sender's name will be displayed on messages
- Office 365 tenant domain will not be enabled or out of scope for this book.

Default Accepted Domain Policy

General policy	Domain name	Authoritative
Accepted domain	superplaneteers.com	Yes

E-mail Address Polices

In this section, you will configure E-mail address policies. As a standard practice you can configure e-mail address firstname.lastname@superplaneteers.com as the email address policy unless you specify otherwise. You can apply this email address policy to a managed OU in Active Directory Domain or entire forest.

Transport Rules

In this Section, you can configure Transport rules that relevant to your organization. Sample configuration is shown below.

New-MessageClassification -Name NewMessageClassification - DisplayName "New Message Classification" - SenderDescription "This is the description that explains to the sender when to use this classification" - RecipientDescription "This is the description that explains to the recipient the intent of the classification and how they should handle the message"	• Non-business • Public • Unrestricted • Restricted • Confidential • Privileged
./Export-OutlookClassification.ps1 c:\exports\Classifications.xml	The classifications will be exported to classifcations.xml for use by Outlook 2013.

Global Settings in Send Connectors

The following is the Sample global Policy settings for send connector

Sending Message Size Limit 10240Kb (13500Kb)
Receiving Message Size Limit 10240Kb (13500Kb)
Recipient Limit 5000

Receive Connectors

In Exchange 2013 one receive connector is installed by default. However you can create multiple receive connector based on your need. The following is the receive connector settings sample.

Receive Connector Setting

Client <server name> protocol logging level: None
FQDN: <servername>.superplaneteers.com
Maximum message size (Kb): 13500
Use all local addresses on port 587 to receive mail
Receive Mail from 0.0.0.0-255.255.255.255
Authentication: TLS, Basic & Integrated Windows.
Permission Group: Exchange users

Default <server name> protocol logging level: None
FQDN: <servername>.superplaneteers.com
Maximum message size (Kb): 13500
Use all local addresses on port 25 to receive mail
Receive Mail from 0.0.0.0 – 255.255.255.255
Authentication: TLS, Basic, Exchange Server authentication,
Integrated Windows
Permission Group: Exchange users, Exchange Servers, Legacy
Exchange Servers

Relay <server name>
In this section you will configure receive connector as relay for printers, scanner, other devices and web applications. Add printers and application servers into the whitelist to allow them send print, scanned documents via the relay.

Protocol logging level: None
FQDN: <servername>.superplaneteers.com
Maximum message size (Kb): 13500
Use all local addresses on port 25 to receive mail

Receive Mail from <see whitelist>
Authentication: TLS, Externally Secured.
Permission Group: Exchange Servers

2.18 Publishing Exchange for External Client

You have to change external DNS or CNAME if you are changing webmail.superplaneteers.com to mail.supperplaneteers.com or you have situation where you are moving from one ISP to another to host your MX and CNAME record. These changes must be performed before you start migrating and deploying a new exchange farm otherwise all external Mail flow will be stopped. You must also consider external smart host or business continuity options if you have one. If so then you must amend necessary configuration via service provider web site to get your external email working as expected.

Forefront Threat Management Gateway 2010

As part of Exchange 2013 deployment, you can configure access to OWA via Forefront TMG 2010. For example all access can be over https using https://webmail.superplaneteers.com. The same address can be used for OWA, ActiveSync and Outlook Anywhere. OWA, ActiveSync and Outlook Anywhere will be shortened to just https://webmail.superplaneteers.com. If a user tries to use http, it will be redirected to https.

I would highly recommend utilizing TMG cluster and an EMS server to manage TMG servers. Clustered TMG configuration will avoid any single point of failure in Exchange Web Access.

Computer Groups in TMG 2010

Exchange 2013 Public IP	Internet Routable IPv4 Public IP
Computer Group Name	GRP_EXCHSRV2013 (EXCHCASSRV1,EXCHCASSRV2)

Access Policies

Policy Name Details	Exchange 2013 Inbound Access Policy
VIP	Public IP
From	External
To	GRP_EXCHSRV2013
Allow	TCP 80 & 443

Digital Certificates with Subject Alternative Name (SAN)

webmail.superplaneteers.com
autodiscover.superplaneteers.com
superplaneteers.com
EXCHCASSRV1.superplaneteers.com
EXCHCASSRV2.superplaneteers.com

HTTPS Web Listeners

HTTPS Listener Network: External (Public IP – Array VIP if clustered TMG)
Connection port: 443
Certificate: webmail.superplaneteers.com
Authentication: HTML Form Authentication
Forms: Not Set
SSO: Not Set

TMG Firewall Policies

In this section you will configure an important firewall policy that will allow communication from external client, vendor and user to internal users.

Rule Name Details	Publish Exchange 2013 to external network
Action:	Allow
From:	Anywhere
To:	webamail.superplaneteers.com IP: 10.10.10.15
Traffic:	HTTPS
Listener:	HTTPS Listener
Paths:	/public/ /OWA/ /ExchWeb/ /Exchange/
Public name:	webmail.superplaneteers.com
Authentication:	Basic Authentication
Application Settings:	Enabled
Custom HTML Set:	Exchange
Logon Type:	As Selected

Redirect HTTP to HTTPS Policy

Name/Description	Action
Publish Outlook Anywhere Action:	Allow
From:	Anywhere
To:	webmail.Superplaneteers.com (forward header) 10.10.10.15
Traffic:	HTTPS
Listener:	HTTPS Listener

Public name:	webmail.Superplaneteers.com
Paths:	/*
Authentication:	Basic Authentication
Redirect OWA http to https Action:	Deny
From:	http://webmail.Superplaneteers.com
Redirect to	https://webmail.Superplaneteers.com

TMG HTTP Filtering Values In this section you will configure Filtering Settings in TMG firewall policies as follows:

Maximum Request Header Length 32768
Request Payload Allow any payload length
Maximum URL Length 10240
Maximum Query Length 10240
Verify Normalization Disabled
Block High Bit Characters Disabled
Block responses containing Windows executable
Content Disabled
Methods Allow All Methods
Extensions Allow All Extensions
Headers Allow All Headers
Server Header: Send original header
Via Header: Send default

2.19 Configure Backup Agent and Schedule
When designing an Exchange Server 2013 farm, always consider backup, schedules and policies based your need and infrastructure you have. The following are the traditional backup agent available in market.

- Exchange Database Agent
- Exchange Mailbox Agent
- Exchange Public Folder Agent
- Exchange Web Folder Agent
- Windows File System Agent
- Exchange Archive Agent

Exchange Archive Storage Policy A storage policy forms the primary logical entity through which an instance is backed up. Its main function is to map data from its original location to a physical media. You have to create the following archive storage policies in this Exchange implementation:

- Storage Policy Name
- Storage Policy Type
- Library Details
- Media Agent
- Streams and Retention for Policy
- Archive Rules
- Stub Management

Exchange Backup Schedules

The following backup schedules is for sample only. You have to create a practical backup schedule which align your business needs.

Agent Job Type	Times	Schedule	Pattern
Public Folders	18:00	Friday	Full
Public Folders	18:00	Monday, Tuesday, Wednesday, Thursday	Incremental
Web Folders	18:00	Friday	Full
Web Folders	18:00	Monday, Tuesday, Wednesday, Thursday	Incremental
Exchange Database	18:00	Monday, Tuesday, Wednesday, Thursday, Friday	Full
Journal Mailboxes	18:00	Friday	Full
Exchange Mailbox	18:00	Monday, Tuesday, Wednesday, Thursday,	Incremental
Journal Mailboxes	18:00	Monday, Tuesday, Wednesday, Thursday	Incremental

2.20 Designing Security in Exchange Server 2013

Exchange 2013 installation creates several roles and AD security groups to manage Organization.

Service Desk Members of this management role group have rights to create, manage and remove Exchange recipient objects in the Exchange organization.

Discovery Members of this management role can perform exchange server discovery.

Management searches of Mailboxes in the Exchange organization for data that meets specific criteria. Assigned roles are Legal Hold and Mailbox search. Membership will be assigned as required. By default this group will be empty.

Administrator Logging Administrator audit logging in Exchange Server 2013 can be enabled to log when a user or administrator executes an Exchange PowerShell change command in the Exchange 2013 organization. The Audit log can be exported from the Role based access control console.

2.21 Performance Management & monitoring

You can utilize perfmon to measure performance of Exchange Server 2013. you can utilize the following are the base alert:

Processor\% Processor Time 90% for 15 minutes
LogicalDisk\Avg. Disk sec\Read Monitor
LogicalDisk\Avg. Disk sec\write Monitor
Memory\Pages\sec Monitor
MSExchange Store Interface\RPC Latency average (msec) Monitor
MSExchange Store Interface\RPC Latency outstanding Monitor
MSExchange IS\RPC Average Latency Monitor
MSExchange IS\RPC Requests Monitor
MSExchange IS Mailbox\Local delivery rate Monitor
MSExchange Transport Queues\Active Remote Delivery
MSExchange Transport Queues\Retry Remote Delivery
MSExchange Transport SMTP\Messages Received/sec Zero for 10 minutes
MSExchange Transport SMTP\Messages Sent/sec Zero for 10 minutes
Processor\% Processor Time 90% for 15 minutes
LogicalDisk\Avg. Disk sec\Read Monitor
LogicalDisk\Avg. Disk sec\write Monitor
Memory\Pages\sec Monitor
MSExchange IS\RPC Average Latency Monitor
MSExchange IS\RPC Requests Monitor

CHAPTER 3

In This Chapter

- Installing Exchange Server 2013
- Configuring Mailflow and Client Access
- Configure SSL Binding and External Access
- Configure Database Availability Group
- Creating a New Mailbox Database
- Testing External Access

Chapter3. Installing and Configuring Exchange Server 2013 Farm

3.1 Installing Exchange Server 2013

Before you begin installing Exchange Server 2013, read chapter 2.12.1 and prepare Active Directory Domain Services and Schema. Once you have performed the Schema and Active Directory preparation steps, you can install Exchange 2013. The account you use must be a member of the Delegated Setup management role group or the Organization Management role group. In each organization, you must have at least one Mailbox Server and one Client Access Server role installed either in one computer or multiple computers.

Note that co-existence scenario isn't supported until Microsoft release Service Pack 3 for Exchange 2007 and Exchange 2010.

1. Mount/Insert Exchange 2013 DVD on to the Server. Start Exchange 2013 Setup by double-clicking **Setup.exe**
2. On the **Check for Updates** Page, choose whether you want Setup to **connect to the Internet and Check for updates** or **Don't check for updates right now**. Microsoft recommends that you download and install updates now. On the Check for Updates? Page, Click **Next** to continue
3. On the Downloading Updates Page, Click **Next** to continue.
4. On the Copying Files Page, setup copies all the files necessary to install Exchange Server 2013
5. On the Introduction Page, Click **Next** to continue
6. On the **License Agreement** page, review the software license terms. Select **I accept the terms in the license agreement**, and then click **Next**.

7. On the **Recommended settings** page, if you select **Use recommended settings**, Exchange will automatically send error reports to Microsoft. If you select **Don't use recommended settings**, you can enable them at any time after Setup completes. On the Recommended Settings Page, Click **Next** to continue

8. On the **Server Role Selection** page, choose whether you want to install the **Mailbox role**, the **Client Access role**, both roles and just the **Management Tools** on this computer. On the Server Role Selection Page, you have to select your deployment topology for your organization. An organization must have at least one Mailbox role and at least one Client Access server role installed. They can be installed on the same computer or on separate computers. The management tools are installed automatically if you install any other server role.
   Note that if you are installing Exchange Server 2013 for the first time and you don't have any co-existence scenario then you install **Mailbox Server role first** then CAS role later.

9. Select **Automatically install Windows Server roles and features that are required to install Exchange Server** to have the Setup wizard install required Windows prerequisites. You have to reboot the computer to complete the installation of some Windows features. If you don't select this option, you must install the Windows features manually. Click **Next** to continue.

10. On the **Installation Space and Location** page, either accept the default installation location or click **Browse** to choose a new location. Click **Next** to continue.

11. If this is the first Exchange server in your organization, on the **Exchange Organization** page, type a name for your Exchange organization if you haven't created one organization in **chapter 2.12.1**. The Exchange organization name can be alpha numeric and does not contain any space.
   If you want to use the Active Directory split permissions model, select **Apply Active Directory split permission security model to the Exchange organization**.

12. Click **Next** to continue.

13. If you're installing the **Mailbox role**, on the **Malware Protection Settings** page, choose whether you want to enable or disable malware scanning. If you disable malware scanning, it can be enabled in the future. Click **Next** to continue.

14. On the **Readiness Checks** page, view the status to determine if the organization and server role prerequisite checks completed successfully. If they haven't completed successfully, you must resolve any reported errors before you can install Exchange 2013. You don't need to exit Setup when resolving some of the prerequisite errors. After resolving a reported error, click **Back** and then click **Next** to run the prerequisite check again.

15. Be sure to also review any warnings that are reported. If all readiness checks have completed successfully, click **Next** to install Exchange 2013.

16. On the **Completion** page, click **Finish**. Restart the computer after Exchange 2013 has completed.
17. Complete your deployment by performing the tasks provided in Exchange 2013 Post-Installation Tasks.
18. Repeat the entire steps to install more **CAS Servers** and **Mailbox Servers** based on your deployment topology.

3.2 Install Exchange 2013 Using Unattended Mode

To automate Exchange Server 2013 installation use Setup.exe command line with several parameters added to setup.exe. Log on to the computer on which you want to install Exchange 2013. Open Elevated command prompt, navigate to the location of the Exchange 2013 installation files and run the following command.

The following PowerShell command install Client Access and Mailbox in a single server to a default directory.

Setup.exe /mode:Install /role:ClientAccess,Mailbox /OrganizationName:MyOrg /IAcceptExchangeServerLicenseTerms

You can add /TirgetDir parameter with setup.exe to point installation location to "E:\Exchange Server" folder. You can also add /AnswerFile:c:\ExchangeConfig.txt parameter to create an answer file.

Setup.exe /mode:Install /role:ClientAccess,Mailbox /OrganizationName:MyOrg /TargetDir:"E:\Exchange Server 2013" /IAcceptExchangeServerLicenseTerms

You can use CA, MB instead of ClientAccess or Mailbox.

Setup.exe /r:CA,MB /IAcceptExchangeServerLicenseTerms

This command completely removes Exchange 2013 from the server and removes this server's Exchange configuration from Active Directory.

Setup.exe /mode:Uninstall

This command adds the Client Access server role to an existing Exchange 2013 server using "E:\Exchange Server" source directory.

E:\ExchangeServer\bin\Setup.exe /m:Install /r:ClientAccess /SourceDir:"E:\Exchange Server"

This command updates ExchangeServer.msi with patches from the specified directory, and then installs the Client Access server role, Mailbox server role, and the management tools.

Setup.exe /role:ClientAccess,Mailbox /UpdatesDir:"E:\ExchangeServer\New Patches"

To add a language pack in existing installation. Run the following command.

Setup.exe /AddUmLanguagePack: da-DK

3.3 Configure Basic Mail Flow in Exchange Server 2013
A default inbounds Receive Connector is created when Exchange 2013 is installed. This Receive connector accepts anonymous SMTP connections from external servers. Before you can send mail to the Internet, you need to create a Send connector on the Mailbox server. Follow the steps to create send connector.

1. Open the (EAC) by browsing to https://<fully qualified domain name (FQDN) of Client Access server>/ECP.
2. Enter your user name and password in **Domain\user name** and **Password** and then click **Sign in**.
3. Go to **Mail flow** , Click **Send connectors**. On the **Send Connectors** page, click **Add+**.
4. In the **New send connector** wizard, specify a name for the Send connector and then select **Internet**. Click **Next**.
5. Verify that **MX record associated with recipient domain** is selected. Click **Next**.
6. Under **Address space**, click **Add+**. In the **Add domain** window, make sure **SMTP** is selected in the **Type** field. In the **Fully Qualified Domain Name (FQDN)** field, enter . Click **Save**.
7. Make sure **Scoped send connector** isn't selected and then click **Next**.
8. Under **Source server**, click **Add+**. In the **Select a server** window, select a Mailbox server that will be used to send mail to the Internet via the Superplaneteers Access server. After you've selected the server, click **Add** and then click **OK**.
9. Click **Finish**.

3.4 Adding additional accepted domains

If you have multiple domains in your organisation and you would like them to send/receive email via your Exchange Server, you can add accepted domain in your organization for those domains. This domain is also added as the primary SMTP address on the default email address policy in the next step. A public Domain Name System (DNS) MX resource record is required for each SMTP domain for which you accept email from the Internet. Each MX record should resolve to the Internet-facing server that receives email for your organization.

1. Open the EAC by browsing to https://<FQDN of Client Access Server>/ECP.
2. Enter your user name and password in **Domain\user name** and **Password** and then click **Sign in**.
3. Go to **Mail flow** , Click **Accepted domains**. On the **Accepted domains** page, click **Add**.
4. In the **New accepted domain** wizard, specify a name for the accepted domain.
5. In the **Accepted domain** field, specify the SMTP recipient domain you want to add. For example, superplaneteers.com.
6. Select **Authoritative domain** and then click **Save**.

3.5 Configure the default email address policy

Once you added an accepted domain in Exchange Organization and you have to add every recipient in the organization, you need to update the default email address policy. Before you configure email policy make sure that a user principal name (UPN) matches the primary email address of each user. If you don't provide a UPN that matches the email address of a user, the user will be required to manually provide their domain\user name or UPN in addition to their email address. If their UPN matches their email address, Outlook Web App, ActiveSync, and Outlook will automatically match their email address to their UPN.

1. Open the EAC by browsing to https://<FQDN of Client Access server>/ECP.
2. Enter your user name and password in **Domain\user name** and **Password** and then click **Sign in**.
3. Go to **Mail flow** , Click **Email address policies**. On the **Email address policies** page, Click **Add+**.
4. On the New **Email Address Policy** page, Type the name of email policy on **Policy Name:** click **Email Address Format**.
5. Under **Email address format**, click **Add+** to add SMTP address type.

6. On the **Email address format** page in the **Email address parameters** field, specify the accepted domain you want to apply to all recipients in the Exchange organization. You can specify a custom domain in this section. This domain must match the accepted domain you added in the previous step. Select **Email Address Format:** John.Smith@superplaneteers.com Click **Save**.
7. Click **Save**
8. In the **New Email Address Policy** details pane, click **Apply**.

3.6 Configure an SSL certificate

Outlook Anywhere and ActiveSync require certificates to be configured on your Exchange 2013 server. The following steps show you how to configure an SSL certificate from a third-party certificate authority (CA):

1. Open the EAC by browsing to https://<FQDN of Client Access server>/ECP.
2. Enter your user name and password in **Domain\user name** and **Password** and then click **Sign in**.
3. Go to **Servers** , Click **Certificates**. On the **Certificates** page, make sure your Superplaneteers Access server is selected in the **Select server EXCHCASSRV01** field, and then click **Add+**.
4. In the **New Exchange certificate** wizard, select **Create a request for a certificate from a certification authority** and then click **Next**.
5. Specify a name for this certificate and then click **Next**.
6. If you want to request a wildcard certificate, select **Request a wild-card certificate** and then specify the root domain of all subdomains in the **Root domain** field (For example .superplaneteers.com). If you don't want to request a wildcard certificate then specify **webmail.superplaneteers.com** and **Autodiscover.superplaneteers.com** as SAN to the certificate. Click **Next**.
7. Click **Browse** and specify an Exchange server to store the certificate on. The server you select should be the Internet-facing Client Access server. Click **Next**. You can store certificaterequest.req file into a shared UNC path (Example \\EXCHCASSRV01\CERT\CertificateRequest.req).
8. For each service in the list shown, specify the external or internal server names that users will use to connect to the Exchange server. For example, for **Outlook Web App (when access from the Internet and intranet)**, you might specify **webmail.superplaneteers.com**. These domains will be used to create the SSL certificate request. Click **Next**.
9. Add any additional domains you want included on the SSL certificate. Click **Next**.

10. Provide information about your organization. This information will be included with the SSL certificate. Click **Next**.
11. Specify the network location where you want this certificate request to be saved. Click **Finish**.

After you've saved the certificate request, submit the request to your certificate authority (CA). This can be an internal CA or a third-party CA, depending on your organization. Client that connect to the Client Access server must trust the CA that you use. In production environment, you should send the request to a third party CA that can be verified in internet. For example verisign, entrust. To submit a certificate request to internal CA, follow the steps.

1. Open Certificaterequest.req using notepad, copy the content.
2. Open internet Explorer, Type Https://<Certificate authority name>/Certsrv and press enter.
3. On the Welcome Page, Click **Request a Certificate,** On the Request a certificate Page, Click **Submit an Advanced Certificate Request**
4. On the Advanced Certificate request page, Click **Submit a Certificate Request by using a base-64-encoded CMC...**
5. On the Submit a certificate request page, paste the copied content on **Saved Certificate:** Select Certificate Template: **Web Template,** Click **Submit.**
6. Click **Yes** to Allow the Operation to continue.
7. Download the certificate and save it on \\EXCHCASRV01\CERT\ folder.

After you receive the certificate from the CA, complete the following steps:

1. In the EAC, Click on the **Server**, Click **Certificates** page, select the pending certificate request you created in the previous steps.
2. In the certificate request details pane, click **Complete** under **Status**.
3. On the complete pending request page, specify the path to the SSL certificate file (\\EXCHCASRV01\CERT\certnew.cer) and then click **OK**.
4. Select the new certificate you just added, and then click **Edit**.
5. On the certificate page, click **Services**.
6. Select the services you want to assign to this certificate. At minimum, you should select **SMTP, POP** and **IIS**. Click **Save**.
7. If you receive the warning **Overwrite the existing default SMTP certificate**, click **OK**.

Assign certificate into Exchange Server. Do the following steps to assign certificates.

1. In the EAC, go to **Servers** , Click **Certificates**.
2. Select the new certificate and then, in the certificate details pane, verify that the following are true: **Status** shows **Valid, Assigned to services** shows **IIS** and **SMTP. Assign to services may show none.**
3. Select the **new certificate and** then Click **Edit,** Click **Services,** Select **SMTP, IMAP, POP, IIS** Click **Save.**
4. On the **Warning Override existing default certificate Page,** Click **Yes.**

Export the certificate and assign to other Exchange Client Access Server in the same organization. Do the following steps to export and assign the certificate.

1. In the EAC, go to **Servers** , Click **Certificates**. Select the Server EXCHCASSRV01 from the list.
2. Now select the newly assigned certificate, Click **Export Exchange Certificate...,**
3. On the Export Exchange Certificate Page, type the UNC path (\\EXCHCASSRV01\CERT\ExchangeCertificate.pfx) and password to export certificate into .pfx format. Click **Save.**

Import the certificate and assign to other Exchange Server in the same organization. Do the following steps to import and assign the certificate.

1. In the EAC, go to **Servers** , Click **Certificates**. Select the Server EXCHCASSRV02 from the list.
2. Click **Import Exchange Certificate...,**
3. On the Export Exchange Certificate Page, type the UNC path (\\EXCHCASSRV01\CERT\ExchangeCertificate.pfx) and password to import certificate into pfx format. Click **Next.**
4. On the Import Certificate Page, to specify the server you want to apply this certificate to, Click **Add +,** Select Server **EXCHCASSRV02.** Click **Add,** Click **Ok.** Click **Finish.**
5. Assign the imported certificate using previous steps.

Now repeat the above steps to import and assign the certificate to other exchange servers in your organization. Save the exported certificate into secure location. This exported certificate will be imported into load balancer and TMG 2010 server to publish Exchange.

3.7 Configure Outlook Web Access for External Users

After you've chosen your external domains and installed your certificate, you need to configure the external domains on the Client Access server's virtual directories and then configure your domain name service (DNS) records. The steps below configure the same external domain on the external URL of each virtual directory. If you want to configure different external domains on one or more virtual directory external URLs, you need to configure the external URLs manually.

1. Open the EAC by browsing to https://<FQDN of Client Access server>/ECP.
2. Enter your user name and password in **Domain\user name** and **Password** and then click **Sign in**.
3. Go to **Servers**, Click **Servers** and then Select CAS Server, click **Configure external access domain**.
4. Under **Select the Client Access servers to use with the external URL**, click **Add+**
5. Select the Client Access servers you want to configure and then click **Add**. After you've added all of the Client Access servers you want to configure, click **OK**.
6. In **Enter the domain name you will use with your external Client Access servers**, type webmail.superplaneteers.com. Click **Save**.
7. Go to **Servers**, Click **Servers**, select all Internet-facing Client Access server and then click **Edit**.
8. Click **Outlook Anywhere**.
9. In the **Specify the external hostname** field, specify the externally accessible FQDN of the Client Access server. For example, webmail.superplaneteers.com. Click **Allow SSL Offloading.**
10. Click **Save**.
11. Repeat step 1 to step 10 for all CAS Server.

After you've configured the external URL on the Client Access server virtual directories, you need to configure DNS records for Autodiscover, Outlook Web App, and mail flow. The DNS records should point to the external IP address of your Internet-facing Client Access server and use the externally accessible FQDNs that you've configured on your Client Access server. The following are examples of recommended DNS records that you should create to enable mail flow and external Client connectivity. Internet facing doesn't mean CAS server directly exposed to internet or in DMZ. Internet facing means you have published webmail using TMG that direct Outlook Anywhere protocol to CAS Server. That means CAS server's IP and location is always hidden from internet and stay in intranet.

FQDN	DNS record	Value

	type	
Superplaneteers.com	MX	webmail.superplaneteers.com
webmail.superplaneteers.com	A	IPv4 Public IP
Autodiscover.superplaneteers.com	A	IPv4 Public IP

This IPv4 Public IP remain same for webmail and Autodiscover. Also this IPv4 Public IP will be configured on the TCP/IP property of the external network interface of TMG 2010 Server or the VIP of the External Network on the TMG 2010 cluster. Make sure this public IP is routed to your premises towards TMG 2010 external NIC from the DNS and MX record Hoster (for example an ISP or Telco).

To verify that you have successfully configured the external URL on the Client Access server virtual directories, do the following:

1. In the EAC, go to **Servers**, Click **Virtual directories**.
2. In the **Select server** field, select the Internet-facing Client Access server.
3. Select a virtual directory and then, in the virtual directory details pane, verify that the **External URL** field is populated with the correct FQDN and service as shown below:

Virtual directory	External URL value
Autodiscover	No external URL displayed
ECP	https://webmail.superplaneteers.com/ecp
EWS	https://webmail.superplaneteers.com/EWS/Exchange.asmx
Microsoft-Server-ActiveSync	https://webmail.superplaneteers.com/Microsoft-Server-ActiveSync
OAB	https://webmail.superplaneteers.com/OAB
OWA	https://webmail.superplaneteers.com/owa
PowerShell	http://webmail.superplaneteers.com/PowerShell

To verify that you have successfully configured DNS, do the following:

1. Open a command prompt and run nslookup.exe.
2. In nslookup, look up the A record of each FQDN you created. Verify that the IP address that's returned for each FQDN is correct.
3. In nslookup, type set type=mx and then look up the accepted domain you added in previous steps. Verify that the value returned matches the FQDN of the Client Access server.

To verify that you have configured mail flow and external Client access, do the following:

1. In Outlook, on an ActiveSync device, or on both, create a new profile. Verify that Outlook or the mobile device successfully creates the new profile.
2. In Outlook, or on the mobile device, send a new message to an external recipient. Verify the external recipient receives the message.
3. In the external recipient's mailbox, reply to the message you just sent from the Exchange mailbox. Verify the Exchange mailbox receives the message.
4. Go to https://webmail.superplaneteers.com/owa and verify that there are no certificate warnings.

3.8 Verify an Exchange 2013 Installation

Open Elevated Windows PowerShell and run the following command to verify exchange installation. Run Get-ExchangeServer

Review the setup log file. By default, the logging method is set to Verbose. Information is available for each installed server role.

You can find the setup log file at %<system drive>%\ExchangeSetupLogs\ExchangeSetup.log. The <system drive> variable represents the root directory of the drive where the operating system is installed.

3.8.1 Configuring server certificates

In Exchange 2013, you can use the Certificate Wizard to request a digital certificate from a certification authority. After you've requested a digital certificate, you'll need to install it on the Client Access server.

You don't need to install digital certificates on the Mailbox servers in your organization. A self-signed certificate is installed by default on the Mailbox servers, and it doesn't need to be replaced. The Client Access servers in your organization implicitly trust the self-signed certificate on the Mailbox servers.

3.8.2 Configuring virtual directories using Windows PowerShell

The following examples show how to configure virtual directory using Windows PowerShell. There are several settings that you can configure on the virtual directories for the Offline Address Book (OAB), Exchange Web Services, Exchange ActiveSync, Outlook Web App, and the Exchange Administration Center. You can configure the virtual directories using the following commands.

- To configure Outlook Anywhere, run the following command.

  Enable-OutlookAnywhere -Server: EXCHCASSRV01 -ExternalHostName:webmail.superplaneteers.com -SSLOffloading $true

- To configure Exchange ActiveSync, run the following command.

  Set-ActiveSyncVirtualDirectory -Identity EXCHCASSRV01\Microsoft-Server-ActiveSync -ExternalUrl "https://webmail.superplaneteers.com/Microsoft-Server-ActiveSync"

- To configure the Exchange Web Services virtual directory, run the following command.

  Set-WebServicesVirtualDirectory -Identity EXCHCASSRV01\Microsoft-Server-ActiveSync -ExternalUrl "https://webmail.superplaneteers.com/EWS/Exchange.asmx"

- To configure the Offline Address Book, run the following command.

  Set-OabVirtualDirectory -Identity EXCHCASSRV01\Microsoft-Server-ActiveSync -ExternalUrl "https://webmail.superplaneteers.com/OAB"

3.9 Configure Exchange Organization

In Exchange 2013 Organisation, you can configure Federated Trust, Apps and Address List. Federated Trust will be discussed later on chapter 8. Apps let you see more in Outlook Client without leaving the outlook. By default, Bing Maps, Action items, Suggested Meeting and Unsubscribe apps are available for Outlook Client.

In the Address list, you will see All users, All Contacts, All Groups, All Rooms, Public Folders, and Default Global Address List.

3.10 Configure High Availability for Resilient Exchange Systems

Before deploying a DAG and creating mailbox database copies, make sure that the following system-wide recommendations are met:

- Domain Name System (DNS) must be running with Active Directory Domain Services. Host (A) record of Exchange server must present in DNS Server. Otherwise, Exchange won't function properly.
- Each Mailbox server in a DAG must be a member server in the same domain.
- Domain Controller must not be a member of DAG.
- NetBIOS of Exchange Server must be unique and available all the time.

3.10.1 Network Requirements

Microsoft recommends that each DAG have at least two networks: a single MAPI network and a single Replication network. This provides redundancy for the network and the network path, and enables the system to distinguish between a server failure and a network failure. Using a single network adapter prevents the system from distinguishing between these two types of failures. The following network requirements must be met before deploying DAG.

- MAPI and Replication networks must be routable, provide connectivity.
- MAPI and Replication Network must be placed in separate VLAN.
- Each network in each DAG member server is on its own network subnet that's separate from the subnet used by each other network in the server.
- Each DAG member server's Replication network can communicate with each other DAG member's Replication network.
- Replication or Heartbeat traffic must not communicate with DAG member MAPI networks or vice versa.

MAPI network adapter configuration

A network adapter intended for use by a MAPI network should be configured as described in the following table.

Networking Features	Setting
Client for Microsoft Networks	Enabled
QoS Packet Scheduler	Optionally enable
File and Printer Sharing for Microsoft Networks	Enabled
Internet Protocol Version 6 (TCP/IP v6)	Enabled
Internet Protocol Version 4 (TCP/IP v4)	Enabled
Link-Layer Topology Discovery Mapper I/O Driver	Enabled
Link-Layer Topology Discovery Responder	Enabled

The TCP/IP v4 properties for a MAPI network adapter are configured as follows:

- MAPI network must use Static IP.
- MAPI network provide connectivity with Active Directory Domain Services.
- The MAPI network typically uses a default gateway
- At least one DNS server address must be configured. Using multiple DNS servers is recommended for redundancy.
- The Register this connection's addresses in DNS check box should be selected.

Replication network adapter configuration

A network adapter intended for use by a Replication network should be configured as described in the following table.

Networking Features	Setting
Client for Microsoft Networks	Disabled
QoS Packet Scheduler	Optionally enable
File and Printer Sharing for Microsoft Networks	Disabled
Internet Protocol Version 6 (TCP/IP v6)	Enabled
Internet Protocol Version 4 (TCP/IP v4)	Enabled
Link-Layer Topology Discovery Mapper I/O Driver	Enabled
Link-Layer Topology Discovery Responder	Enabled

3.10.2 Preparing Base infrastructure

Each location contains the infrastructure elements that are necessary to operate a messaging infrastructure based on Exchange 2013, namely:

- Directory services (Active Directory Domain Services (AD DS))
- Domain Name System (DNS) name resolution
- Multiple Exchange 2013 Client Access servers
- Multiple Exchange 2013 Mailbox servers

3.10.3 TCP/IP Configuration

The settings for each network adapter in each node are detailed in the following table.

Name	IPv4 address	Subnet mask	Default gateway

EXCHMBXSRV1 (MAPI)	10.10.10.5	255.255.255.0	10.10.10.254
EXCHMBXSRV2 (MAPI)	10.10.10.6	255.255.255.0	10.10.10.254
EXCHMBXSRV1 (Replication)	192.168.2.1	255.255.255.0	No Default Gateway
EXCHMBXSRV2 (Replication)	192.168.2.2	255.255.255.0	No Default Gateway

3.10.4 Pre-Stage the Cluster Network Object for a DAG

Automated Cluster configuration may fail depending on the security configured in Active Directory. I strongly recommend that you pre-stage Cluster Object Name (CNO) in Active Directory. Here are the steps to configure CNO.

Pre-stage the CNO

1. Log on to Domain Controller. Open Active Directory Users and Computers.
2. Expand the forest node.
3. Right-click the managed organizational unit (OU) where Exchange Servers are placed, select **New** and then select **Computer**.
4. Type the computer account name for the CNO in the **Computer name** box. Computer name box must not be more than 15 character. For Example **EXCHDAG1** will be computer account in this case. This is the name that you'll use for the DAG itself. Click **OK** to create the account.
5. Right-click the new computer account, and then click **Disable Account**. Click **Yes** to confirm the disable action, and then click **OK**.

Assign permissions to the CNO

1. Log on to domain controller. Open Active Directory Users and Computers.
2. If Advanced Features aren't enabled, turn them on by clicking **View**, and then clicking **Advanced Features**.
3. Right-click the new computer account **EXCHDAG1** and then click **Properties**.
4. In **Properties**, on the **Security** tab, click **Add** to add the computer account for the first node (Example: EXCHMBXSRV01 mailbox server) and Exchange Trusted Subsystem Built in security group.
5. To add the Exchange Trusted Subsystem, type **Exchange Trusted Subsystem** in the **Enter the object names to select** field. Click **OK** to add the USG. Then select the Exchange Trusted Subsystem USG and in

Permissions for Exchange Trusted Subsystem field, select **Full Control** in the **Allow** column. Click **OK** to save the permission settings.

6. To add the computer account for the first node to be added to the DAG, click **Object Types**. In the **Object Types** dialog box, clear the **Built-in security principals, Groups**, and **Users** check boxes. Select the **Computers** check box. Click **OK**. In the **Enter the object names to select** field, type the name of the first Mailbox server to be added to the DAG, and then click **OK**. Then, select the first node's computer account, and in the **Permissions for EXCHMBXSRV01** field, select **Full Control** in the **Allow** column. Click **OK** to save the permission settings.

3.10.5 Database Availability Group Creation

Use the EAC to create a database availability group

1. In the EAC, Go to **Servers**, Click **Database Availability Group**.

2. Click **New+** to create a DAG.

3. On the **new database availability group** page, provide the following information for the DAG:

    - **Database availability group name** Use this field to type a valid and unique name for the DAG of up to 15 characters. The name is the corresponding Cluster Network Object (CNO) created in Active Directory during **Pre-Stage**.

    - **Witness server** Use this field to specify a witness server for the DAG. If you leave this field blank, the system will attempt to automatically select a Client Access server in the local Active Directory site that is not installed on a computer with the Mailbox server to be used as the witness server. If you specify a witness server, you must use either a host name or a fully-qualified domain name (FQDN). In addition, the witness server cannot be a member of the DAG.

    - **Witness directory** Use this field to type the path to a directory on the witness server that will be used to store witness data. If the directory doesn't exist, the system will create it for you on the witness server. If you leave this field blank, the default directory (%SystemDrive%\DAGFileShareWitnesses\<DAG FQDN>) will be created on the witness server.

- **Database availability group IP addresses** Use this field to assign one or more static IPv4 addresses to the DAG. Enter an IPv4 address and click to **add** it.

4. Click **Save** to create the database availability group.

You can use the following Windows PowerShell command to create and set properties of DAG member.

PowerShell Command	Purpose
New-DatabaseAvailabilityGroup	Create the DAG
Set-DatabaseAvailabilityGroup	Preconfigure an alternate witness server and alternate witness directory
Add-DatabaseAvailabilityGroupServer	Add Mailbox servers to the DAG.
Set-DatabaseAvailabilityGroup	Configure properties of the DAG

This example creates a DAG named EXCHDAG1 that is configured to use the witness server EXCHCASSRV1 and the local directory C:\DAGWitness.

New-DatabaseAvailabilityGroup -Name EXCHDAG1 -WitnessServer EXCHCASSRV01 -WitnessDirectory C:\DAGWitness -DatabaseAvailabilityGroupIPAddresses 10.10.10.10

This example creates a DAG named EXCHDAG2. EXCHDAG2 is configured to use the witness server EXCHCASSRV2 and the local directory C:\DAGWitness. EXCHDAG2 is assigned multiple static IP addresses because its DAG members have MAPI networks on different subnets.

New-DatabaseAvailabilityGroup -Name EXCHDAG2 -WitnessServer EXCHCASSRV2 - WitnessDirectory C:\DAGWitness2 -DatabaseAvailabilityGroupIPAddresses 10.10.10.9,192.168.2.10

Use the EAC to configure database availability group properties

1. In the EAC, go to **Servers**, Click **Database Availability Group**.

2. Select the DAG you want to configure and click **Edit**.

3. Use the **General** page to view DAG membership and operational status, and to configure the DAG's witness server, witness directory, and automatic network configuration:

    - Witness server
    - Witness directory
    - Operational servers
    - Configure the database group network manually

4. Use the **IP Addresses** page to view and modify the IP addresses assigned to the DAG.
    - Select an existing IP address and click to modify it.
    - Select an existing IP address and click the minus icon (delete) to remove it.
    - Enter an IP address and click to add it to the DAG.

5. Click **Save** to save any changes that were made.

The following command create a DAG with two static IP from two different subnets.

New-DatabaseAvailabilityGroup -Name EXCHDAG1 -WitnessServer EXCHCASSRV1 -WitnessDirectory C:\DAGWitness\EXCHDAG1.superplaneteers.com -DatabaseAvailabilityGroupIPAddresses 10.10.10.10,192.168.2.10

The following command create a DAG with alternative witness server.

Set-DatabaseAvailabilityGroup -Identity EXCHDAG1 -AlternateWitnessDirectory C:\DAGWitness\EXCHDAG1.superplaneteers.com -AlternateWitnessServer EXCHCASSRV2

You can use PowerShell command add DAG member into the DAG.

Add-DatabaseAvailabilityGroupServer -Identity EXCHDAG1 -MailboxServer EXCHMBXSRV1

Add-DatabaseAvailabilityGroupServer -Identity EXCHDAG1 -MailboxServer EXCHMBXSRV2

This example removes a Mailbox server named EXCHMBXSRV1 from a DAG named EXCHDAG1

Remove-DatabaseAvailabilityGroupServer -Identity EXCHDAG1 -MailboxServer
EXCHMBXSRV1

This example removes the configuration settings for Mailbox server named
EXCHMBXSRV1 from a DAG named EXCHDAG1.

Remove-DatabaseAvailabilityGroupServer -Identity DAG2 -MailboxServer
EXCHMBXSRV1 -ConfigurationOnly

The preceding command enables DAC mode for the DAG.

Set-DatabaseAvailabilityGroup -Identity EXCHDAG1 -DatacenterActivationMode
DagOnly

Use the EAC to manage database availability group membership

1. In the EAC, go to **Servers**, Click **Database Availability Group**.

2. Select the DAG you want to configure, and then click **Edit**.

   - To add one or more Mailbox servers to the DAG, click **Add**, select
     the server(s) from the list, click **Add**, and then click **OK**.
   - To remove one or more Mailbox servers from the DAG, select the
     server(s) and then click the minus (-) icon.

3. Click **Save** to save the changes. When the task has completed successfully,
   click **Close**.

To verify that you have successfully managed DAG membership, follow the steps:

- In the EAC, navigate to **Servers**, Click **Database Availability Groups**. The
  current DAG membership is displayed in the **Member Servers** column.

- In the PowerShell, run the following command to display DAG membership
  information: Get-DatabaseAvailabilityGroup <DAGName> | FL Servers

Use EAC to Add Mailbox Database Copies

1. In the EAC, go to **Servers** , Click **Databases,** Select the Database you want
   to add a copy

2. Click **More,** Click Add Database Copies, Type the Name of the Database same as the database you want to create a copy, select Mailbox Server where database will be copied. Click **Save.**

3.10.6 Mailbox Databases and Mailbox Database Copies

In chapter 2, section 2.12.4 we have discussed having four servers for DR purpose. In this section you will configure that DR scenario using for mailbox servers.

A lagged mailbox database copy is a mailbox database copy configured with a replay lag time value greater than 0. After creating the DAG and adding the Mailbox servers to the DAG, you can prepare to create mailbox databases and mailbox database copies. To meet criteria of failure resistance, you can configure each mailbox database with three non-lagged database copies, and one lagged database. The lagged will have a configured log replay delay of three days.

This configuration provides a total of four copies for each database (one active, two non-lagged passives, and a lagged passive). In this scenario you can have four active databases per server. With four active databases per server, and three passive copies of each database, you can have up to 16 database copies.

Each Mailbox server hosts an active mailbox database, two non-lagged passive database copies, and one lagged passive database. The lagged of each active mailbox database is hosted on a Mailbox server in the DR site.

To create this configuration, you have to run the following PowerShell command.

On EXCHMBXSRV1A, run the following commands.

Add-MailboxDatabase -Identity MANAGER-DB -MailboxServer EXCHMBXSRV2A
Add-MailboxDatabaseCopy -Identity MANAGER-DB -MailboxServer
EXCHMBXSRV2B
Add-MailboxDatabaseCopy -Identity MANAGER-DB -MailboxServer
EXCHMBXSRV1B -ReplayLagTime 3.00:00:00 -SeedingPostponed

You can utilize Suspend-MailboxDatabase and Resume-Mailboxdatabase command to see the functionality of DAG.

Suspend-MailboxDatabase -Identity MANAGER-DB\EXCHMBXSRV1B –
SuspendComment "Seed from EXCHMBXSRV2B" -Confirm:$False

Update-MailboxDatabase -Identity MANAGER-DB\EXCHMBXSRV1B -SourceServer EXCHMBXSRV2B

You can utilize Suspend-MailboxDatabase and Resume-Mailboxdatabase command to see the functionality of DAG.

Suspend-MailboxDatabase -Identity MANAGER-DB\EXCHMBXSRV1B -ActivationOnly

On EXCHMBXSRV2A, run the following commands.

Add-MailboxDatabase -Identity ASSISTANT-DB -MailboxServer EXCHMBXSRV1A
Add-MailboxDatabaseCopy -Identity ASSISTANT-DB -MailboxServer EXCHMBXSRV1B
Add-MailboxDatabaseCopy -Identity ASSISTANT-DB -MailboxServer EXCHMBXSRV2B -ReplayLagTime 3.00:00:00 —SeedingPostponed

You can utilize Suspend-MailboxDatabase and Resume-Mailboxdatabase command to see the functionality of DAG.

Suspend-MailboxDatabase -Identity ASSISTANT-DB\EXCHMBXSRV2B -SuspendComment "Seed from EXCHMBXSRV1B" -Confirm:$False

Update-MailboxDatabase -Identity ASSISTANT-DB\EXCHMBXSRV2B -SourceServer EXCHMBXSRV1B

You can utilize Suspend-MailboxDatabase and Resume-Mailboxdatabase command to see the functionality of DAG.

Suspend-MailboxDatabase -Identity ASSISTANT-DB\EXCHMBXSRV2B -ActivationOnly

On EXCHMBXSRV1B, run the following commands.

Add-MailboxDatabase -Identity GENERAL-DB -MailboxServer EXCHMBXSRV2B
Add-MailboxDatabaseCopy -Identity GENERAL-DB -MailboxServer EXCHMBXSRV2A
Add-MailboxDatabaseCopy -Identity GENERAL-DB -MailboxServer EXCHMBXSRV1A -ReplayLagTime 3.00:00:00 —SeedingPostponed

You can utilize Suspend-MailboxDatabase and Resume-Mailboxdatabase command to see the functionality of DAG.

Suspend-MailboxDatabase -Identity GENERAL-DB\EXCHMBXSRV1A -SuspendComment "Seed from EXCHMBXSRV2A" -Confirm:$False

Update-MailboxDatabase -Identity GENERAL-DB\EXCHMBXSRV1A -SourceServer EXCHMBXSRV2A

You can utilize Suspend-MailboxDatabase and Resume-Mailboxdatabase command to see the functionality of DAG.

Suspend-MailboxDatabase -Identity GENERAL-DB\EXCHMBXSRV1A -ActivationOnly

On EXCHMBXSRV2B, run the following commands.

Add-MailboxDatabase -Identity EXECUTIVE-DB -MailboxServer EXCHMBXSRV1B
Add-MailboxDatabaseCopy -Identity EXECUTIVE-DB -MailboxServer EXCHMBXSRV1A
Add-MailboxDatabaseCopy -Identity EXECUTIVE-DB -MailboxServer EXCHMBXSRV2A -ReplayLagTime 3.00:00:00 -SeedingPostponed

You can utilize Suspend-MailboxDatabase and Resume-Mailboxdatabase command to see the functionality of DAG.

Suspend-MailboxDatabase -Identity EXECUTIVE-DB\EXCHMBXSRV2A – SuspendComment "Seed from EXCHMBXSRV1A" -Confirm:$False

Update-MailboxDatabase -Identity EXECUTIVE-DB\EXCHMBXSRV2A -SourceServer EXCHMBXSRV1A

You can utilize Suspend-MailboxDatabase and Resume-Mailboxdatabase command to see the functionality of DAG.

Suspend-MailboxDatabase -Identity EXECUTIVE-DB\EXCHMBXSRV2A -ActivationOnly

Note that you can use Add-MailboxDatabase, Update-MailboxDatabase and Suspend-MailboxDatabase, and Resume-MailboxDatabase PowerShell command to create, update, suspend and resume a mailbox database.

3.10.7 Creating a Database Availability Group Network

Use the EAC to create a database availability group network

1. In the EAC, go to **Servers** , Click **Database Availability Group**.

2. Select the DAG you want to configure and then click **Add**.

3. On the **new database availability group network** page, provide the following information:

   - **Database availability group network name** Use this field to type a name for the network that is unique in the DAG.

   - **Description** Use this field to provide a text description of the DAG network.

   - **Subnets** Use this field to associate one or more subnets with the DAG network. Click + to add a subnet, click to edit a subnet, and click minus (-) to remove a subnet.

4. Click **Save** to create the database availability group network.

You can use PowerShell to create and verify a database availability group network

New-DatabaseAvailabilityGroupNetwork -DatabaseAvailabilityGroup EXCHDAG1 -Name ReplicationDagNetwork02 -Description "Replication network 2" -Subnets 192.168.2.0/24 -ReplicationEnabled:$True

Get-DatabaseAvailabilityGroupNetwork <DAGNetworkName> | FL

Use the EAC to configure database availability group network properties

1. In the EAC, go to **Servers**, Click **Database Availability Group**.

2. Select the DAG you want to configure, and in the Details pane, under the DAG network you want to configure, choose:

   - **Disable Replication** or **Enable Replication** Use these options to configure the replication settings for the DAG network.

- o **Remove** Use this option to remove a DAG network. Before you can remove a DAG network, you must first remove all associated subnets from the DAG network.

- o **View details** Use this option to configure DAG network properties, such as the name, description and associated subnets for the DAG network, to view the network interfaces associated with those subnets, and to enable or disable replication for the DAG network.

You can use the PowerShell to configure database availability group network properties

Set-DatabaseAvailabilityGroupNetwork -Subnets 10.10.10.0/24 -Identity EXCHDAG1\MapiDagNetwork

Get-DatabaseAvailabilityGroupNetwork <DAGNetworkName> | FL

3.10.8 Test Database Availability Group and Database Copy

To verify that you have successfully configured the DAG, run the following command: Get-DatabaseAvailabilityGroup <DAGName> | FL

To verify the overall health of the DAG, run Test-ReplicationHealth cmdlet.

To verify replication and replay activity, run the Get-MailboxDatabaseStatus cmdlet.

Run Move-ActiveMailboxDatabase cmdlet to perform a series of database switchovers and server switchovers.

3.10.9 Recover a Database availability Group member
Before you run the following command, troubleshoot Exchange Server 2013 to find out any issue within Exchange. You should recover a server as a last option that means when Mailbox Server isn't responding to DAG or CAS array at all, use Setup /m:RecoverServer to recover a server.

3.10.10 Configuring Root Path of Database and Volumes

Use the following example to configure the root path for the databases.

Set-DatabaseAvailabilityGroup EXCHDAG1 -AutoDagDatabasesRootFolderPath "H:\EXCHData"

Use the following example to configure the root path for the storage volumes.

Set-DatabaseAvailabilityGroup EXCHDAG1 -AutoDagVolumesRootFolderPath
"H:\EXCHVOLS"

To verify that you have successfully configured the root paths for databases and volumes, run the following command:

Get-DatabaseAvailabilityGroup EXCHDAG1 | fl auto

Use the following example to configure AutoReseed setting for a DAG that is configured with 4 databases per volume.

Set-DatabaseAvailabilityGroup EXCHDAG1 -AutoDagDatabaseCopiesPerVolume 4

To verify that you have successfully configured the number of databases per volume, run the following command:

Get-DatabaseAvailabilityGroup EXCHDAG1 | fl auto

Next, create the directories that correspond to the root directories you configured in previous steps. The following example shows how to create the default directories using the command prompt:

md H:\EXCHDATA
md H:\EXCHVOLS

To verify that you have successfully configured the root directories for databases and volumes, run the following command: Dir H:\

For every volume that will be used for databases (including spare volumes), use the Windows Disk Management application (diskmgmt.msc) to mount each volume in a mounted folder under H:\EXCHVOLS. For example, if there are 2 volumes with databases and 1 spare volume, then mount the volumes to the following mounted folders:

- H:\EXCHVOLS\Volume1
- H:\EXCHVOLS\Volume2
- H:\EXCHVOLS \Volume3

To verify that you have successfully mounted the volume folders, run the following command: Dir H:\

Next, create the database directories under the root path H:\EXCHDATA. The following example illustrates how to create directories for 4 databases.

md H:\EXCHDATA\db001
md H:\EXCHDATA\db002
md H:\EXCHDATA\db003
md H:\EXCHDATA\db004

To verify that you have successfully mounted the database folders, run the following command: Dir H:\ExchData

Next, create two directories underneath the folders you created in previous steps, one for each database and one for each database's log stream that will be stored on the same volume. The following example illustrates how to create directories for 4 databases that will be stored on Volume 1.

md H:\EXCHVOLS\Volume1\db001.db
md H:\EXCHVOLS \Volume1\db001.log
md H:\EXCHVOLS\Volume1\db002.db
md H:\EXCHVOLS \Volume1\db002.log
md H:\EXCHVOLS\Volume1\db003.db
md H:\EXCHVOLS \Volume1\db003.log
md H:\EXCHVOLS\Volume1\db004.db
md H:\EXCHVOLS \Volume1\db004.log

Repeat the above commands for databases on every volume.

To verify that you have successfully created the database directory structure, run the following command: Dir H:\ExchVols\Volume1

Create the mount points for each database and link the mount point to the correct volume.

Mountvol.exe H:\EXCHDATA\db001 db001

To verify that you have successfully created the mount points for the database, run the following command: Mountvol.exe H:\EXCHDATA\db001 /L

Create the databases in the appropriate folder. The following example illustrates how to create a database that is stored in the newly created directory and mount point structure.

New-MailboxDatabase -Name db001 -Server EXCHMBXSRV1 -LogFolderPath H:\ExchData\db001\db001.log -EdbFilePath H:\ExchData\db001\db001.db\db001.edb

To verify that you have successfully created mount points for the database, run the following command: Get-MailboxDatabase db001 | fl path

Database properties that are returned should indicate that the database file and log files are being stored in the above folders.

To verify that you have configured AutoReseed for a DAG, do the following:

Get-DatabaseAvailabilityGroup DAG1 | fl auto

Run the following command to verify the directory structure is configured correctly (below are the default paths; if necessary, substitute the paths for the paths you are using):

Dir H:\EXCHDATA /s
Dir H:\EXCHVOLS /s

3.10.11 Removing Database Availability Group

Use the EAC to remove a database availability group

1. Navigate to **Servers**, Click **Database availability groups**.
2. Select the DAG you want to remove and click **Delete**
3. Click **Yes** to confirm the warning and remove the DAG.

You can use the PowerShell to remove a database availability group

Remove-DatabaseAvailabilityGroup -Identity DAG1 -Confirm:$False

3.11 Configure Mailbox Database and Database Properties

3.11.1 Configure mailbox database properties

1. In the EAC, go to **Servers** , Click **Databases**.

2. Select the database you want to configure.

3. In the Details pane, under Database Copies, click **View details** for the desired database.

- **Database** Displays the name of the selected database.

- **Mailbox server** Displays the name of the Mailbox server that hosts the selected database .

- **Content index state** Displays the current state of the content index for the selected database .

- **Status** Displays the current status of the selected database .

- **queue length** Indicates the number of log files waiting to be copied to the selected database . This field is relevant only for passive database copies.

- **Replay queue length** Indicates the number of log files waiting to be replayed into the selected database. This field is relevant only for passive database copies.

- **Error messages** Displays any error messages for database copies that have a status of Failed or Failed and Suspended.

- **Latest available log time** Date and time stamp of the most recently generated log file on the active of the database. This field is relevant only for passive database copies. On active database copies (replicated and standalone), this field will say **never**.

- **Last inspected log time** Date and time stamp of the last log file that was inspected by the LogInspector on the selected database . This field is relevant only for passive database copies. On active database copies (replicated and standalone), this field will say **never**.

- **Last copied log time** Date and time stamp of the last log file that was copied by the LogCopier on the selected database. This field is relevant only for passive database copies. On active database copies (replicated and standalone), this field will say **never**.

- **Last replayed log time** Date and time stamp of the last log file that was replayed by the LogReplayer into the selected database. This field is relevant only for passive database copies. On active database copies (replicated and standalone), this field will say **never**.

- **Activation preference number** The activation preference number is used as part of Active Manager's best selection process and to balance the DAG by redistributing active mailbox databases throughout the DAG using the RedistributeActiveDatabases.ps1 script. The value for activation preference is a number equal to or greater than 1, where 1 is at the top of the preference order. The number cannot be larger than the number of copies of the mailbox database.

- **Replay lag time (days)** The amount of time that the Microsoft Exchange Information Store service should wait before replaying log files that have been copied by the Microsoft Exchange Replication service to the passive database. Setting this parameter to a value greater than 0 creates a lagged database. The default setting for this value is 0 days. The maximum allowable value for this setting is 14 days.

3.11.2 Configure mailbox database properties using PowerShell

This example configures a mailbox database with an activation preference number of 3.

Set-MailboxDatabase -Identity GENERAL-DB\EX3 -ActivationPreference 3

This example configures a of a database named MANAGER-DB that is hosted on EXCHMBXSRV1 with a replay lag time and truncation lag time of 1 day, and an activation preference number of 2.

Set-MailboxDatabase -Identity MANAGER-DB\Server1 -ReplayLagTime 1.0:0:0 - TruncationLagTime 1.0:0:0 -ActivationPreference 2

3.11.3 Enable, Disable circular logging

As a best practice, do not enable circular logging, however you can turn the circular logging on in the following scenario:

- Moving Database to new location
- Local or remote migration of bulk mailboxes

To enable circular logging follow the steps in PowerShell prompt.

Get-MailboxDatabase MANAGER-DB | fl lag

Set-MailboxDatabase MANAGER-DB -CircularLoggingEnabled $false

Set-MailboxDatabase MANAGER-DB -CircularLoggingEnabled $true

3.11.4 Configuring the activation policy for a mailbox database

1. In the EAC, go to **Servers** , Click **Databases**.

2. Select the database that you want to configure.

3. In the Details pane, under Database Copies, locate the database you want to configure and click **Suspend**.

4. Optionally, add a comment, and check the box that says **This can only be activated by manual intervention**.

5. Click **Save** to save the configuration changes for the mailbox database .

3.11.4 Suspend or resume a database for activation

This example blocks the database MANAGER-DB on the server EXCHMBXSRV2 for activation.

Suspend-MailboxDatabase -Identity MANAGER-DB\EXCHMBXSRV2 -ActivationOnly

This example resumes the database MANAGER-DB on the server EXCHMBXSRV2 for activation.

Resume-MailboxDatabase -Identity MANAGER-DB\EXCHMBXSRV2

3.11.5 Configure the activation policy for a server

This example configures the database copies on server EXCHMBXSRV2 as blocked for activation.

Set-MailboxServer -Identity EXCHMBXSRV2 -DatabaseAutoActivationPolicy Blocked

This example configures the database copies on server EXCHMBXSRV2 as blocked for out-of-site activation.

Set-MailboxServer -Identity EXCHMBXSRV2 -DatabaseAutoActivationPolicy IntrasiteOnly

This example configures the database copies on server EXCHMBXSRV1 as unblocked for activation.

Set-MailboxServer -Identity EXCHMBXSRV1 -DatabaseAutoActivationPolicy Unrestricted

3.11.6 Update a mailbox database
1. In the EAC, go to **Servers**, Click **Databases**.
2. Select the mailbox database whose passive you want to update.
3. In the Details pane, under Database Copies, click **Suspend** under the passive database you want to seed. Provide any optional comments, and click save.
4. In the Details pane, under Database Copies, click **Update** under the passive database you want to seed.
5. By default, the active of the database is used as the source database for seeding. If you prefer to use a passive of the database for seeding, click browse... to select the server containing the passive database you want to use for the source.
6. Click save to update the passive database.

3.11.7 Update a mailbox database using Windows PowerShell

This example shows how to seed a database named MANAGER-DB on EXCHMBXSRV1.

Update-MailboxDatabase -Identity MANAGER-DB\EXCHMBXSRV1

This example shows how to seed a database named MANAGER-DB on EXCHMBXSRV1 using EXCHMBXSRV2 as the source Mailbox server for the seed.

Update-MailboxDatabase -Identity MANAGER-DB\EXCHMBXSRV1 -SourceServer EXCHMBXSRV2

This example shows how to seed a database named MANAGER-DB on EXCHMBXSRV1 without seeding the content index catalog.

Update-MailboxDatabase -Identity MANAGER-DB\EXCHMBXSRV1 -DatabaseOnly

This example shows how to seed the content index catalog for a database named MANAGER-DB on EXCHMBXSRV1 without seeding the database file.

Update-MailboxDatabase -Identity MANAGER-DB\EXCHMBXSRV1 -CatalogOnly

3.11.8 Manually moving a database

In this example you will move MANAGER-DB to a different server. To do that follow steps mentioned here.

If circular logging is enabled for the database, it must be disabled before proceeding.

Set-MailboxDatabase MANAGER-DB -CircularLoggingEnabled $false

Dismount the database using the Dismount-Database cmdlet in source server, as shown in this example. Dismount-Database MANAGER-DB -Confirm $false

Mount the database using Mount-Database cmdlet to the destination server, as shown in this example. Mount-Database MANAGER-DB

On the destination server that will host the database files from the external drive or network share to the same path as the active database. For example, if the active database path is G:\MANAGER-DB\MANAGER-DB.edb and log file path is G:\MANAGER-DB, then you would move the database files to G:\MANAGER-DB on the server that will host the database.

Add the mailbox database using the Add-MailboxDatabase cmdlet with the SeedingPostponed parameter, as shown in this example.

Add-MailboxDatabase -Identity MANAGER-DB -MailboxServer EXCHMBXSRV2 -SeedingPostponed

If circular logging was enabled for the database in source server for any reason, enable it again by using the Set-MailboxDatabase cmdlet, as shown in this example.

Set-MailboxDatabase MANAGER-DB -CircularLoggingEnabled $true

To verify that you have successfully seeded a mailbox database, run the following command: Get-MailboxDatabaseStatus MANAGER-DB

3.11.9 Suspend a mailbox database
1. In the EAC, go to **Servers**, Click **Databases**.
2. Select the database whose you want to suspend.
3. In the Details pane, under Database Copies, click **Suspend** under the database you want to suspend.
4. In the Comments field, add an optional comment of up to 512 characters specifying the reason for the suspension.
5. To suspend the database for automatic activation, check the box that says This can only be activated by manual intervention.
6. Click save to suspend the database .

3.11.10 Resume a mailbox database
1. In the EAC, go to **Servers** , Click **Databases**.
2. Select the database whose you want to resume.
3. In the Details pane, under Database Copies, click **Resume** under the database you want to resume.
4. Click yes to resume the database .

3.11.11 Move the active mailbox database
1. In the EAC, go to **Servers** , Click **Databases**.
2. Select the database whose you want to activate.
3. In the Details pane, under Database Copies, click **Activate** under the database you want to activate.
4. Click yes to activate the database .

3.11.12 Move/switchover the active mailbox database to different server

In this example the database EXECUTIVE-DB hosted on EXCHMBXSRV2 is activated and mounted as the new active mailbox database. This command makes EXECUTIVE-DB the new active mailbox database and it doesn't override the database mount dial settings on EXCHMBXSRV2.

Move-ActiveMailboxDatabase EXECUTIVE-DB -ActivateOnServer EXCHMBXSRV2 - MountDialOverride:None

This example performs a switchover of the database ASSISTANT-DB to the Mailbox server EXCHMBXSRV1. When the command completes, EXCHMBXSRV1 hosts the active of ASSISTANT-DB. Because the MountDialOverride parameter is set to None, EXCHMBXSRV1 mounts the database using its own defined database auto mount dial settings.

Move-ActiveMailboxDatabase ASSISTANT-DB -ActivateOnServer EXCHMBXSRV1 -MountDialOverride:None

This example performs a switchover of the database MANAGER-DB to the Mailbox server EXCHMBXSRV2. When the command completes, EXCHMBXSRV2 hosts the active of MANAGER-DB. Because the MountDialOverride parameter is specified with a value of Good Availability, EXCHMBXSRV2 mounts the database using a database auto mount dial setting of GoodAvailability.

Move-ActiveMailboxDatabase MANAGER-DB -ActivateOnServer EXCHMBXSRV2 -MountDialOverride:GoodAvailability

This example performs a server switchover for the Mailbox server EXCHMBXSRV1. All active mailbox database copies on EXCHMBXSRV1 will be activated on one or more other Mailbox servers with healthy copies of the active databases on EXCHMBXSRV1. Move-ActiveMailboxDatabase -Server EXCHMBXSRV1

3.11.13 Activating a lagged mailbox database to a specific point in time
You can't use the Exchange Administration Center (EAC) to activate a lagged mailbox database to a specific point in time. Instead, you perform a series of steps using the PowerShell and the command line.

Suspend replication for the lagged database being activated by using the Suspend-MailboxDatabase cmdlet, as shown in this example.

Suspend-MailboxDatabase MANAGER-DB\EXCHMBXSRV1 -SuspendComment "Activate lagged of MANAGER-DB on Server EXCHMBXSRV1" -Confirm:$false

Optionally (to preserve a lagged), take a file system-based (non-Exchange aware) Volume Shadow Service (VSS) snapshot of the volumes containing the database and its log files. You can use the vssadmin.exe tool that's included in Windows to take a VSS snapshot, as shown in this example.

vssadmin create shadow /For=H:\mountpoints\db01
vssadmin create shadow /For=H:\mountpoints\db01_logs

At this point, you have shadow copies outstanding for the database and log volumes. Continuing to perform this procedure on the existing volume would incur a on write performance penalty. If this isn't desirable, you can use the database and log files to another volume to perform the recovery.

Determine which log files are required to replay into the database to meet your point-in-time requirement for this recovery (based on log file date and time, as shown in Windows Explorer). All logs created after this point should be moved to a different directory, until the recovery process is completed, and the logs are no longer needed.

Delete the checkpoint (.chk) file for the database.

Use Eseutil to perform the recovery operation, as shown in this example.

This step may take a considerable amount of time, depending on several factors, such as the length of the replay lag time, the number of log files generated during that period, and the speed at which your hardware can replay those logs into the database being recovered. To replay log file you can Eseutil.exe /r e*XX* /a command.

After log replay is finished, the database is in a clean shutdown state and can be copied and used for recovery purposes. After the recovery process is complete, resume replication for the database that was used as part of the recovery process, as shown in this example.

Resume-MailboxDatabase MANAGER-DB\EXCHMBXSRV1

3.11.14 Activating a lagged mailbox database by replaying log files

Optionally (to preserve a lagged), take a file system-based (non-Exchange aware) Volume Shadow Service (VSS) snapshot of the volumes containing the database and its log files.

Suspend replication for the lagged database being activated by using the Suspend-MailboxDatabase cmdlet, as shown in this example.

Suspend-MailboxDatabase MANAGER-DB\EX3 -SuspendComment "Activate lagged of MANAGER-DB on Server EX3" -Confirm:$false

You can use the vssadmin.exe tool that's included in Windows to take a VSS snapshot, as shown in this example.

vssadmin create shadow /For=H:\mountpoints\db01
vssadmin create shadow /For=H:\mountpoints\db01_logs

At this point, you have shadow copies outstanding for the database and log volumes. Continuing to perform this procedure on the existing volume would incur a write performance penalty. If this isn't desirable, you can use the database and log files to another volume to perform the recovery.

Activate the lagged mailbox database using the Move-ActiveMailboxDatabase cmdlet with the SkipLagChecks parameter, as shown in this example:

Move-ActiveMailboxDatabase MANAGER-DB -ActivateOnServer EX3 -SkipLagChecks

3.11.16 Remove a mailbox database
1. In the EAC, go to **Servers**, Click **Databases**.
2. Select the mailbox database whose you want to remove.
3. In the Details pane, locate the passive you want to remove and click **Remove**.
4. Confirm the removal on the warning dialog by clicking **yes**.
5. Click **Ok** to confirm the removal after reviewing any messages.
6. Manually delete any database and transaction log files from the server from which the database is being removed.

3.11.17 Remove a mailbox database using PowerShell

This example removes a database named MANAGER-DB from a Mailbox server named EXCHMBXSRV1.

Remove-MailboxDatabase -Identity MANAGER-DB\EXCHMBXSRV1 -Confirm:$False

3.11.18 Monitoring Database Availability Group and Exchange Server

Monitors have various states. In addition, monitors define how much time after a failure that a responder is executed, as well as the workflow of the recovery action. From a system state perspective, monitors have two states:

- Healthy
- Unhealthy

From an administrative perspective, monitors have additional states that will appear in PowerShell:

- Degraded
- Disabled
- Unavailable
- Repairing

You can use the Get-MailboxDatabaseStatus cmdlet to view status information about mailbox database copies. The following table describes possible values for the status of a mailbox database.

Database status	Description
Failed	The mailbox database is in a Failed state and it isn't able to replay log files. The status will automatically change to Healthy once the issue has been resolved.
Seeding	The mailbox database is being seeded, the content index for the mailbox database is being seeded, or both are being seeded. Upon successful completion of seeding, the status should change to Initializing.
SeedingSource	The mailbox database is being used as a source for a database seeding operation.
Suspended	The mailbox database is in a Suspended state as a result of a manual intervention suspending the database by running the Suspend-MailboxDatabase cmdlet.
Healthy	The mailbox database is successfully working and replaying log files.
ServiceDown	The Microsoft Exchange Replication service isn't available or running on the server that hosts the mailbox database.
Initializing	The mailbox database will be in an Initializing state when a database has been created, when the Microsoft Exchange Replication service is starting or has just been started.
Resynchronizing	The mailbox database and its log files are being compared with the active of the database to check for any divergence between the two

	copies.
Mounted	The database is online and accepting client connections.
Dismounted	The database is offline and not accepting client connections.
Mounting	The database is coming online and not yet accepting client connections.
Dismounting	The database is going offline and terminating client connections.
DisconnectedAndHealthy	The mailbox database is no longer connected to the active database and it was in the Healthy state when the loss of connection occurred.
Disconnected AndResynchronizing	The mailbox database is no longer connected to the active database, and it was in the Resynchronizing state.
FailedAndSuspended	The Failed and Suspended states have been set simultaneously by the system because a failure was detected, and because resolution of the failure explicitly requires manual intervention.
SinglePageRestore	This state indicates that a single page restore operation is occurring on the mailbox database.

You can use the Test-ReplicationHealth cmdlet to view continuous replication status information about mailbox database copies. This cmdlet can be used to check all aspects of the replication and replay status to provide a complete overview of a specific Mailbox server in a DAG.

Test name	Description
ClusterService	Verifies that the Cluster service is running and reachable on the specified DAG member
ReplayService	Verifies that the Microsoft Exchange Replication service is running and reachable on the specified DAG member.
ActiveManager	Verifies that the instance of Active Manager running on the specified DAG member
TasksRpcListener	Verifies that the tasks remote procedure call (RPC) server is running and reachable on the specified DAG member
TcpListener	Verifies that the TCP log listener is running and reachable on the specified DAG member

DagMembersUp	Verifies that all DAG members are available, running, and reachable.
ClusterNetwork	Verifies that all cluster-managed networks on the specified DAG member is available.
QuorumGroup	Verifies that the default cluster group (quorum group) is in a healthy and online state.
FileShareQuorum	Verifies that the witness server and witness directory and share configured for the DAG are reachable.
DBSuspended	Checks whether any mailbox database copies are in a state of Suspended on the specified DAG member
DBFailed	Checks whether any mailbox database copies are in a state of Failed on the specified DAG member
DBInitializing	Checks whether any mailbox database copies are in a state of Initializing on the specified DAG member, or if no DAG member is specified, on the local server.
DBDisconnected	Checks whether any mailbox database copies are in a state of Disconnected on the specified DAG member, or if no DAG member is specified, on the local server.
DBLogKeepingUp	Verifies that logging and inspection by the passive copies of databases on the specified DAG member is able to keep up with log generation activity on the active .
DBLogReplayKeepingUp	Verifies that replay activity for the passive copies of databases on the specified DAG member (or if no DAG member is specified, on the local server) is able to keep up with logging and inspection activity.

Windows includes two categories of event logs: Windows logs, and Applications and Services logs. The Windows logs category includes the event logs available in previous versions of Windows: Application, Security, and System event logs.

Applications and Services logs are a new category of event logs. These logs store events from a single application or component rather than events that might have system-wide impact. This new category of event logs is referred to as an application's crimson channel.

Exchange 2013 logs events to crimson channels in the Applications and Services logs area. You can view these channels by performing these steps:

1. Open Event Viewer. In the console tree, navigate to **Applications and Services Logs** , Click **Microsoft** , Click **Exchange**.

2. Under **Exchange**, select a crimson channel: **HighAvailability** or **MailboxDatabaseFailureItems**.

Exchange 2013 includes a script called CollectOverMetrics.ps1, which can be found in the Scripts folder. CollectOverMetrics.ps1 reads DAG member event logs to gather information about database operations (such as database mounts, moves, and failovers) over a specific time period. For each operation, the script records the following information:

- Identity of the database
- Time at which the operation began and ended
- Servers on which the database was mounted at the start and finish of the operation
- Reason for the operation
- If the operation was successful, including the error details if the operation failed

The following example collects metrics for all databases that match DB (which includes a wildcard character) in a DAG named EXCHDAG1. After the metrics are collected, an HTML report is generated and displayed.

CollectOverMetrics.ps1 -DatabaseAvailabilityGroup EXCHDAG1 -Database:"DB" -GenerateHTMLReport -ShowHTMLReport

The following examples demonstrate ways that the summary HTML report may be filtered. The first uses the Database parameter, which takes a list of database names.

CollectOverMetrics -SummariseCsvFiles (dir .csv) -Database MailboxDatabase123,MailboxDatabase456

CollectOverMetrics -SummariseCsvFiles (dir .csv) -ReportFilter { $_.DatabaseName -notlike "Mailbox Database" }

CollectOverMetrics -SummariseCsvFiles (dir .csv) -ReportFilter { ($_.ActiveOnStart -like "EXCHCASSRV1") -and ($_.ActiveOnEnd -notlike "EXCHCASSRV1") }

CollectReplicationMetrics.ps1 is another health metric script included in Exchange 2013. This script provides an active form of monitoring because it collects metrics in real time, while the script is running. The following example gathers one hour's worth of data from all the servers in the DAG "EXCHDAG1", sampled at one minute intervals, and then generates a summary report.

CollectReplicationMetrics.ps1 -DagName EXCHDAG1 -Duration "01:00:00" - Frequency "00:01:00" –ReportPath

CHAPTER 4

In This Chapter

- Create and configure advanced mail flow
- Create and configure mail routing
- Configure accepted domain
- Configure Anti-Spam Agent
- Publish Exchange 2013 via TMG 2010
- Redirect Exchange OWA from HTTP to HTTPS

Chapter4. Advanced Configuration of Mail Flow and Message Delivery

4.1 Configure Exchange Mail Routing Settings in Active Directory

As discussed earlier in **chapter2**, it is an important design factor that you configure Active Directory Sites with optimum and least cost routing path because Microsoft Exchange Server 2013 references the IP site link objects in Active Directory to find the least-cost routing path. If your Active Directory IP site link costs and traffic flow aren't designed according to Microsoft best practice you should design AD Sites before deploying Exchange Server 2013. Designing and implanting Active Directory using Microsoft best practices guidelines is out of scope for this book. Visit http://microsoftguru.com.au to obtain a free design best practices.

Configure an Exchange-specific cost on an Active Directory IP site link

A lower cost value indicates a more preferred route. To set an Exchange-specific cost on an Active Directory site link, run the following command:

Set-AdSiteLink <ADSiteLinkIdentity> -ExchangeCost <Integer | $null>

This example sets an Exchange-specific cost of 10 on the IP site link named IPSiteLinkPerthAlbany.

Set-AdSiteLink IPSiteLinkPerthAlbany -ExchangeCost 10

This example clears the Exchange cost from the IP site link named IPSiteLinkPerthAlbany.

Set-AdSiteLink IPSiteLinkPerthAlbany -ExchangeCost $null

To verify that you have successfully set an Exchange cost on an Active Directory site link, run the following command:

Get-AdSiteLink | Format-List Name,ExchangeCost

Configure an Active Directory site as a hub site

When a hub site exists along the least cost routing path for a message, the message must be routed through the hub site. If this isn't the case, you need to assign Exchange-specific costs to the IP site links to make the least cost routing path go through the selected sites.

To configure an Active Directory site as a hub site, run the following command:

Set-AdSite <ADSiteIdentity> -HubSiteEnabled $true

This example configures the Active Directory site named Site A as a hub site.

Set-AdSite "Albany" -HubSiteEnabled $true

This example removes the hub site attribute from the Active Directory site named Site B.

Set-AdSite "Kalbarri" -HubSiteEnabled $false

To verify that you have successfully configured an Active Directory site as a hub site, run the following command:

Get-AdSite | Format-List Name,HubSiteEnabled

4.2 Create a Send Connector for Email (Sent to the Internet)

By default, Microsoft Exchange Server 2013 create a receive connector not send connector meaning you cannot send mail outside of your domain when you install

Exchange 2013 first time. To send mail outside your domain, you need to create a Send connector.

Use the EAC to create a send connector for email sent to the Internet

1. In the EAC, navigate to **Mail flow**, Click **Send connectors**, and then click **Add +**.
2. In the **New send connector** wizard, specify a name for the send connector and then select **Internet** for the **Type**. Click **Next**.
3. Verify that **MX record associated with recipient domain** is selected, which specifies that the connector uses the domain name system (DNS) to route mail. Click **Next**.
4. Under **Address space**, click **Add +**. In the **Add domain** window, make sure SMTP is listed as the **Type**. For **Fully Qualified Domain Name (FQDN)**, enter * which indicates that this send connector applies to messages addressed to any domain. Click **Save**.
5. Make sure **Scoped send connector** is not selected and then click **Next**.
6. For **Source server**, click **Add +**. In the **Select a server** window, select a Mailbox server that will be used to send mail to the Internet via the Client Access server and click **Add +**. After you've selected the server, click **Add +**. Click **OK**.
7. Click **Finish**.

Use the PowerShell to route mail through the Client Access server

If you are working in an environment with a large number of messaging servers then setting up mail route consolidate route email by the following cmdlet.

This example sets the FrontendProxyEnabled parameter to $true on a Send connector.
Set-SendConnector "Internal Send Connector" -FrontendProxyEnabled $true

4.3 Create a Send Connector to Route Outbound Email through a Smart Host

A smart host act like a secondary mail server when primary server goes down. Smart host keeps all the email until primary server is back online. Once primary mail server is back online then smart host resends all the email back to primary server in the organization. This is sometimes referred a "Email business continuity" options in technology market place. The third-party smart host must use SMTP for transport. If it does not, you should use a Foreign connector or Delivery Agent connector.

Use the EAC to create a Send connector to route outbound email through a smart host

1. In the EAC, navigate to **Mail flow**, Click **Send connectors**, and then click **Add+**.
2. In the **New send connector** wizard, specify a name for the send connector and then select **Custom** for the **Type**. You typically choose this selection when you want route messages to computers not running Microsoft Exchange Server 2013. Click **Next**.
3. Choose **Route mail through smart hosts**, and then click **Add +**. In the **Add smart host** window, specify the IP address, such as 192.168.5.1, or the fully qualified domain name (FQDN). Here FQDN is the FQDN of SMTP server of the smart host provider. Click **Save**.
   For **Smart host authentication**, choose the type of authentication required by the smart host. If you choose **Basic authentication**, you must provide a user name and password.
4. Under **Address space**, click **Add+**. In the **Add domain** window, make sure SMTP is listed as the **Type**. For **Fully Qualified Domain Name (FQDN)**, enter * to specify that this send connector applies to messages sent to any domain. Click **Save**.
5. For **Source server**, click **Add+**. In the **Select a server** window, select a Mailbox server that will be used to send mail to the Internet via the Client Access server and click **Add+**. After you have selected the server, click **Add+**. Click **OK**.
6. Click **Finish**.

4.4 Create a Send Connector to Send Email to a Partner

In this section you will configure send connection with TLS. TLS provides a secure communication over the Internet. If you want to ensure secure, encrypted communication with a partner, you can create a Send connector that is configured to enforce Transport Layer Security (TLS) for messages sent to a partner domain.

1. In the EAC, navigate to **Mail flow**, Click **Send connectors**, and then click **Add+**.
2. In the **New send connector** wizard, specify a name for the send connector and then select **Partner** for the **Type**. When you select **Partner**, the connector is configured to allow connections only to servers that authenticate with TLS certificates. Click **Next**.

3. Verify that **MX record associated with recipient domain** is selected, which specifies that the connector uses the domain name system (DNS) to route mail. Click **Next**.
4. Under **Address space**, click **Add+**. In the **Add domain** window, make sure SMTP is listed as the **Type**. For **Fully Qualified Domain Name (FQDN)**, enter the name of your partner domain. Click **Save**.
5. For **Source server**, click **Add+**. In the **Select a server** window, select a Mailbox server that will be used to send mail to the Internet via the Client Access server and click **Add+**. After you've selected the server, click **Add+**. Click **OK**.
6. Click **Finish**.

4.5 Configuring Receive Connector Authentication

The Receive connector authentication mechanisms are the following:

Authentication mechanism	Description
None	No authentication.
TLS	Requires a server certificate to offer TLS.
Integrated	NTLM and Kerberos (Integrated Windows authentication).
BasicAuth	Basic authentication.
BasicAuthRequireTLS	Basic authentication over TLS.
ExchangeServer	Exchange Server authentication
ExternalAuthoritative	Internet Protocol security (IPsec) association or a virtual private network (VPN).

Create a Receive Connector to Receive Email from the Internet

This topic shows you how to configure a Receive connector to receive email from the Internet. Use the EAC to Create a Receive Connector to Receive Messages from the Internet

1. In the EAC, navigate to **Mail flow**, Click **Receive connectors**. Click **Add+** to create a Receive connector.
2. On the **New receive connector** page, specify a name for the Receive connector and then select **Frontend transport** for the **Role**.
3. Choose **Internet** for the type. The Receive connector will receive mail from Internet senders.

4. For the **Network adapter bindings**, observe that **All available IPV4** is listed in the **IP addresses** list and the **Port** is 25. (Simple Mail Transfer Protocol (SMTP) uses port 25.) This indicates that the connector listens for connections on all IP addresses assigned to network adapters on the local server.
5. Click the **Finish** button to create your connector.

Create a Secure Receive Connector to Receive Email from a Partner

This topic shows you how to configure a Receive connector to receive secure email from a partner. Use the EAC to Create a Receive Connector to Receive Secure Messages from a Partner

1. In the EAC, navigate to **Mail flow**, Click **Receive connectors**. Click **Add+** to create a new Receive connector.
2. On the **New receive connector** page, specify a name for the Receive connector and then select **Frontend Transport** for the **Role**.
3. Choose **Partner** for the type. The Receive connector will receive mail from a trusted third party.
4. For the **Network adapter bindings**, observe that **All available IPV4** is listed in the **IP addresses** list and the **Port** is 25. (Simple Mail Transfer Protocol uses port 25.) This indicates that the connector listens for connections on all IP addresses assigned to network adapters on the local server. Click **Next**.
5. If the Remote network settings page lists 0.0.0.0-255.255.255.255, which means that the Receive connector receives connections from all IP addresses, click **Remove-** to remove it. Click **Add+**, add the IP address for your partner's server, and click **Save**.
6. Click **Finish** to create the connector.

Create a Receive Connector to Receive Email from a System Not Running Exchange

You may have a situation where you want to receive messages from a system not running Exchange. For example, if you have a network appliance and devices that routes messages to your Exchange server. Use the EAC to Create a Receive Connector to Receive Messages from a Messaging Appliance.

1. In the EAC, navigate to **Mail flow**, Click **Receive connectors**. Click **Add+** to create a Receive connector.
2. On the **New receive connector** page, specify a name for the Receive connector and then select **Hub Transport** for the **Role**. In this case, you

want your Mailbox server running the Transport service to receive messages from the appliance.

3. Choose **Custom** for the type, since the Receive connector will receive mail from an appliance not running Microsoft Exchange Server 2013.
4. For the **Network adapter bindings**, observe that **All available IPV4** is listed in the **IP addresses** list. Click **Next**.
5. For **Remote network settings**, click **Remove-** to remove **0.0.0.0-255.255.255.255** from the **IP addresses** list, since you want to specify that the connector accepts mail from a specific appliance. Click **Add+** to add a new IP address, and in the **Add IP address** window, add the IP address of your appliance. Click **Save**.
6. Click the **Finish** button to create your connector.

Create a Receive Connector to Receive Messages from an Internal Exchange Server

When you want to route mail from the Transport service on a Mailbox server to a specific Edge Transport server, or from one Mailbox server to another with your internal organization. Create a Receive Connector to Receive Messages from an Internal Exchange Server.

1. In the EAC, navigate to **Mail flow**, Click **Receive connectors**. Click **Add+** to create a new Receive connector.
2. On the **New receive connector** page, specify a name for the Receive connector and then select **Hub transport** for the **Role**. In this case we assume you want to route mail within your network, not into and out of the organization.
3. Choose **Internal** for the type. The connector is configured with Exchange server authentication.
4. If the Remote network settings page lists 0.0.0.0-255.255.255.255, which means that the Receive connector receives connections from all IP addresses, click **Remove-** to remove it. Click **Add+**, add the IP address for the server you want to receive mail from, such as 192.168.5.5, and click **Save**.
5. Click **Finish** to create the connector.

4.6 Create a Foreign Connector for a non-SMTP Fax Gateway

You may have a scenario where you want to send messages to and receive messages from a fax-gateway server that doesn't use SMTP as its primary transport mechanism. Follow the steps outlined in this procedure to create a Foreign connector that delivers messages to and receives messages from the foreign system.

4.6.1 Create a Foreign connector to a non-SMTP gateway server

Run the following command to create the Foreign connector:

New-ForeignConnector -Name "Foreign Connector" -AddressSpaces "X400:c=US;a=Superplaneteers;P=Superplaneteers;5" -SourceTransportServers EXCHHUB1,EXCHHUB02

In this example, EXCHHub01 and EXCHHub02 are source servers in your organization that you designate to deliver messages to the foreign system. Using more than one source server provides fault tolerance.

Once you have created the Foreign Connector, you can configure the Drop Pickup, and Replay directories, depending on the requirements for your organization.

4.6.2 Configure the Drop directory for a Mailbox server

The Drop directory for a Mailbox server running the Transport service is used to deliver outbound messages from your Foreign connector. Run the following command to specify the Drop directory for your Foreign connector

Set-ForeignConnector "Foreign Connector" -DropDirectory "C:\Drop Directory"

4.7 Delivery Agents and Delivery Agent Connectors

A Delivery Agent connector in Exchange 2013 is similar to the Delivery Agent connector introduced in Exchange 2010. They route messages addressed to foreign systems that do not use the SMTP protocol. When a message is routed to a Delivery Agent connector, the associated delivery agent performs the content conversion and message delivery. Typically, delivery agents are created by a third-party and configured to work with a Delivery Agent connector in your organization. You create a Delivery Agent connector in the Exchange Management PowerShell with the New-DeliveryAgentConnector cmdlet and edit the Delivery Agent connector's properties with Set-DeliveryAgentConnector.

4.8 Configure an Accepted Domain within Exchange Organization

If a domain belonging to your organization hosts mailboxes for all the recipients within an SMTP namespace, that domain is considered to be authoritative. By default, one accepted domain is configured as authoritative for the Exchange organization. If your organization has more than one SMTP namespace, you can configure more than one accepted domain as authoritative.

4.8.1 Configure an accepted domain as authoritative

1. In the EAC, navigate to **Mail flow**, Click **Accepted domains**, and click **Add+**.
2. In the **Name** field, enter the display name for the accepted domain.
3. In the **Accepted domain** field, enter the accepted domain. Specify an SMTP namespace for which your organization accepts email messages. (For example, **martianspirit.com**).
4. Select **Authoritative domain**. This option is for email relayed to servers within your Exchange organization for an accepted domain that hosts mailboxes for all the recipients within an SMTP namespace.
5. Click **Save**.

4.8.2 Configure an Accepted Domain for an Independent Business Unit

In some situations you may want to configure an accepted domain for an independent business unit with email servers outside your Exchange organization. You may want to configure an accepted domain for a business unit with email servers outside your Exchange organization.

1. In the EAC, navigate to **Mail flow**, Click **Accepted domains**, select the domain you wish to configure, and click **Edit**.
2. In the **Name** field, enter the display name for the accepted domain. Each accepted domain for your organization must have a unique display name. This may be different than the accepted domain. For example, the domain martianspirit.com could have a display name of martianspirit Local Accepted Domain.
3. Select **External Relay Domain**. This option is for email is relayed to a server outside your Exchange organization. Click **Save**.

4.8.3 Configure an Accepted Domain outside Exchange Organization

When an organization shares the same SMTP address space between two or more different email systems. For such scenarios, you can configure an accepted domain as an internal relay domain.

1. In the EAC, navigate to **Mail flow**, Click **Accepted domains**, select the domain you wish to configure, and then click **Edit**.
2. In the **Name** field, enter the display name for the accepted domain. Each accepted domain for your organization must have a unique display name. This may be different than the accepted domain. For example, the domain martianspirit.com could have a display name of martianspirit Local Accepted Domain.
3. Select **Internal Relay Domain**.
4. Click **Save**.

4.9 Configure Remote Domain Out of Office Replies

You can use the Exchange Management PowerShell to configure the way emails are sent and received through remote domains. The following shows how to use the Exchange Management PowerShell to configure the way Exchange handles out of office replies.

4.9.1 Configure out-of-office replies

You can use the **Set-RemoteDomain** cmdlet to configure the properties of a remote domain. This example disables out-of-office messages for the remote domain named martianspirit.

Set-RemoteDomain martianspirit -AllowedOOFType None

This example allows only external out-of-office messages.

Set-RemoteDomain martianspirit -AllowedOOFType External

4.9.2 Configure Remote Domain Automatic Replies

You can use the Exchange Management PowerShell to configure the way emails are sent and received through remote domains. The following shows how to use the Exchange Management PowerShell to configure the way Exchange handles automatic replies.

You can use the Set-RemoteDomain cmdlet to configure the properties of a remote domain. This example allows automatic replies to the remote domain named martianspirit. This setting is disabled by default.

Set-RemoteDomain martianspirit -AutoReplyEnabled $true

This example allows automatic forwards to the remote domain. This setting is disabled by default.

Set-RemoteDomain martianspirit -AutoForwardEnabled $true

4.9.3 Configure Remote Domain Message Reporting

The following shows how to use the Exchange Management PowerShell configure the way Exchange handles delivery and non-delivery reports.

You can use the Set-RemoteDomain cmdlet to configure the properties of a remote domain. This example disables delivery reports to the remote domain named martianspirit. This setting is enabled by default.

Set-RemoteDomain martianspirit -DeliveryReportEnabled $false

This example disables non-delivery reports to the remote domain. This setting is enabled by default.

Set-RemoteDomain martianspirit -NDREnabled $false

4.10 Enable Support for Legacy Transport Agents

In Microsoft Exchange Server 2013, transport agents that were created using the Microsoft .NET Framework version 4.0 are supported by default. Exchange 2013 supports transport agents that were created using previous versions of the .NET Framework, but support for these legacy transport agents isn't enabled by default.

To enable support for legacy transport agents, you need to modify the appropriate XML application configuration file. Use the following procedure to enable support for legacy transport agents:

In a Command prompt window, on the Exchange 2013 server where you want to configure the legacy transport agent support, open the appropriate application configuration file in Notepad by running the following command:

Notepad %ExchangeInstallPath%\Bin\<AppConfigFile>

For example, to open the EdgeTransport.exe.config file on a Mailbox server, run the following command:

Notepad %ExchangeInstallPath%\Bin\EdgeTransport.exe.config

Locate the </configuration> key at the end of the file, and paste the following keys before the </configuration>:

```
<startup useLegacyV2RuntimeActivationPolicy="true">
  <supportedRuntime version="v4.0" />
  <supportedRuntime version="v3.5" />
  <supportedRuntime version="v3.0" />
  <supportedRuntime version="v2.0" />
</startup>
```

When you are finished, save and close the application configuration file. Repeat Steps to modify the other application configuration files. Restart the associated Windows service by running the following command:

net stop MSExchangeTransport
net start MSExchangeTransport

Repeat to restart services associated with the other modified application configuration files.

4.11 Manage Transport Agents

Transport agents use SMTP events to operate on messages as the messages move through the transport pipeline. Most of the built-in transport agents that are included with Microsoft Exchange Server 2013 are invisible and unmanageable.

However, you can install and configure third-party transport agents on Exchange servers in your organization.

Installing a transport agent

When you install a transport agent, Exchange only registers the DLLs associated with the transport agent. Transport agents are installed in a disabled state to make sure mail flow isn't affected by transport agents that haven't been configured. Therefore, you need to enable the transport agent.

Use the following syntax to install a transport agent.

Install-TransportAgent -Name <TransportAgentIdentity> -TransportAgentFactory "TransportAgentFactory" -AssemblyPath "FilePath"

This example installs a fictitious transport agent named martianspirit Transport Agent in the Transport service on a Mailbox server.

Install-TransportAgent -Name "martianspirit Transport Agent" - TransportAgentFactory "vendor.exchange.TransportAgentfactory" -AssemblyPath "C:\Program Files\Vendor\TransportAgent\TransportAgentFactory.dll"

To verify that you have successfully installed the transport agent, run the command Get-TransportAgent and verify the transport agent is listed.

Enable a transport agent

Use the following syntax to enable a transport agent.

Enable-TransportAgent <TransportAgentIdentity>

This example enables the transport agent named Superplaneteers Transport Agent in the Transport service on a Mailbox server.

Enable-TransportAgent "martianspirit Transport Agent"

To verify that you have successfully enabled a transport agent, run the command Get-TransportAgent | Format-List Name,Enabled and verify the transport agent is enabled.

Disable a transport agent

Use the following syntax to disable a transport agent:

Disable-TransportAgent <TransportAgentIdentity>

This example disables the transport agent named martianspirit Transport Agent in the Transport service on a Mailbox server.

Disable-TransportAgent "martianspirit Transport Agent"

To verify that you have successfully disabled a transport agent, run the command Get-TransportAgent | Format-List Name,Enabled and verify the transport agent is disabled.

View transport agents

To view a summary list of transport agents, run the following command:

Get-TransportAgent

To view the detailed configuration of a specific transport agent, run the following command:

Get-TransportAgent <TransportAgentIdentity> | Format-List

This example provides detailed configuration of the transport agent named Transport Rule Agent.

Get-TransportAgent "Transport Rule Agent" | Format-List

Configure the priority of a transport agent

Transport agents with a priority closest to 0 process email messages first. However, the SMTP event in the transport pipeline where the transport agent is registered may cause a lower priority agent to act on the message before a higher priority agent. To modify the priority of an existing transport agent, run the following command:

Set-TransportAgent <TransportAgentIdentity> -Priority <Integer>

This example sets the priority agent value of 3 for the existing transport agent named Superplaneteers Transport Agent in the Transport service on a Mailbox server.

Set-TransportAgent "martianspirit Transport Agent" -Priority 3

To verify that you have successfully configured the priority of a transport agent, run the command Get-TransportAgent | Format-List Name,Priority and verify the priority value of the transport agent.

Uninstall a transport agent

When the transport agent is uninstalled, Exchange unregisters the DLL files used with the agent. Exchange doesn't remove any files, registry keys, or other objects added by the installation of the transport agent.

To uninstall a transport agent, run the following command:

Uninstall-TransportAgent <TransportAgentIdentity>

This example uninstalls the transport agent named Superplaneteers Transport Agent from the Transport service on a Mailbox server.

Uninstall-TransportAgent "martianspirit Transport Agent"

To verify that you have successfully uninstalled the transport agent, run the command Get-TransportAgent and verify the transport agent isn't listed.

4.12 Configure Anti-Spam Agent Logging

Agent logging records the actions performed by specific Exchange anti-spam agents. The information written to the agent log depends on the agent, the SMTP event, and the action performed on the message. Use the PowerShell to configure anti-spam agent logging, run the following command:

Set-TransportService <ServerIdentity> -AgentLogEnabled <$true | $false> -AgentLogMaxAge <dd.hh:mm:ss> -AgentLogMaxDirectorySize <Size> -AgentLogMaxFileSize <Size> -AgentLogPath <LocalFilePath>

This example sets the following agent log settings on the Mailbox server named EXCHMBXSRV1:

- Sets the location of the agent log files to L:\Anti-Spam Agent Log.
- Sets the maximum size of an agent log file to 20 MB.
- Sets the maximum size of the agent log directory to 400 MB.
- Sets the maximum age of an agent log file to 14 days.

Set-TransportService EXCHMBXSRV1 -AgentLogPath "L:\Anti-Spam Agent Log" -AgentLogMaxFileSize 20MB -AgentLogMaxDirectorySize 400MB -AgentLogMaxAge 14.00:00:00

To verify that you have successfully configured anti-spam agent logging, do the following, run the following command:

Get-TransportService <ServerIdentity> | Format-List

4.13 Configure Connectivity Logging

Connectivity logging records the outbound connection activity that's used to transmit messages from a transport service on an Exchange server. Connectivity logging records the connection source, destination, number of messages and bytes transmitted, and connection failure information.

Use the EAC to configure connectivity logging in the Transport service

1. In the EAC, navigate to **Servers**, Click **Servers**.
2. Select the Mailbox server you want to configure, and then click **Edit**.
3. On the server properties page, click **Transport Logs**.
4. In the **Connectivity log** section, change any of the following:

   - **Enable connectivity log** To disable connectivity logging on the server, clear the check box. To enable connectivity logging on the server, select the check box.
   - **Connectivity log path** The value you specify must be on the local Exchange server. If the folder doesn't exist, it will be created for you when you click **Save**.

5. When you are finished, click **Save**.

Configure connectivity logging

To configure connectivity logging, run the following command:

Set-TransportService | Set-MailboxTransportService | Set-FrontEndTransportService <ServerIdentity> -ConnectivityLogEnabled <$true | $false> -ConnectivityLogMaxAge <dd.hh:mm:ss> -ConnectivityLogMaxDirectorySize <Size> -ConnectivityLogMaxFileSize <Size> -ConnectivityLogPath <LocalFilePath>

This example sets the following connectivity log settings in the Transport service on the Mailbox server named EXCHMBXSRV1:

- Sets the location of the connectivity log files to L:\Hub Connectivity Log.
- Sets the maximum size of a connectivity log file to 20 MB.
- Sets the maximum size of the connectivity log directory to 1.5 GB.
- Sets the maximum age of a connectivity log file to 45 days.

Set-TransportService EXCHMBXSRV1 -ConnectivityLogPath "L:\Hub Connectivity Log" -ConnectivityLogMaxFileSize 20MB -ConnectivityLogMaxDirectorySize 1.5GB -ConnectivityLogMaxAge 45.00:00:00

4.14 Configure Protocol Logging

Protocol logging records the SMTP conversations that occur on Send Connectors and Receive connectors as part of message delivery. Don't perform this steps on an Edge Transport server that has been subscribed to the Exchange organization by using EdgeSync. Instead, make the changes in the Transport service on the Mailbox server. The changes are then replicated to the Edge Transport server next time EdgeSync synchronization occurs

Use the EAC to configure protocol logging

Use the EAC to enable or disable protocol logging on a Send connector or a Receive connector in the Transport service on a Mailbox server, or on a Receive connector in the Front End Transport service on a Client Access server, do the following:

1. In the EAC, navigate to **Mail flow**, Click **Send connectors** or **Mail flow**, Click **Receive connectors**.
2. Select the connector you want to configure, and then click **Edit**.
3. On the **General** tab in the **Protocol logging level** section, select one of the following options:

    - **None** Protocol logging disabled on the connector.

- **Verbose** Protocol logging is enabled on the connector.

4. When you are finished, click **Save**.

Use the EAC to configure the protocol log paths for the Send connectors and Receive connectors in the Transport service on a Mailbox server, do the following:

1. In the EAC, navigate to **Servers**, Click **Servers**.
2. Select the Mailbox server you want to configure, and then click **Edit**.
3. On the server properties page, click **Transport logs**.
4. In the **Protocol log** section, change any of the following settings:

   - **Send protocol log path** The value you specify must be on the local Exchange server. If the folder doesn't exist, it will be created for you when you click **Save**.
   - **Receive protocol log path** The value you specify must be on the local Exchange server. If the folder doesn't exist, it will be created for you when you click **Save**.

5. When you are finished, click **Save**.

Enable or disable protocol logging on a Send connector or a Receive connector

To enable or disable protocol logging on a Send connector or a Receive connector, run the following command:

Set-SendConnector |Set-ReceiveConnector <ConnectorIdentity> - ProtocolLoggingLevel <Verbose | None>

This example enables protocol logging for the Receive connector named Connection from martianspirit.com.

Set-ReceiveConnector "Connection from martianspirit.com" -ProtocolLoggingLevel Verbose

Enable or disable protocol logging on the intra-organization Send connector

To enable or disable protocol logging on the implicit and invisible intra-organization Send connector that exists in the Transport service on a Mailbox server and in the Front End Transport service on a Client Access server, run the following command:

Set-TransportService | Set-FrontEndTransportService -IntraOrgConnectorProtocolLoggingLevel <Verbose | None>

This example enables protocol logging on the intra-organization Send connector in the Transport service on a Mailbox server named EXCHMBXSRV02.

Set-TransportService EXCHMBXSRV02 -IntraOrgConnectorProtocolLoggingLevel Verbose

Enable or disable protocol logging on the mailbox delivery Send connector

To enable or disable protocol logging on the implicit and invisible mailbox delivery Send connector that exists in the Mailbox Transport service on a Mailbox server, run the following command:

Set-MailboxTransportService -MailboxDeliveryConnectorProtocolLoggingLevel <Verbose | None>

This example enables protocol logging on the mailbox delivery Receive connector in the Mailbox Transport service on a Mailbox server named EXCHMBXSRV02.

Set-MailboxTransportService EXCHMBXSRV02 -MailboxDeliveryConnectorProtocolLoggingLevel Verbose

Configure protocol logging settings

To configure the protocol log settings, run the following command:

Set-TransportService | Set-MailboxTransportService | Set-FrontEndTransportService <ServerIdentity> -ReceiveProtocolLogPath <LocalFilePath> -SendProtocolLogPath <LocalFilePath> -ReceiveProtocolLogMaxFileSize <Size> -SendProtocolLogMaxFileSize <Size> -ReceiveProtocolLogMaxDirectorySize <Size> -SendProtocolLogMaxDirectorySize <Size> -ReceiveProtocolLogMaxAge <dd.hh:mm:ss> -SendProtocolLogMaxAge <dd.hh:mm:ss>

This example sets the following protocol log settings in the Transport service on the Mailbox server named EXCHMBXSRV02:

- Sets the location of all Receive connector protocol logs to L:\Hub Receive SMTP Log and all Send connector protocol logs to L:\Hub Send SMTP Log.
- Sets the maximum size of a Receive connector protocol log file and a Send connector protocol log file to 20 MB.
- Sets the maximum size of the Receive connector protocol log folder and the Send connector protocol log folder to 400 MB.
- Sets the maximum age of a Receive connector protocol log file and a Send Connector protocol log file to 45 days.

Set-TransportService EXCHMBXSRV02 -ReceiveProtocolLogPath "L:\Hub Receive SMTP Log" -SendProtocolLogPath "L:\Hub Send SMTP Log" - ReceiveProtocolLogMaxFileSize 20MB -SendProtocolLogMaxFileSize 20MB - ReceiveProtocolLogMaxDirectorySize 400MB -SendProtocolLogMaxDirectorySize 400MB -ReceiveProtocolLogMaxAge 45.00:00:00 -SendProtocolLogMaxAge 45.00:00:00

4.15 Configure a Moderated Recipient

When you configure a recipient for moderation, all messages sent to that recipient are subject to approval by the designated moderators. For more information about how Microsoft Exchange Server 2013 handles recipient moderation

Use the EAC to configure a recipient for moderation

This example configures the following moderation settings for the distribution group named All Employees:

- Enable moderation for the distribution group.
- Designate Raihan Al-Beruni as moderators.
- Allow the members of the distribution group named HR to bypass moderation.
- Notify internal senders if their message to the distribution group is rejected, but do not send any notifications to external senders.

1. In the EAC, navigate to **Recipients**, Click **Groups**.
2. In the result pane, select the **All employees** distribution group and click **Edit**.
3. On the properties page, click **Message approval**, and complete the following:

- Select the **Messages sent to this group have to be approved by a moderator** check box.
- In the **Group moderators** list, click **Add+**.
- In the **Select group moderators** dialog, find and select Raihan Al-Beruni, click **Add**. When you are finished, click **OK**.
- In the **Senders who don't require message approval** list, click **Add+**.
- In the **Select senders** dialog, find and select HR from the list and click **Add**. When you are finished, click **OK**.
- In **Select moderation notifications**, select **Notify all senders when their messages aren't approved**.

4. Click **Save**.

Use the PowerShell to configure a recipient for moderation

Run the following command:

Set-RecipientType <Identity> -ModerationEnabled $true -ModeratedBy <recipient1,recipient2> -ByPassModerationFromSendersOrMembers <recipient1,recipient2> -SendModerationNotifications <Never | Always | Internal>

This example configures the following moderation settings for the distribution group named All Employees:

- Enable moderation for the distribution group.
- Designate Raihan Al-Beruni and John as moderators.
- Allow the members of the distribution group named HR to bypass moderation.
- Notify internal senders if their message to the distribution group is rejected, but do not send any notifications to external senders.

To accomplish the tasks in this example scenario, run the following command:

Set-DistributionGroup "All Employees" -ModerationEnabled $true -ModeratedBy "Raihan","John" -ByPassModerationFromSendersOrMembers HR - SendModerationNotifications Internal

This example configures the following moderation settings for the distribution group named All Employees:

- Add the user John@superplaneteers.com to the list of existing moderators.
- Remove the user Shane@superplaneteers.com from the list of existing senders who bypass moderation.

Set-DistributionGroup "All Employees" -ModeratedBy @{Add="John@superplaneteers.com"} -ByPassModerationFromSendersOrMembers @{Remove="Shane@superplaneteers.com"

4.16 Configure Content Transfer Encoding

Content transfer encoding defines encoding methods for transforming binary email message data into the US-ASCII plain text format. This transformation allows the message to travel through older SMTP messaging servers that only support messages in US-ASCII text. In Microsoft Exchange Server 2013, the following content transfer encoding methods are available:

- 7-bit
- Quoted-printable (QP)
- Base64

You can configure the transfer encoding method using the ByteEncoderTypeFor7BitCharsets parameter on the **Set-OrganizationConfig** and **Set-RemoteDomain** cmdlets. The content transfer encoding settings you configure with **Set-OrganizationConfig** apply to all messages in the Exchange organization.

Use the PowerShell to configure the content transfer encoding method for the organization

To configure the content transfer encoding method for the organization, run the following command:

Set-OrganizationConfig -ByteEncoderTypeFor7BitCharsets <Integer>

For example, to set the content transfer encoding method to Base64, run the following command:

Set-OrganizationConfig -ByteEncoderTypeFor7BitCharsets 2

Use the PowerShell to configure the content transfer encoding method for a remote domain

To configure the content transfer encoding method for all the recipients in a remote domain, run the following command:

Set-RemoteDomain -ByteEncoderTypeFor7BitCharsets <Value>

For example, to set the content transfer encoding method to Base64, run the following command:

Set- RemoteDomain -ByteEncoderTypeFor7BitCharsets UseBase64

4.17 Message Encoding Options

The message encoding options that are available in Exchange specify message characteristics, such as MIME and non-MIME character sets, binary encoding, and attachment formats. You can specify message encoding options in the following locations:

- Remote domain settings
- Mail user and mail contact settings
- Microsoft Outlook settings

Message encoding options for mail users and mail contacts

When you configure message encoding options for a mail contact or a mail user, that option is applied to all messages sent to that specific recipient. For mail contacts and mail users in your organization, you have the following configuration options for message encoding:

- UsePreferMessageFormat
- MessageFormat
- MessageBodyFormat
- MacAttachmentFormat

You need to use the following cmdlets to set the message encoding options for mail users and mail contacts with the above parameters.

- Enable-MailContact
- New-MailContact

- Set-MailContact
- Enable-MailUser
- New-MailUser
- Set-MailUser

Message encoding options in Outlook As a sender, you can specify message encoding options in Outlook at any of the following stages:

- By configuring the default message format to be either plain text or HTML.
- By setting the message format as you're composing it to either plain text or HTML using the **Format** area in the **Options** tab.

4.18 DSN Message Identity

You can identify a customized delivery status notification (DSN) message based on its syntax. The identity is the customized DSN message's GUID or a string that consists of the following values:

- **Locale** For a list of locale codes that you can use with the **New-SystemMessage** command.
- **Internal or External**
- **DSN code**

Track Messages with Delivery Reports

Delivery Reports is a message tracking tool in the Exchange Administration Center (EAC) that you can use to search for delivery status on email messages sent to or from users in your organization's address book, with a certain subject. You can track messages for up to 14 days after they were sent or received.

1. In the EAC, navigate to **Mail Flow**, Click **Delivery Reports**.
2. Enter the following information: **Mailbox to search:** Click **Browse** to select the mailbox from the address book and then click **OK**. Selecting the mailbox to search is required. Select one of the following:
   - Search for messages sent to
   - Search for messages received from
   - Search for these words in the subject line
3. When you are finished, click **Search**. If you want to start over, click **Clear**.

Use the EAC to review a delivery report

To view delivery information, select a message in the **Search results** pane and click **Details**. The delivery report shows delivery status and detailed delivery information for the message you have selected from the **Search results** pane. At the top of the report, you'll see the following fields:

- **Subject** The subject line of the message appears as the heading of the report.
- **From** Alias, display name, or email address of the person who sent the message.
- **To** Alias, display name, or email address for each recipient of the message.
- **Sent** Date and time the message was sent.

Summary to date section

This section appears in the delivery report if a message was sent to more than one person or recipient. The top of this section tells you the total number of recipients that the message was sent to and gives brief delivery information for each recipient.

- Summary to date
- Search box
- Status

Detailed report information

This section contains detailed delivery information for a message sent to the recipient you select in the Summary to date section.

- Delivery Report for
- Submitted
- Delivered
- Deferred
- Pending
- Moderator
- Groups Expanded
- Failed

4.19 Viewing Mailflow Queue

When you use Queue Viewer in the Exchange Toolbox on a Microsoft Exchange Server 2013 server that's located inside the Exchange organization, you can connect to other Mailbox servers. Use the Exchange Toolbox to specify the server you want to manage in Queue Viewer

1. Click **Start**, Click **Search,** Type **Exchange,** Right Click on **Exchange Toolbox.** Click **run as Administrator.**
2. In the **Mail flow tools** section, double-click **Queue Viewer**.
3. In the action pane, click **Connect to server**.
4. In the **Connect to Server** window, click **Browse** to view a list of the available Mailbox servers.
5. In the **Select Exchange Server** window, select a Mailbox server. To search for a Mailbox server, use one of the following procedures:

   - Enter the exact server name or the first few letters of the server name in the **Search** field, and then click **Find Now**. Select a server from the result pane.
   - Select the **View** menu, and then click **Show Filter**. In the **Name** column or **Version** column, click the filter icon, and then select the filter operator. Type the filter criteria in the **Enter text here** field. Press ENTER. Select a server from the result pane.

6. Click **OK** to close the **Select Exchange Server** window.
7. After you select a server, in the **Connect to server** window, select the **Set as default server** check box if you want Queue Viewer to focus on this server first whenever Queue Viewer is opened.
8. In the **Connect to server** window, click **Connect**.

Use the Exchange Toolbox to specify the server that Queue Viewer uses to run Remote PowerShell

1. Click **Start**, Click **Search,** Type **Exchange,** Right Click on **Exchange Toolbox.** Click **run as Administrator**.
2. In the **Mail flow tools section**, double-click **Queue Viewer**.
3. In the action pane, click **Properties**.
4. In the **Queue Viewer,** Select **Mailbox Server, Properties** dialog box, select **Connect to the automatically selected server** or **Specify a server to connect to** Select this option to specify a server to run Remote PowerShell.

If you select this option, click **Browse** to open the **Select Exchange Server** dialog box. Select the server where you want to run Remote PowerShell
5.   click **OK**.

Set Queue Viewer Options

You can set options in Queue Viewer to adjust the number of items that are displayed on the page and adjust the auto-refresh interval. The auto-refresh interval determines how frequently the results in Queue Viewer are updated.

Use the Exchange Toolbox to set Queue Viewer options

1.   Click **Start**, Click **Search**, Type **Exchange**, Right Click on **Exchange Toolbox**. Click **run as Administrator**.
2.   In the **Mail flow tools** section, double-click **Queue Viewer**.
3.   In Queue Viewer, click **View** , Click **Options** to configure the following settings in the **Queue Viewer Options** dialog box:
     1.   In the **Refresh interval (seconds)** field, enter the frequency at which Queue Viewer should update the display.
     2.   In the **Number of items to display on each page** field, enter the maximum number of items to display in Queue Viewer. This number must be from 1 through 10,000.
4.   When you are finished, click **OK**.

View Queued Message Properties

You can use the Queue Viewer in the Exchange Toolbox or the Exchange Management PowerShell to view the properties of a message that is queued for delivery.

1.   Click **Start**, Click **Search**, Type **Exchange**, Right Click on **Exchange Toolbox**. Click **run as Administrator**.
2.   In the **Mail flow tools** section, double-click **Queue Viewer** to open the tool in a new window.
3.   In Queue Viewer, select the **Messages** tab to see the list of messages that are currently queued for delivery in your organization.
4.   Right-click the message whose properties you want to view and then select **Properties**.
5.   The **General** tab displays **Identity, Subject, Internet Message ID,From Address, Status, Size (KB)...**

6. The **Recipient Information** tab displays **Address, Status.**

Use the PowerShell to view the properties of a message

Use the **Get-Message** cmdlet to view the properties of a message that is currently queued for delivery. The following example presents the sender address, recipients, subject, and received date information for all messages that are currently in retry state:

Get-Message -IncludeRecipientInfo -Filter {Status -eq "Retry"} | Format-Table FromAddress,Recipients,Subject,DateReceived

Filter Messages in Queues

Use Queue Viewer in the Exchange Toolbox or the Exchange Management PowerShell to filter messages in queues on a Microsoft Exchange Server 2013 Mail server or Edge Transport server. You can then perform the following operations that modify the status of those messages.

1. Click **Start**, Click **Search,** Type **Exchange,** Right Click on **Exchange Toolbox.** Click **run as Administrator**
2. In the **Mail flow tools** section, double-click **Queue Viewer**.
3. In Queue Viewer, click the **Messages** tab. A list of all messages in all queues on the server to which you are connected is displayed. To limit the view to a single queue, click the **Queues** tab, double-click the queue name, and then click the Server\Queue tab that appears.
4. Click **Add Expression**, and enter your filter expression
5. (Optional) Click **Add Expression** to specify additional filter criteria. Only messages that meet all filter criteria will be displayed.
6. Click **Apply Filter**. The results of messages that meet the filter criteria are displayed.

Use the PowerShell to filter messages in queues

This example filters all messages that have a spam confidence level (SCL) value equal to or greater than 6 and that were sent from any sender in the superplaneteers.com domain.

Get-Message -Filter {SCL -ge 6 -and FromAddress -eq "superplaneteers.com"}

Export Lists from Queue Viewer

This topic shows how to use Queue Viewer in the Exchange Toolbox to export lists of messages or queues. You can export lists to the following file formats:

- Text (tab delimited)
- Text (comma delimited)
- Unicode text (tab delimited)
- Unicode text (comma delimited)

Export a list from the result pane in Queue Viewer

1. Click **Start**, Click **Search,** Type **Exchange,** Right Click on **Exchange Toolbox**. Click **run as Administrator**.
2. In the **Mail flow** section, double-click **Queue Viewer**.
3. In Queue Viewer, select the **Queues** tab or the **Messages** tab. On either tab, you can click **Create Filter** to restrict the results.
4. In the action pane, click **Export List**. The **Export List** dialog box appears.
5. In **Export List**, type the name of the file in the **File name** box, and then select the file format from the **Save as type** list.
6. Click **Save**.

4.20 Configure the Pickup Directory and the Replay Directory

The Pickup and replay directories are used by the Transport service on Mailbox servers and Edge Transport servers to insert message files directly into the transport pipeline. The Pickup directory is used by administrators for mail flow testing, or by applications that must create and submit their own messages. The Replay directory receives messages from non-SMTP foreign gateway servers and resubmits messages that you exported from the queues of Microsoft Exchange servers.

4.20.1 Configure the Pickup directory

To configure the Pickup directory, use the following syntax.

Set-TransportService <ServerIdentity> -PickupDirectoryPath <LocalFilePath> -PickupDirectoryMaxHeaderSize <Size> -PickupDirectoryMaxRecipientsPerMessage <Integer> -PickupDirectoryMaxMessagesPerMinute <Integer>

This example makes the following changes to the Pickup directory on the Mailbox server named EXCHMBXSRV01:

- The Pickup directory location is set to H:\Pickup Directory.
- The maximum size allowed for message headers in a message file is increased to 96 KB.
- The maximum number of recipients allowed in a message file is increased to 250.
- The maximum rate of message processing for the Pickup and Replay directories is increased to 200 messages per minute.

Set-TransportService EXCHMBXSRV01 -PickupDirectoryPath "H:\Pickup Directory" -PickupDirectoryMaxHeaderSize 96KB -PickupDirectoryMaxRecipientsPerMessage 250 -PickupDirectoryMaxMessagesPerMinute 200

4.20.2 Configure the Replay directory

To configure the Replay directory, use the following syntax.

Set-TransportService <ServerIdentity> -ReplayDirectoryPath "H:\Replay Directory" <LocalFilePath> -PickupDirectoryMaxMessagesPerMinute <Integer>

This example makes the following changes to the Replay directory on the Mailbox server named EXCHMBXSRV01:

- The Replay directory location is set to D:\Replay Directory.
- The maximum rate of message processing for the Pickup and Replay directories is increased to 200 messages per minute.

Set-TransportService EXCHMBXSRV01 -ReplayDirectoryPath "H:\Replay Directory" -PickupDirectoryMaxMessagesPerMinute 200

4.21 Publish Exchange Server 2013 using Forefront TMG 2010

Before you publish Exchange OWA and ActiveSync you must install and assign the digital certificate on to CAS Servers (OWA, ActiveSync, ECP,OAB). Export the certificate from CAS Server you have created in chapter 3.6 (Open EAC>Servers>certificates>Select CAS Server>Export Certificates...) and import Certificate into TMG 2010 server(s). To import certificate, follow the steps.

1. Open Elevated command prompt, type **MMC** and press **Enter**.
2. From the **File**, Click **Add/Remove Snap-in**, Click **Certificates**, Click **Add,** Click **Computer Account**, Click **Finish,** Click **Ok.**

3. Select the **Personal** store under **Certificates (Local Computer)**.

4. On the **Action** menu, point to **All Tasks** and then click **Import** to start the Certificate Import Wizard.

5. Type the file name containing the certificate to be imported. click **Browse** and navigate to the file. Select PKCS **#12 (.PFX)** file, Type the password used to encrypt the private key.

   - (Optional) If you want to be able to use strong private key protection, select the **Enable strong private key protection** check box.

   - (Optional) If you want to back up or transport your keys at a later time, select the **Mark key as exportable** check box.

6. Follow the screen and install the certificate.

4.21.1 Publish OWA using Exchange Web Client Access Wizard

Before you begin configuring TMG 2010 make sure TMG 2010 is configured with **Edge Topology**. External Network Interface of TMG must have routable public IP (VIP for TMG cluster) configured in TCP/IP property. This public IP has been routed from internet to TMG external NIC. Make sure webmail.superplaneteers.com resolve the public IP from external network. I assume that you have configured TCP/IP properties of TMG Server NICs and all Initial configuration of TMG Server is completed.

1. Log on to TMG 2010 Server or TMG 2010 Array from the Array Manager or EMS using Administrator Account.
2. Open TMG Console. In the Forefront TMG Management console, in the tree, click the **Firewall Policy** node.
3. In the **Tasks** pane, click the **Toolbox** tab.
4. On the **Toolbox** tab, click **Network Objects**, click **New**, and then select **Web Listener** to open the New Web Listener Wizard.

5. On the Web Listener Wizard Type the name of **Web Listener Name**: **Exchange2013OWAListener**, Click **Next**.

6. On the **Client Connection Security Page,** Select **Require SSL secured connections with clients,** Click **Next**

7. **On the Web Listener IP Addresses,** Select the **External** network. Click **Select IP Addresses**, and select **Specified IP Addresses on the Forefront TMG computer in the selected network**. Under **Available IP Addresses**, select the IP address for the Web site, click **Add**, and then click **OK**. This IP Address must be publicly routable IP address and resolve webmail.superplaneteers.com from internet. That means your ISP/Telco must host webmail.superplaneteers.com to the corresponding public IP you assigned on the external NIC or VIP of TMG external NIC. **Click Next**

8. On the **Listener SSL Certificates,** Select **Use a single certificate for this Web listener**, click **Select Certificate**, and select a certificate for which the host name that users use to access the published Web site appears in the **Issued To** field. You have imported this certificate in previous section of this chapter. Click **Next**

9. On the **Authentication Settings page,** select **HTML Form Authentication from the drop down list**. On the **Select how Forefront TMG will validate client credentials, select Windows (Active Directory),** Click **Next**. If you would like to use LDAP (Active Directory) then add Domain Controller name DC, UPN (superplaneteers*) and search criteria superplaneteers.com.

10. On the **Single Sign On Settings Page,** leave **Enable SSO for Web sites published with this listener unchecked,** Click **Next**

11. **Completing the New Web Listener Wizard,** Review the settings and click **Finish**. If a message box appears, click **Yes** to enable the system policy rule Allow All HTTP Traffic from Forefront TMG to All Networks (for CRL downloads).

12. In the **Tasks** pane, click the **Tasks** tab.

13. On the **Tasks** tab, click **Publish Exchange Web Client Access** to open the New Exchange Publishing Rule Wizard.

14. On the New Exchange Publishing Rule Wizard, Type the name **Exchange 2013 OWA,** Click **Next.**

15. On the **Select Services Page,** select **Exchange Server 2010** from drop down list as exchange 2013 isn't available in TMG 2010. On the **Web client mail services,** Select **Outlook Web Access**. Click **Next.**

16. On the **Publishing Type,** Select **Publish a single Web site or load balancer,** Click **Next.**

17. On the **Server Connection Security,** Select **Use SSL to connect the published Web server or Web farm**. Click **Next**

18. **On the Internal Publishing Details,** Type the host name that Forefront TMG will use in HTTP request messages sent to the published server. In this case **VIP of the F5 Load balancer** that is 10.10.10.15 and **Internal site name : webmail.superplaneteers.com.** If you are using Microsoft NLB cluster for CAS Servers, 10.10.10.15 is the IP address of NLB cluster.
19. On the next screen type **Public name: webmail.superplaneteers.com.** The public name **must be a fully qualified domain name (FQDN).** Click **Next**
20. On the **Select Web Listener,** In the drop-down list, select the Web listener that you created in Step 4. You can then click **Edit** to modify properties of the Web listener selected. In this case web listener is **Exchange2013OWAListener**
21. On the **Authentication Delegation,** Select **Basic authentication.** Click **Next**
22. **On the User Sets,** If you are using Windows credentials validation, do not change the default **All Authenticated Users.** Click **Next.**
23. **Completing the New Exchange Publishing Rule Wizard.** Review the settings and click **Finish.**
24. In the details pane, click the **Apply** button to save and update the configuration, and then click **OK.**

4.21.2 Configuring the idle session time-out period for OWA clients

Before performing this task, you must have a Web listener that uses forms-based authentication for Outlook Web Access.

1. Log on to TMG 2010 Server or TMG 2010 Array from the Array Manager or EMS using Administrator Account.
2. Open TMG Console, In the Forefront TMG Management console, in the tree, click the **Firewall Policy** node.
3. In the **Tasks** pane, click the **Toolbox** tab.
4. On the **Toolbox** tab, click **Network Objects**, expand **Web Listeners**, and select the applicable Web listener. In this case **Exchange2013OWAListener**.
5. On the toolbar beneath **Network Objects**, click **Edit**.
6. On the **Forms** tab, click **Advanced**.
7. Under **Client Security Settings**, select **Treat as maximum idle time**.
8. In **Timeout for public computers (minutes)**, set the maximum time that users can remain idle on public computers before they are disconnected.
9. In **Timeout for private computers (minutes)**, set the maximum time that users can remain idle on trusted private computers before they are disconnected.

10. Click **OK** to close **Advanced Form Options**, and then click **OK** again to close the Web listener properties.
11. In the details pane, click the **Apply** button to save and update the configuration, and then click **OK**.

4.21.3 Publish ActiveSync using Exchange Web Client Access Wizard

By publishing Exchange ActiveSync, you allow users to access their Exchange mailboxes from Windows Mobile and handheld devices. Users can then synchronize the e-mail messages, appointments, contact information and tasks in their mailboxes and use any of this information when the mobile device is offline.

1. Log on to TMG 2010 Server or TMG 2010 Array from the Array Manager or EMS using Administrator Account.
2. Open TMG Console, In the Forefront TMG Management console, in the tree, click the **Firewall Policy** node.
3. In the **Tasks** pane, click the **Toolbox** tab.
4. On the **Toolbox** tab, click **Network Objects**, click **New**, and then select **Web Listener** to open the New Web Listener Wizard. Follow **Step5 to Step11 on Chapter 4.21.1** to create **Web Listener**. Complete the New Web Listener Wizard as outlined in the previous step. **Skip step 4** if you already created a Web Listener.
5. In the **Tasks** pane, click the **Tasks** tab.
6. On the **Tasks** tab, click **Publish Exchange Web Client Access** to open the New Exchange Publishing Rule Wizard.
7. On the **Welcome to the New Exchange Publishing Rule Wizard** Type the Name of new ActiveSync Policy: **Exchange 2013 ActiveSync**. Click **Next**.
8. On the **Select Services Page,** Select **Exchange version: Exchange Server 2010.** Select **Web client mail services : Exchange ActiveSync,** Click **Next**
9. On the **Publishing Type page,** Select **Publish a single Web site or load balancer**. Click **Next.**
10. On the **Server Connection Security Page,** Select **Use SSL to connect the published Web server or Web farm**. Click **Next.**
11. On the **Internal Publishing Details page,** select **Internal site name webmail.superplaneteers.com,** Click **Next**. On the **select Use a computer name or IP address to connect to the published server**, and type 10.10.10.15 which is load balancer VIP or Microsoft NLB cluster IP of CAS servers.
12. On the **Public Name Details Page,** Select **This domain name (type below)**. Type **webmail.superplaneteers.com**. Click **Next**

13. On the **Select Web Listener Page,** In the drop-down list, select the Web listener: **Exchange2013OWA** that you created in Step 4 on **chapter 4.21.1**. Click Next

14. On the **Authentication Delegation Page,** For forms-based authentication, select **Basic Authentication**. Click **Next**

15. On the **User Sets Page,** If you are using Windows credentials validation, do not change the default **All Authenticated Users**. Click **Next**

16. Completing the New Exchange Publishing Rule Wizard**.** Review the settings and click **Finish**.

17. In the details pane, click the **Apply** button to save and update the configuration, and then click **OK**.

4.21.4 Redirect OWA Traffic from HTTP to HTTPS using TMG 2010

This is a crucial procedure to secure OWA traffic and redirect them to use SSL instead of non-secure HTTP. Follow the steps to redirect OWA traffic from HTTP to HTTPS.

1. Log on to TMG 2010 Server or TMG 2010 Array from the Array Manager or EMS using Administrator Account.

2. Open TMG Console, In the Forefront TMG Management console, in the tree, click the **Firewall Policy** node.

3. Click on **Firewall Policy**, In the **Tasks Pan**, Click **Publish Web Sites,** Type the name of the policy as **Redirect OWA**. Click **Next**

4. On the **Select Rule Action Page,** Click **Allow,** Click **Next**

5. On the **Publishing Type Page,** Select **Publish a Single Web Site or Load Balancer,** Click **Next**

6. On the **Server Connection Security Page,** Select **Use SSL to connect to the published Web Servers,** Click **Next**

7. On the **Internal Publishing Details page, select Internal site name webmail.superplaneteers.com,** Click **Next**. On the **select Use a computer name or IP address to connect to the published server**, and type 10.10.10.15 which is load balancer VIP or Microsoft NLB cluster IP. Click **Next**. On the **Internal Publishing Details Page,** Click **Next**

8. On the **Public Name Details Page,** type **webmail.superplaneteers.com** and Leave **Path (Optional)** Blank. Click **Next.**

9. On the **Web Listener Page,** Select **Exchange2013OWA** from the drop down list. Click **Next**

10. On the **Authentication Delegation Page,** Select **No Delegation but client may authenticate directly,** Click **Next**

11. On the **User Set Page,** Remove **All Authenticated Users,** Add **All Users, Ignore Warning** Click **Ok.** Click **Finish.**

12. Right Click on **Redirect OWA Policy, Click Property,** Click **Action Tab,** Select **Deny,** Check **Redirect HTTP request to this Web Page,** Type https://webmail.superplaneteers.com/owa. On the **Listener Tab, Click Properties,** Click **Connections,** Check **Enable HTTP Connect on Port: 80,** Check **Redirect Authenticated Traffic from HTTP to HTTPS,** Click **Apply,** Click **OK.** Click **Apply,** Click **Ok.**

13. Click **Apply** to Finish the Configuration. Click **Ok.**

4.22 Redirect OWA traffic from HTTP to HTTPS in CAS Servers

For security and encryption of Exchange OWA traffic, you must redirect all incoming HTTP request to HTTPS. Follow the steps redirect OWA traffic from HTTP to HTTPS.

1. Log on to Exchange CAS Server using Administrator Account.
2. Click **Server Manager,** Click **Tools,** Click **Internet Information Services (IIS) Manager**
3. Click **Default Web Site**, Double Click on **HTTP Redirect,** Check **Redirect Request to this destination,** Type the name of the URL where you want to redirect OWA client, for example: https://webmail.superplaneteers.com/owa . Check **Only redirect request to content in this directory (not subdirectories)**, Click **Apply.**
4. Go back to **Default Web Site,** Click **SSL Settings,** uncheck **Require SSL,** Click **Apply.**
5. Manually configure redirect HTTP and SSL settings for the subdirectories under default web site (excluding OWA subdirectory) as mentioned below:

Subdirectories	SSL Settings	Redirect HTTP
aspnet_client	Enable SSL	Uncheck
Autodiscover	Enable SSL	Uncheck
ecp	Enable SSL	Uncheck
EWS	Enable SSL	Uncheck
Microsoft-Server-ActiveSync	Enable SSL	Uncheck
OAB	Enable SSL	Uncheck
PowerShell	DISABLE SSL	Uncheck
Rpc	Enable SSL	Uncheck

6. Finally, open a command prompt window and run "**iisreset /noforce**"in order for the changes to be applied.
7. Repeat step 1 to step 6 for all CAS Servers in Exchange Organization.

4.23 Configure Mail Apps for Outlook Client

Since Outlook Web App Customization isn't supported in Exchange 2013, you can install a customized Outlook Mail Apps using EAC of Exchange 2013. Mail apps provide a single interface and programming model that use web standards to create a custom experience for your users. Your mail app can be simple or complex, use data from an Exchange server or from any service on the web, and fully integrate with both Outlook Web App and Outlook 2013.

You can install mail apps on an internal server to limit access to authorized users, or you can put your mail app on the **Office Store and Apps** for sale to the general public. Anyone who is running Outlook Web App or Outlook 2013 can download, install, and use mail apps from the marketplace. Mail apps use HTM5, JavaScript and XML.

To install a mail app

1. Open the EAC by using a URL that resembles the following:

   https://<FQDN of exchange CAS server>/ecp/

2. Log on to the Exchange server by using a valid user name and password.
3. Click **Organization**, Click **Apps.**
4. Click **Add+** a new mail app.
5. From the drop-down list, select **Add from URL**.
6. Enter the fully qualified URL of the manifest file that you deployed earlier to your web server, and then choose **Install**.
7. Select the user name in the upper-right corner of the window and select My Mail to switch to your email to test the mail app.

Visit http://msdn.microsoft.com/en-us/library/exchange/jj190894.aspx for more information.

CHAPTER 5

In This Chapter

- Configure Role Based Administration for Exchange Server 2013
- Create a Mailbox using Exchange EMC
- Create a Room Mailbox using Exchange EMC
- Create a Shared Mailbox using Exchange EMC
- Configure Transport Rules
- Create Recipient Policy
- Create Email Policy
- Create an Authoritative Domain in Exchange
- Configure Mailbox Journaling
- Configure Mailbox Audit Logging
- Create Public Folder and Assign Permission
- Configure Offline Address Book
- Configure Outlook Web Access Policy
- Migrate Exchange mailbox from local server

Chapter5. Administering Exchange Server 2013

5.1 Configure Role Based Administration for Exchange Server 2013

A management role group is a universal security group (USG) used in the Role Based Access Control (RBAC) permissions model in Exchange Server 2013. The following list describes the layers that make up the role assignment policy model:

- Mailbox
- Management role assignment policy
- Management role assignment
- Management role
- Management role entry

Role Based Groups

- Compliance Management
- Delegated Setup

- Discovery Management
- Help Desk
- Hygiene Management
- Organization Management
- Public Folder Management
- Recipient Management
- Records Management
- Server Management
- UM Management
- View-Only Organization Management

5.2 Creating Recipients in Exchange Server 2013

Mailboxes are the most common recipient type you will be working on as an Exchange Administrator. All internal users can send/receive messages, voice mail, schedule tasks and appoints via OWA or ActiveSync. Each mailbox is associated with an Active Directory user account. Use the Exchange Administration Center (EAC) or PowerShell to create and manage user mailboxes.

5.2.1 Creating a user mailbox

1. In the EAC, navigate to **Recipients, Click Mailboxes**.
2. Click **New**, Click **User mailbox**.
3. On the **New user mailbox** page, in the **Alias** box, type the user's alias, which specifies the email alias for the user.
4. Select one of the following options:

    - **Existing user,** Click **Browse** to open the **Select User – Entire Forest** dialog box. Select the user account you want to mail-enable, and then click **OK**.
    - **New user** Select to create a new user account in Active Directory and create a mailbox for this user.

5. If you selected **New User** in Step 4, complete the following boxes on the **New user mailbox** page. Otherwise skip Step 5 and go to Step 7.

    - **First name**
    - **Initials**
    - **Last name**
    - **Display name**
    - **Name**

- **Organizational unit** you can select an organizational unit (OU) where you would like to store Active Directory user. To select a different OU, click **Browse**. Select the desired OU, and then click **OK**.
- **User logon name**
- **New Password**
- **Confirm password**

6. **Require password change on next logon** Select this check box if you want the user to reset the password when they first log on to the mailbox.
7. Click **More options** to configure the following boxes. Otherwise, skip to Step 7 to save the new user mailbox.

- **Specify the mailbox database** Use this option to specify a mailbox database instead of allowing Exchange to select a database for you. Click **Browse** to open the **Select Mailbox Database** dialog box. Select the mailbox database you want to use, and then click **OK**.
- **Create local archive storage for this user** Select this check box to create an archive mailbox for the mailbox. Click **Browse** to select a database that resides in the local forest to store the archive mailbox.
- **Address book policy** Use this option to specify an address book policy (ABP) for the mailbox.

8. When you're finished, click **Save** to create the mailbox.

This example creates a new user account and mailbox with the following details:

New-Mailbox -Alias Raihan -Name "Raihan Al-Beruni" -FirstName Raihan -LastName Al-Beruni -DisplayName " Raihan Al-Beruni" -UserPrincipalName raihan@superplaneteers.com -Password (ConvertTo-SecureString -String 'P@ssw0rd1' -AsPlainText -Force)

Get-Mailbox <Name> | FL Name,RecipientTypeDetails,PrimarySmtpAddress

5.2.2 Change user mailbox properties

After you create a user mailbox, you can make changes and set additional properties by using the Exchange Administration Center (EAC) or the Exchange Management PowerShell.

1. In the EAC, navigate to **Recipients, Click Mailboxes**.
2. In the list of user mailboxes, click the mailbox that you want to change the properties for, and then click **Edit**.
3. On the mailbox properties page, click one of the following sections to view or change properties.

  - General
  - Mailbox Usage
  - Contact Information
  - Organization
  - Email Address
  - Mailbox Features
  - Member Of
  - MailTip
  - Mailbox Delegation

5.2.3 Change user mailbox properties

Use the **Get-Mailbox** and **Set-Mailbox** cmdlets to view and change properties for user mailboxes. One advantage of using the PowerShell is the ability to change the properties for multiple mailboxes. For information about what parameters correspond to mailbox properties, type the following command:

  - Get-help Get-Mailbox -Examples
  - Get-Help Set-Mailbox -Examples

Here are some examples of using the PowerShell to change user mailbox properties. This example shows how to forward John's email messages to Raihan (Raihan@superplaneteers.com) mailbox.

Set-Mailbox -Identity John -DeliverToMailboxAndForward $true -ForwardingAddress raihan@superplaneteers.com

This example uses the **Get-Mailbox** command to find all user mailboxes in the organization, and then uses the **Set-Mailbox** command to set the recipient limit to 500 recipients allowed in the To:, Cc:, and Bcc: boxes of an email message.

Get-Mailbox -ResultSize unlimited -Filter {(RecipientTypeDetails -eq 'UserMailbox')} | Set-Mailbox -RecipientLimits 200

5.2.4 Bulk edit user mailboxes

Here's a list of the user mailbox properties and features that can be bulk edited. Note that not all properties in each area are available to be changed.

- Contact Information
- Organization
- Custom attributes
- Mailbox quota
- Email connectivity
- Archive
- Retention policy, role assignment policy, and sharing policy
- Move mailboxes to another database

Uses the EAC to bulk edit user mailboxes

1. In the EAC, navigate to **Recipients, Click Mailboxes**.
2. In the list of mailboxes, select two or more mailboxes.
3. In the Details pane, under **Bulk Edit**, select the mailbox properties or feature that you want to edit.
4. Make the changes on the properties page and then save your changes.

5.3 Configure Shared Mailbox

5.3.1 Create a Shared mailbox

Use the EAC to create a shared mailbox

1. Navigate to **Recipients** , Click **Shared**, and then click **Add+**.
2. Complete the following required fields:

   - Display name
   - Email address

3. To grant Full Access or Send As permissions, click **Add+**, and then select the users you want to grant permissions for.
4. Click **Save** to save your changes and create the shared mailbox.

5.3.2 Create a shared mailbox

This example creates the shared mailbox of Sales Department and grants Full Access and Send on Behalf permissions for the security group Marketing. Users who are members of the security group will be granted the permissions to the mailbox.

New-Mailbox -Shared -Name "Sales Department" -DisplayName "Sales Department" -Alias Sales | Set-Mailbox -GrantSendOnBehalfTo Marketing | Add-MailboxPermission -User MarketingSG -AccessRights FullAccess -InheritanceType All

5.3.3 Convert a User Mailbox into a Shared Mailbox
Use the PowerShell to convert a user mailbox to a shared mailbox. This example converts the user mailbox MarketingDepartment@superplaneteers.com to a shared mailbox.

Set-Mailbox -Identity MarketingDepartment@superplaneteers.com -Type Shared

To verify that you have successfully converted the mailbox, run the following PowerShell command:

Get-Mailbox -Identity MarketingDepartment@superplaneteers.com | Format-List RecipientTypeDetails

5.4 Configure Public Folder in Exchange Server

5.4.1 Create Public Folders

Public folders are designed for shared access and provide an easy and effective way to collect, organize, and share information within organization. By default, a public folder inherits the settings of its parent folder, including the permissions settings.

Use the EAC to create a public folder

When creating a public folder from the EAC, you'll only be able to set the name and the path of the public folder. To configure additional settings, you'll need to edit the public folder.

1. In the EAC, go to **Public Folders,** Click **Public Folders**.

2. If you want to create this public folder as a child to an existing public folder, select the existing public folder in the List view. If you want to create a top-level public folder, skip this step.
3. From the tool bar, click **Add+**.
4. In the new public folder form, type the name of the public folder that you are creating.
5. Verify the path that you are creating this public folder under. If this isn't the desired path, click **cancel** and follow step 2 above.
6. Click **save** to save your public folder.

Use the PowerShell to create a public folder

This example creates a public folder named Reports in the Marketing\2013 public folder path.

New-PublicFolder -Name Reports -Path \Marketing\2013

To verify that you've successfully created a public folder, do the following:

- In the EAC, click **Refresh** to refresh the list of public folders. Your new public folder should display in the list.
- In the PowerShell, run any of the following commands:

  Get-PublicFolder -Identity \Marketing\2013\Reports | Format-List
  Get-PublicFolder -Identity \Marketing\2013 -GetChildren
  Get-PublicFolder -Recurse

5.4.2 Create a public folder hierarchy mailbox

1. Go to **Public Folders,** Click **Public Folder Mailboxes**, and then click **Add+**.
2. In the New Public Folder Mailbox page, provide a name for the new public folder mailbox.
3. Click **Save**.

Use the PowerShell to create a public folder hierarchy mailbox

This example creates the master public folder hierarchy mailbox.

New-Mailbox -PublicFolder -Name MasterHierarchy

This example creates a secondary public folder hierarchy mailbox.

New-Mailbox -PublicFolder -Name PERTH -Database ResourceDB

To verify that you have successfully created the master hierarchy folder, do the following:

Get-OrganizationConfig | Format-List DefaultPublicFolderMailbox

5.4.3 Configure quota limits and retention settings for public folders

The default quota limits and deleted item retention settings are set at the organizational level by using the Set-OrganizationConfig cmdlet in the PowerShell.

This example sets the issue warning quota to 1.9 GB, the prohibit post quota to 2.3 GB, and the maximum items size that can be sent or received to 200 MB. It also changes the default deleted item retention to 30 days.

Set-OrganizationConfig -DefaultPublicFolderIssueWarningQuota 1.9GB -DefaultPublicFolderProhibitPostQuota 2.3GB -DefaultPublicFolderMaxItemSize 200MB -DefaultPublicFolderDeletedItemRetention 30.00:00:00

5.4.4 Create the primary public folder mailbox

The primary public folder hierarchy mailbox will be the first public folder mailbox that you create for your organization. Subsequent public folder mailboxes will be secondary public folder mailboxes. The primary public folder mailbox contains the writeable of the public folder hierarchy.

1. In the EAC, navigate to **Public folders,** Click **Public folder mailboxes**.
2. Click **Add+**.
3. In **New public folder mailbox**, type a name for the mailbox, for example **Primary**.
4. Click **Save** to save your public folder mailbox.

5.4.5 Assign permissions to the public folder

After you create the public folder, you'll need to assign the Owner permissions level so that at least one user can access the public folder from the client and create subfolders. Any public folders created after this one will inherit the permissions of the parent public folder.

1. In the EAC, navigate to **Public folders, Click Public folders**.
2. In the list view, select the public folder.
3. In the details pane, under **Folder Permissions**, click **Manage**.
4. In **Public Folder Permissions**, click **Add+**.
5. Click **Browse** to select a user.
6. In the **Permission level** list, select a level. At least one user should be an **Owner**.
7. Click **Save**.
8. You can add multiple users by clicking **Add+** and assigning the appropriate permissions using the steps above. You can also customize the permission level by selecting or clearing the check boxes. When you edit a predefined permission level such as **Owner**, the permission level will change to **Custom**.

5.4.6 Mail-enable or Mail-Disable the public folder

If you want users to send mail to the public folder, you can mail-enable it. This step is optional. If you don't mail-enable the public folder, users can post messages to the public folder by dragging items into it from within Outlook.

Use the EAC to mail-enable or mail-disable a public folder

1. Go to **Public Folders, Click Public Folders**.
2. In the list view, select the public folder that you want to mail-enable or mail-disable.
3. In the details pane, go to **Mail settings**, and then click **Enable** or **Disable** depending on the mail settings status.
4. A warning box will display asking if you are sure you want to enable or disable email for the public folder. Click **Yes** to continue.

Use the PowerShell to enable email for a public folder

Enable-MailPublicFolder -Identity "\IT Help Desk"

This example mail-enables the public folder Reports under the Marketing public folder, but hides the folder from address lists.

Enable-MailPublicFolder -Identity "\Marketing\Reports" -
HiddenFromAddressListsEnabled $True

This example disables email on the public folder Marketing\Reports.

Disable-MailPublicFolder -Identity "\Marketing\Reports"

5.4.7 View Statistics for Public Folders and Public Folder Items

This topic explains how you use the Exchange Management PowerShell to retrieve
statistics about a public folder, such as the display name, creation time, last user
modified time, last user access, and item size.

This example returns the statistics for the public folder Marketing with a piped
command to format the list.

Get-PublicFolderStatistics -Identity \Marketing | Format-List

This example returns default statistics for all items in the public folder 2013 under
the \Marketing\ path. Default information includes item identity, creation time,
and subject.

Get-PublicFolderItemStatistics -Identity "\Marketing\2013" | Format-List

Use the PowerShell to export the output of the Get-PublicFolderItemStatistics and
Export-csv cmdlet to a .csv file

Get-PublicFolderItemStatistics -Identity "\Marketing\2013" | Select
Subject,LastModificationTime,HasAttachments,ItemType,MessageSize | Export-
CSV C:\2013.csv

5.5 Remove Public Folders in Exchange 2013

You may need to remove public folders that are no longer being used in your
organization

Use the EAC to remove public folders

1. Go to **Public Folders, Click Public Folders**.
2. In the list view, select the public folder that you want to delete, and then
   click **Delete**.

3. A warning box will display asking if you are sure you want to delete the public folder. Click **Yes** to continue.

Use the PowerShell to delete public folders

This example deletes the public folder Help Desk\Resolved. This command assumes that the Resolved public folder doesn't have any sub-folders.

Remove-PublicFolder -Identity "\IT Help Desk\Resolved"

This example tests the previous command without making any modifications.

Remove-PublicFolder -Identity "\IT HelpDesk\Resolved" -WhatIf

This example removes the public folder Marketing and all of its subfolders because the command runs recursively.

Remove-PublicFolder -Identity "\Marketing" -Recurse: $True

5.6 Manage Site Mailbox Provisioning Policies in Exchange 2013

Site mailbox provisioning policies apply only to email that's sent to and from the site mailbox and to the size of the site mailbox on the Exchange server.

Create a site mailbox provisioning policy

This example creates the default provisioning policy SM_ProvisioningPolicy with the following settings:

- The warning quota for the site mailboxes is 9 GB.
- The site mailboxes are prohibited from receiving messages when the mailbox size reaches 10 GB.
- The maximum size of email messages that can be sent to site mailboxes is 50 MB.

New-SiteMailboxProvisioningPolicy -Name SM_ProvisioningPolicy -IsDefault - IssueWarningQuota 9GB -ProhibitSendReceiveQuota 10GB -MaxReceiveSize 50MB

View the settings of a site mailbox provisioning policy

This example returns detailed information about all site mailbox provisioning policies in your organization. Get-SiteMailboxProvisioningPolicy | Format-List

This example returns all policies in your organization, but only displays the IsDefault information to identify which policy is the default policy.

Get-SiteMailboxProvisioningPolicy | Format-List IsDefault

Make changes to an existing site mailbox provisioning policy

This example changes the site mailbox provisioning policy named Default to allow the maximum size of email messages that can be received by the site mailbox to 25 MB.

Set-SiteMailboxProvisioningPolicy -Identity Default -MaxReceiveSize 25MB

This example changes the warning quota to 9.5 GB and the prohibit send and receive quota to 10 GB.

Set-SiteMailboxProvisioningPolicy -Identity Default -IssueWarningQuota 9GB -ProhibitSendReceiveQuota 10GB

Delete a site mailbox provisioning policy

This example deletes the default site mailbox policy that was created during Exchange Setup. Remove-SiteMailboxProvisioningPolicy -Identity Default

5.7 Create a Distribution Group Naming Policy

5.7.1 Create a Group Naming Policy

1. In the EAC, select **Groups, Click More,** Click **Configure group naming policy**.
2. Under **Group Naming Policy**, configure the prefix by selecting either **Attribute** or **Text** in the pull-down menu.
3. Click **Add** to add additional prefixes.
4. For the suffix, in the pull-down menu, select either **Attribute** or **Text**, and configure the suffix.

5. Click **Add** to add additional suffixes.
   After you add a prefix or suffix, notice that a preview of the group naming policy is displayed.
6. To delete a prefix or suffix from the policy, click **Remove**.
7. Click **Blocked Words** to **add+** or **remove-** or **Edit** blocked words.
8. When you are finished, click **Save**.

5.7.2 Manage Dynamic Distribution Groups

Use the EAC to create a dynamic distribution group

1. In the EAC, navigate to **Recipients,** Click **Groups,** Click **New,** Click **Dynamic distribution group**.
2. On the **New dynamic distribution group** page, complete the following boxes:

   - **Display name** (mandatory field)
   - **Alias** (mandatory field)
   - **Description**
   - **Organizational unit** To select a different OU, click **Browse**. The dialog box displays all OUs in the forest that are within the specified scope. Select the OU you want, and then click **OK**.
   - **Owner** An owner for a dynamic distribution group is optional. You can add owners by clicking **Browse** and then selecting users from the list.

3. Use the **Members** section to specify the types of recipients for the group and set up rules that will determine membership. Select one of the following boxes:

   - **All recipient types**
   - **Only the following recipient types** Messages that meet the criteria defined for this group will be sent to one or more of the following recipient types:

     - Users with Exchange mailboxes
     - Users with external email addresses
     - Resource mailboxes
     - Contacts with external email addresses
     - Mail-enabled groups

4. Click **Add a rule** to define the criteria for membership in this group.
5. Select one of the following recipient attributes from the drop-down list and provide a value. If the value for the selected attribute matches that value you define, the recipient receives a message sent to this group.

Use the PowerShell to create a dynamic distribution group

This example creates the dynamic distribution group "Sales DDG" that contains only mailbox users.

New-DynamicDistributionGroup -IncludedRecipients MailboxUsers -Name "Sales DDG" -OrganizationalUnit Users

This example creates a dynamic distribution group with a custom recipient filter. The dynamic distribution group contains all mailbox users that have a value of "FullTimeEmployee" in the CustomAttribute10 property.

New-DynamicDistributionGroup -Name "Full Time Employees" -RecipientFilter {(RecipientTypeDetails -eq 'UserMailbox') -and (CustomAttribute10 -eq 'FullTimeEmployee')}

5.7.3 Change dynamic distribution group properties

Use the EAC to change dynamic distribution group properties

1. In the EAC, navigate to **Recipients, Click Groups**.
2. In the list of groups, click the dynamic distribution group that you want to view or change, and then click **Edit**.
3. On the group's properties page, click one of the following sections to view or change properties.

   - General
   - Ownership
   - Membership
   - Delivery management
   - Message approval
   - Email options
   - MailTip
   - Group delegation

5.8 Manage Mail Contacts

5.8.1 Create a mail contact

Use the EAC to create a mail contact

1. In the EAC, navigate to **Recipients, Click Contacts**.
2. Click **New+, Click Mail contact**.
3. Complete the following boxes on the **New mail contact** page:

   - First name
   - Initials
   - Last name
   - Display name (mandatory field)
   - Name (mandatory field)
   - Alias (mandatory field)
   - External email address (mandatory field)
   - Organizational unit

4. When you've finished, click **Save**.

Use the PowerShell to create a mail contact

This example creates a mail contact for Raihan Al-Beruni.

New-MailContact -Name " Raihan Al-Beruni" -ExternalEmailAddress raihan@superplaneteers.com -OrganizationalUnit Users

Enable-MailContact -Identity "Raihan Al-Beruni" -ExternalEmailAddress raihan@superplaneteers.com

5.8.2 Manage Mail Users

Use the EAC to create a mail user

1. In the EAC, click **Recipients, Click Contacts, Click New, Click Mail user**.
2. On the **New mail user** page, in the **Alias** box, type the alias for the mail user. The alias can't exceed 64 characters and must be unique in the forest. This box is required.

3. To specify an SMTP email address for the mail user's external email address, click **SMTP**.
4. In the **External email address** box, type the mail user's external email address. Email sent to this mail user is forwarded to this email address. This box is required.
5. Select one of the following options:

   - Existing user
   - New user

6. If you selected **New User** in Step 5, complete the following boxes on the **New mail user** page. Otherwise skip to Step 7.

   - First name
   - Initials
   - Last name
   - Display name
   - Name
   - Organizational unit
   - User logon name
   - New Password
   - Confirm password
   - Require password change on next logon

7. When you've finished, click **Save** to create the mail user.

Use the PowerShell to create a mail user

This example creates a mail-enabled user account for Raihan Al-Beruni with the following details:

New-MailUser -Name "Raihan Al-Beruni" -Alias Raihan -ExternalEmailAddress raihan@superplaneteers.com -FirstName Raihan -LastName Al-Beruni - UserPrincipalName Raihan@superplaneteers.com -Password (ConvertTo- SecureString -String 'P@ssw0rd1' -AsPlainText -Force)

5.9 Manage Room Mailboxes

Use the EAC to create a room mailbox

1. In the EAC, navigate to **Recipients, Click Resources**.
2. Click **New, Click Room mailbox**.
3. Complete the following boxes on the **New room mailbox** page:

   - Room name
   - Email address
   - Organizational unit
   - Location, Phone, Capacity
   - Booking requests
   - Delegates

4. Click **More options** to configure the following fields. Otherwise, skip to Step 5 to save the new room mailbox.

   - Alias
   - Specify the mailbox database
   - Address book policy

5. When you're finished, click **Save** to create the room mailbox.

Use the PowerShell to create a room mailbox

This example creates a room mailbox with the following configuration:

New-Mailbox -Database "Resource DB" -Name ConfRoom1 -OrganizationalUnit "Conference Rooms" -DisplayName "ConfRoom1" -Room

5.10 Manage Equipment Mailboxes

Use the EAC to create an equipment mailbox

1. In the EAC, navigate to **Recipients, Click Resources**.
2. Click **New, Click Equipment mailbox**.
3. Complete the following boxes on the **New equipment mailbox** page:

   - Equipment name
   - Email address
   - Organizational unit
   - Booking requests
   - Delegates

4. Click **More options** to configure the following fields. Otherwise, skip to Step 5 to save the new equipment mailbox.

   - Alias
   - Specify the mailbox database
   - Address book policy

5. When you're finished, click **Save** to create the equipment mailbox.

Use the PowerShell to create an equipment mailbox

New-Mailbox -Database "Resource DB" -Name VEHICLE1BXATGT -OrganizationalUnit Equipment -DisplayName "VEHICLE1BXATGT" –Equipment

Where VEHICLE1BXATGT started with first word "vehicle" and "1BXATGT" is the registration number of the vehicle.

5.11 Creating and Configuring Address List

Use the EAC to create an address list

1. Navigate to **Organization, Click Address lists**, and then click **Add**.
2. In **Address List**, type a name and specify the types of recipients to include in the list.
3. By default, Exchange creates address lists that contain all members of your organization. To create a unique custom address list, click **Add a rule**.
4. In the list, select a filtering option (for example, **Custom attribute 1**).
5. In **Specify words or phrases**, type words or phrases to filter by, click **Add+**, and then click **OK**.
   You can continue to add several phrases or words by repeating Step 4. The filter is a Boolean **OR** statement. For example, you can create a filter that will apply the address list to users whose Custom 1 attribute equals **Perth or Canberra**.
6. (Optional) Click **Add a rule** again to add additional filters. Additional filters create a Boolean **And** statement. The more filters you add, the fewer number of users the address list will apply to.
7. Click **Preview recipients the address lists includes** to see the recipients that this address list is going to apply to.
8. Click **Save**.
9. You'll get a warning that the address list won't be applied until you update it. Updating address lists can impact your resources, so you may want to

update the address during off-peak hours.

Use the PowerShell to create an address list

This example creates the address list MyAddressList by using the RecipientFilter parameter and includes recipients that are mailbox users and have StateOrProvince set to Perth or Canberrea.

New-AddressList -Name MyAddressList -RecipientFilter {((RecipientType -eq 'UserMailbox') -and ((StateOrProvince -eq 'Perth') -or (StateOrProvince -eq 'Oregon')))}

This example creates the child address list Building 1ADT in the All Rooms parent container, using built-in conditions.

New-AddressList -Name "Building 1ADT" -Container "\All Rooms" - IncludedRecipients Resources -ConditionalCustomAttribute1 "Building 1ADT"

Use the EAC to update an address list

1. Navigate to **Organization, Click Address lists**.
2. In the list view, select the address list that you want to update.
3. In the details pane, click **Update**.

Use the PowerShell to update an address list

This example updates the address list Perth State.

Update-AddressList "Adddress List Name"
Move-AddressList -Identity GUID -Target "\All Users\Sales"

Use the EAC to remove an address list

1. Navigate to **Organization, Click Address lists**.
2. In the list view, select the address list you want to remove, and then click **Delete**.
3. In the warning, click **Yes** to remove the address list.

Use the PowerShell to remove an address list

This example removes the address list Sales Department, which doesn't contain child address lists. Remove-AddressList -Identity "Sales Department"

5.12 Create a Global Address List

Use the PowerShell to create a GAL using conditional filter properties

This example creates a GAL named GAL_Superplaneteers that includes recipients who are mailbox users and have their company listed as Superplaneteers.

New-GlobalAddressList -Name "GAL_Superplaneteers" -IncludedRecipients MailboxUsers -ConditionalCompany Superplaneteers

Use the PowerShell create a GAL using a recipient filter

This example creates a GAL named GAL_AgencyA that includes recipients for which the CustomAttribute15 parameter has a value of AgencyA.

New-GlobalAddressList -Name "GAL_AgencyA" -RecipientFilter {CustomAttribute15 -like "AgencyA"}

Use the PowerShell to configure GAL properties

This example assigns a new name, Superplaneteers, to the GAL that has the GUID.

Set-GlobalAddressList -Identity GUID -Name Superplaneteers

This example changes the recipients who will be included in the Superplaneteers global GAL to those whose company is set to Superplaneteers.

Set-GlobalAddressList -Identity Superplaneteers -RecipientFilter {Company -eq "Superplaneteers"}

Update-GlobalAddressList -Identity "Superplaneteers"

5.13 Deploying Address Book Policies

Address Book Policies are deployed in the following circumstances.

1. One single Exchange organization offering email systems for multiple divisions and organization within a big enterprise via accepted domain name.
2. One single organization offering email systems for different group of user isolating the visibility of address book within their own address list
3. Two companies sharing one exchange organization restricting visibility of address book within their own organization.

Use the PowerShell to create an address book policy

This example creates an ABP with the following settings:

- **Name:** All Superplaneteers ABP
- **GAL:** All Superplaneteers
- **OAB:** Superplaneteers-All-OAB
- **Room list:** All Superplaneteers Rooms
- **Address lists:** All Superplaneteers, All Superplaneteers Mailboxes, All Superplaneteers DLs, and All Superplaneteers Contacts.

New-AddressBookPolicy -Name "All Superplaneteers ABP" -AddressLists "\All Superplaneteers","\All Superplaneteers Mailboxes","\All Superplaneteers DLs","\All Superplaneteers Contacts" -OfflineAddressBook \Superplaneteers-All-OAB -GlobalAddressList "\All Superplaneteers" -RoomList "\All Superplaneteers Rooms"

Use the EAC to assign an ABP to a mailbox user

1. Navigate to **Recipients, Click Mailboxes**.
2. In the list view, select the user that you want to assign the policy to, and then click **Edit**.
3. Click **Mailbox features**.
4. In the **Address book policy** list, select the ABP that you want to apply to this user.
5. Click **Save**.

Use the EAC to assign an ABP to multiple mailbox users

1. Navigate to **Recipients, Click Mailboxes**.
2. In the list view use the Ctrl key to select multiple users.
3. In the details pane, click **More options**.
4. Under **Address Book Policy**, click **Update**.
5. In the **Select Address Book Policy** list, select the ABP that you want to apply to these users.
6. Click **Save**.

Use the PowerShell to assign an ABP to mailbox users

This example assigns the ABP All Superplaneteers to the existing mailbox user john@superplaneteers.com.

Set-Mailbox -Identity john@superplaneteers.com -AddressBookPolicy "All Superplaneteers"

This example assigns the ABP ABP_SalesDepartment to all mailbox users whose CustomAttribute11 value contains "Engineering Department".

Get-Mailbox -Filter {(CustomAttribute11 -like "Sales Department")} | Set-Mailbox -AddressBookPolicy ABP_SalesDepartment

Change the OAB, Room list, and GAL

This example changes the OAB, room list, and GAL that will be used by mailbox users who are assigned the ABP named All Superplaneteers ABP.

Set-AddressBookPolicy -Identity "All Superplaneteers ABP" -OfflineAddressBook \Superplaneteers-OAB-2 -GlobalAddressList "\All Superplaneteers GAL" -RoomList "\All Superplaneteers Rooms"

Add an address list to an existing ABP

This example adds the address lists Superplaneteers-Perth and Superplaneteers-Albany to the ABP named ABPSuperplaneteers

Set-AddressBookPolicy -Identity "ABPSuperplaneteers" -AddressLists @{Add="Superplaneteers-Perth","Superplaneteers-Seattle"}

Remove an address list from an ABP

This example removes the address lists Superplaneteers-Perth and Superplaneteers-Albany from the ABP named ABPSuperplaneteers

Set-AddressBookPolicy -Identity "ABPSuperplaneteers" -AddressLists @{Remove="Superplaneteers-Perth","Superplaneteers-Albany"}

Replace an address list in an ABP

This example replaces the address lists Joondalup and Bunbury with address lists NorthPerth and SouthPerth for the ABP named ABPSuperplaneteers.

Set-AddressBookPolicy -Identity ABPSuperplaneteers -AddressLists @{Remove=" Joondalup"," Bunbury";Add=" NorthPerth"," SouthPerth"}

5.14 Configure Transport Rules

Use the EAC to create an email address policy

1. Navigate to **Mail flow, Click Email address policies**, and then click **Add+**.
2. In **Email Address Policy**, Complete the following mandatory properties:

   - Policy name
   - Email address format
   - Specify the types of recipients this email address will apply to

3. Click **Add a rule** to further restrict the recipients that this policy will apply to. This creates a Boolean **And** statement.
4. Click **Preview recipients the policy applies to** to view the recipients that policy will apply to.
5. Click **Save** to save your changes and to create the email address policy.
6. You'll get a warning that the email address policy won't be applied until you update it. After it's created, select it, and then, in the details pane, click **Apply**.

Use the PowerShell to create an email address policy

This example creates an email address policy that includes mailbox users in Bunbury and Albany offices who will have email addresses that include their last name combined with the first two letters of their first name.

New-EmailAddressPolicy -Name "South of River Policy" -IncludedRecipients MailboxUsers -ConditionalStateorProvince "Bunbury","Albany" - EnabledEmailAddressTemplates "SMTP:%s%2g@wa.superplaneteers.com"

Use the EAC to remove an email address policy

1. Navigate to **Mail flow, Click Email address policies**.
2. In the list view, select the email address policy that you want to delete and then click **Delete**.
3. In the warning, click **Yes** to remove the policy.

Use the PowerShell to remove an email address policy

This example removes the e-mail address policy South East Offices.

Remove-EmailAddressPolicy -Identity "South River Policy"

5.15 Create an Offline Address Book

This example creates an OAB named OAB_Superplaneteers that uses web-based distribution for Outlook 2007 or later clients on EXCHCASSRV01 by using the default virtual directory.

New-OfflineAddressBook -Name "OAB_Superplaneteers" -AddressLists "\Default Global Address List" -Server EXCHCASSRV01 -VirtualDirectories "EXCHCASSRV01\OAB (Default Web Site)"

When using the AddressLists parameter, any address lists that currently exist will be overwritten. You must include existing address lists when you use the AddressLists parameter to continue to generate those address lists in your OAB.

This example, in which you have AddressList1 and AddressList2, adds AddressList3.

Set-OfflineAddressBook -Identity "My OAB" -AddressLists
AddressList1,AddressList2,AddressList3
Set-OfflineAddressBook -Identity "My OAB" -IsDefault $true

This example sets up the web-based distribution of My OAB for the default mailbox database.

Set-MailboxDatabase -Identity "Mailbox Database" -OfflineAddressBook "My OAB"

Use the PowerShell to specify which OAB will be downloaded by linking the OAB directly to a recipient's mailbox

You need to be assigned permissions before you can perform this procedure or procedures. To specify which OAB is downloaded by linking the OAB directly to a recipient's mailbox, use the following syntax.

Set-Mailbox -Identity <MailboxIDParameter> -OfflineAddressBook
<OfflineAddressBookIdParameter>

This example specifies that the user Raihan will download the OAB My OAB.

Set-Mailbox -Identity Raihan -OfflineAddressBook "My OAB"

Use the PowerShell to specify the OAB that multiple recipients will download

You need to be assigned permissions before you can perform this procedure or procedures. This example specifies that all user mailboxes in Superplaneteers Organization will download the OAB Superplaneteers.

Get-User -ResultSize Unlimited -Filter {Company -eq "Superplaneteers" -and
RecipientType -eq "UserMailbox"} | Where { $_.CountryOrRegion -eq "Australia"} |
Set-Mailbox -OfflineAddressBook "My OAB"

Use the PowerShell to configure OAB properties

This example modifies the time and date at which the OAB generation occurs for the OAB My OAB.

Set-OfflineAddressBook -Identity "My OAB" -Schedule "Sun.1:15 AM-Sun.1:30 AM"

5.16 Configure Mailbox Journaling

5.17 Client Protocol and Mobility Configuration

The following client protocol and mobility services are available in Exchange 2013.

- Outlook Anywhere
- Exchange ActiveSync
- POP3 and IMAP4
- Office Web Apps Server Integration
- Client Protocol Management
- Outlook Web App

5.17.1 Outlook Anywhere

Outlook Anywhere offers Exchange messaging to clients who use Outlook 2013, Outlook 2010, or Outlook 2007.

In Exchange 2013, Outlook Anywhere is enabled by default, because all Outlook connectivity takes place via Outlook Anywhere. The only post-deployment task you must perform to successfully use Outlook Anywhere is to install a valid SSL certificate on your Client Access server. Mailbox servers in your organization only require the default self-signed SSL certificate.

You can test end-to-end client connectivity for Outlook Anywhere and TCP-based connections by using the Test-OutlookConnectivity cmdlet.

5.17.2 Exchange ActiveSync

Exchange ActiveSync provides the following:

- Support for HTML messages
- Support for follow-up flags
- Conversation grouping of email messages
- Ability to synchronize or not synchronize an entire conversation
- Synchronization of Short Message Service (SMS) messages with a user's Exchange mailbox
- Support for viewing message reply status
- Support for fast message retrieval

- Meeting attendee information
- Enhanced Exchange Search
- PIN reset
- Enhanced device security through password policies
- Autodiscover for over-the-air provisioning
- Support for setting automatic replies when users are away, on vacation, or out of the office
- Support for task synchronization
- Direct Push
- Support for availability information for contacts

Managing Exchange ActiveSync

By default, Exchange ActiveSync is enabled. All users who have an Exchange mailbox can synchronize their mobile device with the Microsoft Exchange server.

You can perform the following Exchange ActiveSync tasks:

- Enable and disable Exchange ActiveSync for users
- Set policies such as minimum password length, device locking, and maximum failed password attempts
- Initiate a remote wipe to clear all data from a lost or stolen mobile phone
- Run a variety of reports for viewing or exporting into a variety of formats
- Control which types of mobile devices can synchronize with your organization through device access rules

5.17.3 Change a user's mobile device mailbox policy

You change a single user's mobile device mailbox policy using the EAC.

1. In the EAC, click **Recipients,** Click **Mailboxes** and then select a mailbox.
2. In the Details pane, scroll to **Phone and Voice Features** and select **View details** to display the **Mobile Device Details** screen.
3. The mobile device mailbox policy that's currently assigned is displayed. To change the mobile device mailbox policy, click **Browse**.
4. Choose the appropriate mobile device mailbox policy from the list, click **OK** and then click **Save**.

Use the PowerShell to add a user to a mobile device mailbox policy

You can change a single user's mobile device mailbox policy using the Get-CASMailbox cmdlet in the PowerShell, run the following command.

Get-CASMailbox -Identity raihan@superplaneteers.com -ActiveSyncMailboxPolicy "Sales"

Use the bulk edit tool in the EAC to change the mobile device mailbox policy for multiple users

You can update the mobile device mailbox policy for multiple users at once using the Bulk Edit functionality.

1. In the EAC, click **Recipients,** Click **Mailboxes.**
2. Select multiple users.
3. In the Details pane, scroll down to **Exchange ActiveSync** and click **Update a policy**.
4. Click **Browse** to choose a mobile device mailbox policy.
5. Click **OK** and then click **Save.**

You can use the PowerShell to change the mobile device mailbox policy for a filtered set of users. You can filter users on a variety of attributes.

Get-Mailbox | where { $_.CustomAttribute1 -match "Manager"} | Set-CASMailbox -activesyncmailboxpolicy(Get-ActiveSyncMailboxPolicy "Superplaneteers").Identity

Use the EAC to create a new mobile device mailbox policy

You can create a new mobile device mailbox policy using the EAC.

1. In the EAC, click **Mobile,** Click **Mobile Device Mailbox Policies**, and then click **New**.
2. Use the various check boxes and drop-down lists to configure the settings for the mobile device mailbox policy. Click **Save**.

Use the PowerShell to create a new mobile device mailbox policy

You can create a new mobile device mailbox policy using the New-MobileDeviceMailboxPolicy cmdlet. In the PowerShell, run the following command.

New-MobileDeviceMailboxPolicy -Name:"Management" -AllowBluetooth:$true -AllowBrowser:$true -AllowCamera:$true -AllowPOPIMAPEmail:$false -PasswordEnabled:$true -AlphanumericPasswordRequired:$true -PasswordRecoveryEnabled:$true -MaxEmailAgeFilter:10 -AllowWiFi:$true -AllowStorageCard:$true -AllowPOPIMAPEmail:$false

Use the EAC to view mobile device information for users

The EAC displays a list of mobile devices that are currently synchronizing with a user's mailbox. You can view mobile devices by family, model, phone number, or status.

1. In the EAC, click **Recipients, Click Mailboxes** and choose a mailbox.
2. In the Details pane, scroll to **Phone and Voice Features** and click **View details** to display the **Mobile Device Details** screen.

Use the PowerShell to view mobile device information for users

You can use the Get-MobileDevice cmdlet to view a list of mobile devices for a specific user. Run the following command.

Get-MobileDevice -Mailbox useralias

5.17.4 Exchange 2013 Client Access Server Configuration

After you've installed the Exchange 2013 Client Access server, there are variety of configuration tasks that you can perform. Although the Client Access server in Exchange 2013 doesn't handle processing for the client protocols, several settings need to be applied to the Client Access server, including virtual directory settings and certificate settings.

Configuring server certificates

In Exchange 2013, you can use the Certificate Wizard to generate a digital certificate request and signed by a commercial certificate authority like Geotrust, Entrust, Verisign, Go Daddy. After you've requested a digital certificate, you'll need to install it on the Client Access server.

You don't need to install digital certificates on the Mailbox servers in your organization. A self-signed certificate is installed by default on the Mailbox servers, and it doesn't need to be replaced. The Client Access servers in your organization implicitly trust the self-signed certificate on the Mailbox servers.

Configuring virtual directories

There are several settings that you can configure on the virtual directories for the Offline Address Book (OAB), Exchange Web Services, Exchange ActiveSync, Outlook Web App, and the Exchange Administration Center. You can configure the virtual directories using the following commands.

To configure Outlook Anywhere, run the following command.

Enable-OutlookAnywhere -Server: EXCHCASSRV01 - ExternalHostName:webmail.superplaneteers.com -SSLOffloading $true

To configure Exchange ActiveSync, run the following command.

Set-ActiveSyncVirtualDirectory -Identity EXCHCASSRV01 -ExternalUrl "https://webmail.superplaneteers.com/Microsoft-Server-ActiveSync"

To configure the Exchange Web Services virtual directory, run the following command.

Set-WebServicesVirtualDirectory -Identity EXCHCASSRV01 -ExternalUrl "https://webmail.superplaneteers.com/EWS/Exchange.asmx"

To configure the Offline Address Book, run the following command.

Set-OabVirtualDirectory -Identity EXCHCASSRV01 -ExternalUrl "https://webmail.superplaneteers.com/OAB"

5.17.5 POP3 and IMAP Services

Do one of the following to start or stop Exchange related services in Windows Server 2012.

1. On the computer running the Client Access server role or Mailbox Server Role, Hover mouse on the right hand side top corner, click **Search**, Type **Services**, then right click on **Services,** Click **run as Administrator**. Right-click

Microsoft Exchange POP3, Microsoft Exchange IMAP4, Microsoft Exchange POP3 Backend and then click **Start/Stop**.

2. On the computer running the Client Access server role or Mailbox Server Role, Right Click on **PowerShell**, Click **run as Administrator**, run the following command to start the Microsoft Exchange related service.

Start-service MSExchangePOP3
Stop-service MSExchangePOP34

Use the Microsoft Management Console Services snap-in to set start type Automatic

On the computer running the Client Access server role and Mailbox Role:

1. In the **Services** snap-in, in the console tree, click **Services (Local)**.
2. In the result pane, right-click on any **Microsoft Exchange Services**, and then click **Properties**.
3. On the **General** tab, under **Startup type**, select **Automatic**, and then click **Apply**.
4. Under **Service status**, click **Start**, and then click **OK**.

Set the Microsoft Exchange IMAP4 service to start automatically using Windows PowerShell. Set-service msExchangeIMAP4 -startuptype automatic

Use the EAC to enable or disable POP3 for a user

1. In the EAC, navigate to **Recipients, Click Mailboxes**.
2. In the result pane, select the user for which you want to enable or disable POP3, and then click **Edit**.
3. In the **User Mailbox** dialog box, in the console tree, click **Mailbox Features**. In the result pane, under **Email Connectivity**, do one of the following:

   - To disable POP3 for the user, under **POP3: Enabled**, click **Disable**.
   - To enable POP3 for the user, under **POP3: Disabled**, click **Enable**.

4. Click **Save**.

Use the PowerShell to enable or disable POP3 for a user

This example enables POP3 for the user Raihan Al-Beruni.

Set-CASMailbox -Identity "Raihan Al-Beruni" -POPEnabled $true

This example disables POP3 for the user Raihan Al-Beruni.

Set-CASMailbox -Identity "Raihan Al-Beruni" -POPEnabled $false

5.18 Office Web Apps Server Integration in Exchange 2013

By default, the following file types are displayed using Office Web Apps Server:

- Word documents (doc, docx, dotx, dot, dotm extensions)
- Excel documents (xls, xlsx, xlsm, xlm, xlsb extensions)
- PowerPoint documents (ppt, pptx, pps, ppsx, potx, pot, pptm, potm, ppsm extensions)

In Exchange 2010, the attachment previews were displayed using the web-ready document viewing technology, which is built in to Exchange. With Office Web Apps Server integration in Exchange Server 2013, when the user wants to preview an Office attachment, Exchange makes a call to the Office Web Apps Server which renders the document instead. This provides a richer preview experience for the user.

Office Web Apps Server integration for attachment previews is available to all Exchange Online customers. Exchange on-premises customers need to deploy an Office Web Apps Server to enable the functionality.

Configure Office Web Apps Server Integration

This section provides detailed steps for configuring Office Web Apps Server integration with Exchange Server 2013 for on-premises customers. This procedure doesn't apply to Exchange Online customers because Microsoft has already enabled the functionality in Exchange Online.

Configure the Office Web Apps Server URL

To use Office Web Apps Server to render attachments in Outlook Web App, you must specify the URL of your Office Web Apps Server. Use the Set-OrganizationConfig cmdlet to configure the URL.

Use the PowerShell to configure the Office Web Apps Server URL

You need to be assigned permissions before you can perform this procedure or procedures. This example sets the Office Web Apps Server URL to https://Server/hosting/discovery.

Set-OrganizationConfig -WACDiscoveryEndPoint https://Server/hosting/discovery

To verify that you have configured the Office Web App Server URL correctly, do the following, Run the following PowerShell command:

Get-OrganizationConfig | Format-List WACDiscoveryEndPoint

Enable or disable Office Web Apps Server rendering

You can enable rendering of attachments using Office Web Apps Server for both public and private computers. Use the Set-OwaVirtualDirectory cmdlet for both options.

Use the PowerShell to enable Office Web Apps Server rendering on private computers

This example enables Office Web Apps Server rendering on the default Outlook Web App virtual directory on server EXCHCASSRV01 for users who logged on to Outlook Web App using the Private option:

Set-OwaVirtualDirectory "EXCHCASSRV01\owa (Default Web Site)" - WacViewingOnPrivateComputersEnabled $true

Use the PowerShell to disable Office Web Apps Server rendering on public computers

This example disables Office Web Apps Server rendering on the default Outlook Web App virtual directory on server EXCHCASSRV01 for users who logged on to Outlook Web App using the Public option.

Set-OwaVirtualDirectory "EXCHCASSRV01\owa (Default Web Site)" - WacViewingOnPublicComputersEnabled $true

To verify that you have configured Office Web Apps server rendering correctly, do the following, Run the following PowerShell command:

Get-OwaVirtualDirectory "EXCHCASSRV01\owa (Default Web Site)" | Format-List Name,WacViewing

Force Office Web Apps Server rendering

You can force users to render attachments using the Office Web Apps Server first before they can open them directly. You need to be assigned permissions before you can perform this procedure or procedures.

Use the PowerShell to force Office Web Apps Server rendering first on private and public computers

This example configures the Outlook Web App virtual directory on EXCHCASSRV01 so that users always first view supported attachments using Office Web Apps Server before they can open them, regardless of the option they chose when logging on to Outlook Web App.

Set-OwaVirtualDirectory "EXCHCASSRV01\owa (Default Web Site)" -
ForceWacViewingFirstOnPublicComputers $true -
ForceWacViewingFirstOnPrivateComputers $true

5.19 Create an Outlook Web App Mailbox Policy

Use the EAC to create an Outlook Web App mailbox policy

1. In the EAC, click **Permissions,** Click **Outlook Web App policies**.
2. Click the **New** button.
3. Enter a name for your policy.
4. Use the check boxes to enable or disable features. By default, the most common features are displayed. To see all features that can be enabled or disabled, click **More options**.
5. Click **Save** to save the policy.

Use the PowerShell to create an Outlook Web App mailbox policy. This example creates an Outlook Web App mailbox policy named "Company Policy".

New-OwaMailboxPolicy -Name "Company Policy"

Use the EAC to apply an Outlook Web App mailbox policy

1. In the EAC, click **Recipients,** Click **Mailboxes**.
2. In the work pane, click to select the mailbox that you want to apply an Outlook Web App mailbox policy to. You can also select multiple mailboxes.
3. **If you've selected one mailbox:**
    1. Scroll down in the details pane to **Email Connectivity** and click **View Details**.
    2. Click **Browse** to view and select from the available mailbox policies.
    3. Click **Save** to assign the selected policy to the selected mailbox.

    If you've selected more than one mailbox:

    4. Scroll down in the details pane to **Outlook Web App** and click **Assign a policy**.
    5. Click **Browse** to view and select from the available mailbox policies.
    6. Click **Save** to assign the selected policy to the selected mailboxes.

Use the PowerShell to apply an Outlook Web App mailbox policy to an existing mailbox This example applies the Outlook Web App mailbox policy named "Calendar" to the mailbox of the user raihan@superplaneteers.com.

Set-CASMailbox -Identity raihan@superplaneteers.com -OwaMailboxPolicy:Calendar

Remove an Outlook Web App mailbox policy

1. In the EAC, click **Recipients,** Click **Mailboxes**.
2. In the work pane, click to select the mailbox that you want to remove an Outlook Web App mailbox policy from.
3. Scroll down in the details pane to **Email Connectivity** and click **View details**.
   If a mailbox policy has been assigned, click **Clear** to remove it from the mailbox.
4. Click **Save** to save your changes.

Use the PowerShell to remove an Outlook Web App mailbox policy from an existing mailbox.

This example removes the Outlook Web App mailbox policy from mailbox of the user raihan@superplaneteers.com.

Set-CASMailbox -Identity raihan@superplaneteers.com -OwaMailboxPolicy:$null

Use the EAC to view or configure Outlook Web App mailbox policies

1. In the EAC, click **Permissions,** Click **Outlook Web App policies**.
2. In the result pane, click to select the mailbox policy you want to view or configure.
3. Click the **Edit** button.
4. On the **General** tab, you can view and edit the name of the policy.
5. On the **Features** tab, use the check boxes to enable or disable features. By default, the most common features are displayed. To see all features that can be enabled or disabled, click **More options**.
6. On the **File Access** tab, use the check boxes to configure the file access and viewing options for users. The following file access options are available in File Access Tab.

   - Direct file access
   - WebReady Document Viewing
   - Force WebReady Document Viewing when a converter is available

7. On the **Offline access** tab, use the option buttons to configure offline access availability. Click **Save** to update the policy.

This example enables calendar access in the default mailbox policy.

Set-OwaMailboxPolicy -Identity Default -CalendarEnabled $true

This example retrieves the properties of the Outlook Web App mailbox policy Executives in the organization Superplaneteers.

Get-OwaMailboxPolicy -Identity Superplaneteers\Executives

CHAPTER 6

In This Chapter

- Overview Exchange 2013 UM Dial Plan
- Deploy Exchange 2013 UM
- Create and configure IP Gateway
- Configure Voice mail
- Install Language pack

Chapter6. Configuring Unified Communication in Exchange 2013

Unified Communication Overview

Unified Communication in Exchange 2013 brings telephony and email in a single platform i.e. within a user's mailbox. In Exchange 2013, the Client Access server is responsible SIP redirection to mailbox Server. Mailbox Server is responsible for handling Media traffic and act as a SIP peer between VoIP gateways, IP PBXs, or SBCs and itself.

How does it work? When a Client Access server receives a SIP invite for an incoming call, the Microsoft Exchange Unified Messaging Call Router service redirects the incoming call to the Mailbox server. Then a media channel (RTP or SRTP) is created between the VoIP gateway, IP PBX, or session border controller (SBC) and the Mailbox server. Although the Client Access server acts as a SIP redirector, it only handles SIP requests from VoIP gateways, IP PBXs, or SBCs. It doesn't receive any media traffic. Media traffic that uses RTP or SRTP is only passed between the Mailbox server and SIP peers such as VoIP gateways, IP PBXs, or SBCs—not to the Client Access server. When you deploy Exchange 2013 and UM, you have to configure your VoIP gateways, IP PBXs, or SBCs to point to the Client Access servers that you've installed so that incoming calls will be routed correctly for UM.

How does a Mailbox Server record voice mail? After a Client Access server redirects an incoming call to a Mailbox server, a media channel is established between the VoIP gateway, IP PBX, or SBC and the Mailbox server. After the media channel is established, the Microsoft Exchange Unified Messaging service on the Mailbox server plays the user's voice mail greeting, processes call answering rules for the user, and invites the caller to leave a voice message. The Mailbox server then records the voice message, creates a transcription of the message, and deposits it in the user's mailbox.

What is the role of Lync/OCS then? If you're integrating Exchange with Office Communications Server 2007 R2 or Lync Server, both the SIP and RTP or SRTP media channels for incoming calls are handled by Lync servers and the Mailbox server. In a Lync integrated environment, you don't have VoIP gateways, IP PBXs, or SBCs. To Lync, the Mailbox server that's running the Microsoft Exchange Unified Messaging service looks just like Exchange 2010 UM server. The Mailbox server and the Client Access server that's running the Microsoft Exchange Unified Messaging Call Router service are considered trusted peers because both servers must be added to a SIP dial plan. Lync routes the incoming call using the Inbound Routing component, which uses SIP to communicate with the Client Access server and then route the call to a Mailbox server.

6.1 UM listening ports

Protocol	TCP port	UDP port	Can the ports be changed?
SIP (CAS Server)	5060 (unsecured), 5061 (secured).	Not applicable	Use the Set-UMCallRouterSettings cmdlet.
SIP (Mailbox server)	5062 (unsecured), 5063 (secured).	Not applicable	Ports can't be changed.
SIP (Mailbox server-UM worker process)	5065 and 5067 for TCP (unsecured). 5066 and 5068 for mutual TLS (secured).	Not applicable	Ports can't be changed.
RTP (Mailbox server - UM worker process)	Not applicable	Ports between 1024 and 65535.	this isn't a supported configuration

6.2 UM dial plans

Mapping or associating UM dial plans to UM servers isn't required in Exchange 2013 the way it was in Exchange 2007 or Exchange 2010. Client Access or Mailbox servers running UM services don't need to be linked to a dial plan because all Client Access and Mailbox servers are expected to receive all incoming calls from VoIP gateways, IP PBXs, or SBCs. The exception is that SIP dial plans that are used with Lync 2013, Lync Server 2010, and Office Communications Server 2007 R2 must be associated with Client Access and Mailbox servers that you've deployed. Both types of Exchange servers must be added to each SIP dial plan to be included as trusted peers from Communications Server 2007 R2 or Lync Server. Otherwise, Communications Server 2007 R2 or Lync Server will reject outbound calls from users.

Linking UM dial plans

The following table summarizes the relationship between Client Access and Mailbox servers and UM dial plans.

Topology	Dial plan
Client Access and Mailbox on the same server (without OCS 2007 R2 or Lync Server 2010 non-SIP dial plans)	You aren't allowed to add the Client Access or Mailbox servers to a dial plan.
Client Access and Mailbox on different servers (without OCS 2007 R2 or Lync Server 2010 non-SIP dial plans)	You aren't allowed to add Client Access or Mailbox servers to a dial plan.
Client Access and Mailbox server on the same physical server (with OCS 2007 R2 and Lync Server 2010 with SIP dial plans)	For a single SIP dial plan, add all Client Access and Mailbox servers to the SIP dial plan. This will make both servers trusted peers of Office OCS 2007 R2 or Lync Server. You must use the same certificate in your Office OCS 2007 R2 or Lync Server deployment as you do on each Client Access and Mailbox server.
Client Access and Mailbox server on different physical servers (with OCS	For a single SIP dial plan, add all Client Access and Mailbox servers to the SIP dial plan. You must use the same certificate in your Office

2007 R2 and Lync Server 2010 with SIP dial plans)	OCS 2007 R2 or Lync Server deployment as you do on each Client Access and Mailbox server.

6.3 Deploy Exchange 2013 UM

Whether you're deploying UM using IP Private Branch Exchanges (IP PBXs), Voice over IP (VoIP) gateways, or Microsoft Lync Server, all the deployment options for Unified Messaging have several steps in common. These steps are required to create a scalable and highly available system to support large numbers of Unified Messaging users. These steps are as follows:

1. Deploy and configure your telephony components (IP PBX, VOIP Gateway and IP Phone) for Unified Messaging.
2. Verify that you've correctly installed the Client Access server running the Microsoft Exchange Unified Messaging Call Router service and Mailbox server running the Microsoft Exchange Unified Messaging service.
3. Create and configure the required Unified Messaging components.
4. Perform any post deployment tasks for Unified Messaging.

6.3.1 Deploy and configure telephony components

Generally, there are three tasks that must be completed successfully to configure the telephony components that are required by Unified Messaging:

1. Provision PBX lines
2. Organize channels
3. Deploy VoIP gateways

When you integrate your organization's telephony and data networks during the deployment of Unified Messaging, you must configure the telephony and data networking components correctly. You must also configure the following components or interfaces to successfully deploy Unified Messaging:

1. Configure the connection from the IP PBXs in your organization to communicate to VoIP gateways or vice-versa
2. Configure the connection from the VoIP gateway interface to the Client Access role and Mailbox servers role or vice-versa.

6.3.2 Installing the Mailbox and Client Access servers

You must deploy your Client Access and Mailbox servers in your Exchange Organization before you proceed configuring UM Dial plan. Visit **Chapter3** to install and configure CAS and Mailbox roles.

6.3.3 Add the required UM language packs if necessary

US English is default language in UM. If you would like to install multiple language for client and vendor you can install in Exchange Server. UM language packs enable callers and Outlook Voice Access users to interact with the voice mail system in multiple languages. After you install an additional language on a Mailbox server, callers and Outlook Voice Access users can hear email messages and interact with the voice mail system in that language. After you install a UM language pack on a Mailbox server, the language associated with the language pack will be listed as an available option when you configure the default language for the dial plan.

6.3.4 Create and configure UM dial plans

UM dial plans are important to the operation of Unified Messaging and are required to successfully deploy Unified Messaging on your network. After you've successfully installed your Client Access and Mailbox servers, a UM dial plan will be the first component that you'll create.

Perform one of the following procedures to create a new UM dial plan.

1. In the Exchange Administration Center (EAC), navigate to **Unified Messaging, Click UM dial plans** and click **Add+**.
2. On the New UM Dial Plan page, complete the following boxes:
    o   **Name**
    o   **Extension length (digits)** The number of digits for extension numbers is based on the telephony dial plan created on an IP PBX or PBX. This is a required field that has a value range from 1 through 20. The typical extension length is from 3 through 7 digits.
    o   **Dial plan type** A Uniform Resource Identifier (URI) is a string of characters that identifies or names a resource. You can select one of the following URI types for the dial plan:
        ▪   **Telephone extension** This is the most common URI type. Example formats: Tel:512345 or 512345@<IP address>. This is the default URI type for dial plans.

- **SIP URI** Use this URI type if you must have a Session Initiation Protocol (SIP) URI dial plan such as an IP PBX that supports SIP routing or if you're integrating Microsoft OCS 2007 R2 or Lync Server and Unified Messaging. Example format: sip:raihan@superplaneteers.com:Port.
- **E.164** E.164 is an international numbering plan for public telephone systems in which each assigned number contains a country code, a national destination code, and a subscriber number. Example format: Tel:+610812345678.
  - **VoIP security mode** Use this drop-down list to select the VoIP security setting for the UM dial plan. You can select one of the following security settings for the dial plan:
    - Unsecured
    - SIP secured
    - Secured
    - Country/Region code
3. Click **Save**.

Use the PowerShell to create a UM dial plan

This example creates a new UM dial plan named MyUMDialPlan that uses four-digit extension numbers.

New-UMDialplan -Name MyUMDialPlan -NumberofDigits 4

This example creates a new UM dial plan named MyUMDialPlan that uses five-digit extension numbers and supports SIP URIs.

New-UMDialplan -Name MyUMDialPlan -UriType SIPName -NumberofDigits 5

6.3.5 View or configure UM dial plan settings

1. In the EAC, navigate to **Unified Messaging,** Click **UM dial plans**.
2. In the list view, select the UM dial plan you want to view or modify and click **Edit.**
3. On the **UM Dial Plan** page, click **Configure**. Use the configuration options to view specific dial plan settings and to enable or disable features as described in the following steps.

   - General

- Dial codes
- Outlook Voice Access
- Settings
- Dialing rules
- Dialing authorization
- Transfer & search

4. After you configure the required settings, click **Save** to save your changes.

Use the PowerShell to configure UM dial plan settings

This example configures a UM dial plan named MyDialPlan to use 9 for the outside line access code.

Set-UMDialplan -Identity MyDialPlan -OutsideLineAccessCode 9

This example configures a UM dial plan named MyDialPlan to use a welcome greeting.

Set-UMDialplan -Identity MyDialPlan -WelcomeGreetingEnabled $true -WelcomeGreetingFilename welcome.wav

This example configures a UM dial plan named MyDialPlan with dialing rules.

$csv=import-csv "C:\Groups.csv"
Set-UMDialPlan -Identity MyDialPlan -ConfiguredInCountryGroups $csv
Set-UMDialPlan -Identity MyDialPlan -AllowedInCountryGroups "local, long distance"

Use the PowerShell to view UM dial plan settings

This example displays a list of all the UM dial plans. Get-UMDialplan

This example displays a formatted list of all of the settings on a UM dial plan named MyUMDialPlan. Get-UMDialplan -Identity MyUMDialPlan | Format-List

Use the EAC to delete an existing dial plan

1. In the EAC, navigate to **Unified Messaging, Click UM dial plans**.
2. In the list view, select the UM dial plan you want to delete.
3. On the toolbar, click **Delete**. On the warning page, click **Yes**.

Use the PowerShell to delete an existing dial plan

This example deletes a UM dial plan named MyUMDialPlan.

RemoveUMDialplan -identity MyUMDialPlan

6.3.6 Change the audio codec on a Unified Messaging dial plan

1. In the EAC, navigate to **Unified Messaging, Click UM dial plans**.
2. In the list view, select the UM dial plan you want to modify.
3. On the toolbar, click **Edit**.
4. On the **UM dial plan** page, click **Configure**.
5. In **Settings**, under **Audio codec**, use the drop-down list to select one the following:
   o MP3
   o WMA
   o GSM
   o G711
6. Click **Save**.

Use the PowerShell to change the audio codec on a Unified Messaging dial plan

This example sets the audio codec on a UM dial plan named MyUMDialPlan to G.711.

Set-UMDialPlan -Identity MyUMDialPlan -AudioCodec G711

This example sets the audio codec on a UM dial plan named MyUMDialPlan to WMA.

Set-UMDialPlan -Identity MyUMDialPlan -AudioCodec Wma

6.3.7 Use the EAC to change the primary dial by name method

1. In the EAC, navigate to **Unified Messaging,** Click **UM dial plans**.
2. In the list view, select the UM dial plan you want to change, and then click **Edit**.
3. On the **UM dial plan** page, click **Configure**.

4. In **Settings**, under **Primary way to search for names**, use the drop-down list to select the option you want:

    - Last first (default)
    - First last
    - SMTP address

5. Click **Save**.

Use the PowerShell to change the primary dial by name method

This example sets the primary dial by name method to FirstLast. This enables callers who call the Outlook Voice Access number or a UM auto attendant associated with the dial plan to search for a UM-enabled user by their first and then last name.

Set-UMDialPlan -Identity MyUMDialPlan -DialByNamePrimary FirstLast

This example sets the primary dial by name method to LastFirst. This enables callers who call the Outlook Voice Access number or a UM auto attendant associated with the dial plan to search for a UM-enabled user by their last and then first name.

Set-UMDialPlan -Identity MyUMDialPlan -DialByNamePrimary LastFirst

This example sets the primary dial by name method to SMTP address. This enables callers who call the Outlook Voice Access number or a UM auto attendant associated with the dial plan to search for a UM-enabled user by their SMTP address.

Set-UMDialPlan -Identity MyUMDialPlan -DialByNamePrimary SMTPAddress

6.3.7 Configure the number of sign-in failures

1. In the EAC, navigate to **Unified Messaging,** Click **UM dial plans**.
2. In the list view, select the UM dial plan you want to modify, and on the toolbar, click **Edit**.
3. On the **UM dial plan** page, click **Configure**.
4. In **Settings**, under **Number of sign-in failures before disconnecting**, enter the number of sign-in failures.
5. Click **Save**.

Use the PowerShell to configure the number of sign-in failures before users are disconnected

This example sets the number of sign-in failures before users are disconnected to 5 for a UM dial plan named MyUMDialPlan.

Set-UMDialPlan -identity MyUMDialPlan -LogonFailuresBeforeDisconnect 5

6.3.8 Configure the maximum call duration

1. In the EAC, navigate to **Unified Messaging,** Click **UM dial plans**.
2. In the list view, select the UM dial plan you want to modify, and on the toolbar, click **Edit**.
3. On the **UM dial plan** page, click **Configure**.
4. In **Settings**, under **Maximum call duration (minutes)**, enter the number in minutes.
5. Click **Save**.

Use the PowerShell to configure the maximum call duration

This example sets the maximum call duration to 30 minutes on a UM dial plan named MyUMDialPlan.

Set-UMDialPlan -identity MyUMDialPlan -MaxCallDuration 30

6.3.9 Configure the maximum recording duration

1. In the EAC, navigate to **Unified Messaging,** Click **UM dial plans**.
2. In the list view, select the UM dial plan you want to modify, and then on the toolbar, click **Edit**.
3. On the **UM dial plan** page, click **Configure**.
4. In **Settings**, under **Maximum recording duration (minutes)**, enter the number in minutes.
5. Click **Save**.

Use the PowerShell to configure the maximum recording duration

This example sets the maximum recording duration to 30 minutes for a UM dial plan named MyUMDialPlan.

Set-UMDialPlan -identity MyUMDialPlan -MaxRecordingDuration 30

6.3.10 Configure the recording idle time-out value

1. In the EAC, navigate to **Unified Messaging,** Click **UM dial plans**.
2. In the list view, select the UM dial plan you want to modify, and then on the toolbar, click **Edit**.
3. On the **UM dial plan** page, click **Configure**.
4. On **Settings**, under **Recording idle time out (seconds)**, enter the number in seconds.
5. Click **Save**.

Use the PowerShell to configure the recording idle time-out value

This example sets the recording idle time-out value to 10 for a UM dial plan named MyUMDialPlan.

Set-UMDialPlan -identity MyUMDialPlan -RecordingIdleTimeout 10

6.3.11 Configure the input failures before disconnect

1. In the EAC, navigate to **Unified Messaging, Click UM dial plans**.
2. In the list view, select the UM dial plan you want to modify, and then on the toolbar, click **Edit**.
3. On the **UM dial plan** page, click **Configure**.
4. In **Settings**, under **Number of input failures before disconnecting**, enter the number of input failures.
5. Click **Save**.

Use the PowerShell to configure the input failures before disconnect

This example sets the input failures before disconnect to 5 on a UM dial plan named MyUMDialPlan.

Set-UMDialPlan -identity MyUMDialPlan -InputFailuresBeforeDisconnect 5

6.3.12 Configure VoIP security on a UM dial plan

1. In the EAC, navigate to **Unified Messaging, Click UM Dial Plans**, select the UM dial plan on which you want to change the VoIP security, and then click **Edit**.
2. On the **UM Dial Plan** page, click **Configure**.
3. In **General**, under **VoIP security mode**, select one of the following options:
   - **SIP secured**
   - **Unsecured** (default)
   - **Secured**
4. Click **Save**.

Use the PowerShell to configure VoIP security on a UM dial plan

This example configures a UM dial plan named MySecureDialPlan to encrypt both SIP and RTP traffic.

Set-UMDialPlan -identity MySecureDialPlan -VoIPSecurity Secured

This example configures a UM dial plan named MySecureDialPlan to encrypt SIP but not encrypt RTP traffic.

Set-UMDialPlan -identity MySecureDialPlan -VoIPSecurity SIPsecured

This example configures a UM dial plan named MySecureDialPlan to not encrypt SIP and RTP traffic.

Set-UMDialPlan -identity MySecureDialPlan -VoIPSecurity Unsecured

6.4 Create and configure your UM IP gateways

A UM IP gateway represents either a VoIP gateway hardware device or an IP PBX. The combination of the UM IP gateway and a UM hunt group establishes a link between a VoIP gateway or IP PBX and a UM dial plan. In that case, you must use a fully qualified domain name (FQDN) to create the UM IP gateway, and not an IP address. You must also configure the UM IP gateway to listen on TCP port 5061. To configure a UM IP gateway to listen on TCP port 5061, run the following command: Set-UMIPGateway -identity MyUMIPGateway -Port 5061. You must also verify that any VoIP gateways or IP PBXs have also been configured to listen on port 5061 for mutual TLS.

6.4.1 Create a UM IP gateway

Perform one of the following procedures to create a new UM IP gateway.

1. In the EAC, navigate to **Unified Messaging,** Click **UM IP Gateways**, and then click **Add**.
2. On the **New UM IP gateway** page, enter the following information:

   - **Name** Use this box to specify a unique name for the UM IP gateway.
   - **Address** You can configure a UM IP gateway with either an IP address or a fully qualified domain name (FQDN).
   - **UM dial plan** Click **Browse** to select the UM dial plan that you want to associate with the UM IP gateway.

3. Click **Save**

6.4.2 Create and configure your UM hunt groups

Hunt group is a term that's used to describe a group of PBX or IP PBX resources or extension numbers that are shared by users. Hunt groups are used to efficiently distribute calls into or out of a given business unit.

When you create a UM hunt group, you enable all Mailbox servers that are specified within the UM dial plan to communicate with a VoIP gateway.

1. In the EAC, navigate to **Unified Messaging,** Click **UM dial plans**. In the list view, select the UM dial plan you want to change and then click **Edit**.
2. On the **UM Dial Plan** page, under **UM Hunt Groups**, on the toolbar, click **Add**.
3. On the **New UM Hunt Group** page, complete the following boxes:

   - Associated UM IP gateway
   - Name
   - Dial plan

4. **Pilot identifier** Use this box to specify a string that uniquely identifies the pilot identifier or pilot ID configured on the PBX or IP PBX.
5. Click **Save**.

6.4.3 Create and configure UM auto attendants

Unified Messaging enables you to create one or more UM auto attendants, depending on the needs of your organization. When you create a UM auto attendant, you create a voice menu system for your organization. Callers from outside or inside your organization can then move through the menu system to locate and place or transfer calls to users or departments in your organization.

Creating and using auto attendants is optional in Unified Messaging. However, if you want to create a new UM auto attendant, following procedures below.

1. In the EAC, navigate to **Unified Messaging**, Click **UM dial plans**, select the UM dial plan for which you want to add an auto attendant, and then click **Edit**.
2. On the **UM Dial Plan** page, under **UM Auto Attendants**, click **Add**.
3. On the **New UM auto attendant** page, complete the following fields:
   - **Name** Use this text box to create the display name for the UM auto attendant. A UM auto attendant name is required and must be unique.
   - **Create this auto attendant as enabled** Select this check box to enable the auto attendant to answer incoming calls when you finish creating the UM auto attendant. By default, a new auto attendant is created as disabled.
   - **Set the auto attendant to respond to voice commands** Select this check box to speech-enable the UM auto attendant.
   - **Access numbers** Use this box to enter the extension or telephone numbers that callers will use to reach the auto attendant. Type an extension number or telephone number in the box, and then click **Add+** to add the number to the list. You can edit or remove an existing extension number or pilot identifier. To edit an existing extension number or telephone number, click **Edit**. To remove an existing extension number or telephone number from the list, click **Remove**.
4. Click **Save**.

Use the PowerShell to create a UM auto attendant

This example creates a UM auto attendant named MyUMAutoAttendant that can accept incoming calls but isn't speech-enabled.

New-UMAutoAttendant -Name MyUMAutoAttendant -UMDialPlan MyUMDialPlan -PilotIdentifierList 55000 -Enabled $false

This example creates a speech-enabled UM auto attendant named MyUMAutoAttendant.

New-UMAutoAttendant -Name MyUMAutoAttendant -UMDialPlan MyUMDialPlan -PilotIdentifierList 56000,56100 -SpeechEnabled $true

6.4.4 Add an extension or phone numbers for a UM auto attendant

1. In the EAC, navigate to **Unified Messaging**, Click **UM dial plans**. In the list view, select the UM dial plan you want to edit and click **Edit**.
2. On the **UM Dial Plan** page, under **UM Auto Attendants**, select the UM auto attendant you want to add extension or phone numbers to.
3. On the toolbar, click **Edit**.
4. On the **UM Auto Attendant** page , Click **General**, under **Access numbers**, in the text box, enter the extension or phone number that you want to use and click **Add+**.
5. Click **Save** to add the number.

Use the PowerShell to configure an extension number on a UM auto attendant

This example configures a UM auto attendant named MyUMAutoAttendant with multiple extension numbers.

Set-UMAutoAttendant -Identity MyUMAutoAttendant -PilotIdentifierList "12345, 72000, 75000"

6.4.5 Specify business hours for a UM auto attendant

1. In the EAC, navigate to **Unified Messaging** , Click **UM dial plans**. In the list view, select the UM dial plan you want to change, and then click **Edit**.
2. On the **UM Dial Plan** page, under **UM Auto Attendants**, select the UM auto attendant for which you want to set the business hours, and then click **Edit**.
3. On the **UM Auto Attendant** page, , Click **Business Hours**, under **Business hours**, click **Configure business hours**.
4. On the **Configure Business Hours** page, select the hours you want to use as your business hours for each day of the week.

5. Click **OK**, and then click **Save**.

Use the PowerShell to specify business hours for a UM auto attendant

This example sets the business hours for a UM auto attendant named MyUMAutoAttendant.

Set-UMAutoAttendant -Identity MyUMAutoAttendant -BusinessHoursSchedule 0.10:45-0.13:15,1.09:00-1.17:00,6.09:00-6.16:30

6.4.6 Configure a speech-enabled auto attendant with a DTMF fallback

1. In the EAC, navigate to **Unified Messaging**, Click **UM dial plans**. In the list view, select the UM dial plan you want to change and click **Edit**.
2. On the **UM Dial Plan** page, under **UM Auto Attendants**, select the UM auto attendant for which you want to create a DTMF fallback auto attendant. On the toolbar, click **Edit**.
3. On the **UM Auto Attendant** page , Click **General**, select the check box next to **Use this auto attendant when voice commands don't work correctly**, and then click **Browse**.
4. On the **Select a UM Auto Attendant** page, select the auto attendant you want to use as a DTMF fallback auto attendant, and then click **Save**.

Use the PowerShell to configure a speech-enabled auto attendant with a DTMF fallback auto attendant

This example configures a UM auto attendant named MySpeechEnabledAA to use a DTMF fallback auto attendant named MyDTMFAA.

Set-UMAutoAttendant -Identity MySpeechEnabledAA -
DTMFFallbackAutoAttendant MyDTMFAA

6.4.7 Configure UM auto attendant navigation menus

1. In the EAC, navigate to **Unified Messaging** , Click **UM dial plans**. In the list view, select the UM dial plan you want to change, and then click **Edit**.
2. On the **UM Dial Plan** page, under **UM Auto Attendants**, select the UM auto attendant for which you want to create menu navigation. On the toolbar, click **Edit**.

3. On the **UM Auto Attendant** page, click **Menu navigation**, select either **Enable business hours menu navigation** or **Enable non-business hours menu navigation**, and then click **Add+**.

4. On the **New menu navigation entry** page, configure the following:

- **Prompt** Use this box to type the name of the new navigation menu.
- **When this key is pressed** The key mapping is the number key that a caller presses to have the auto attendant perform a specific operation, for example, forwarding the caller to another auto attendant or to an operator. By default, no entries are defined. Use the drop-down list to select the numeric key (from 1 through 9) that the caller must press. Zero (0) is reserved for the auto attendant operator.
- **Play the following audio file** Use this option to select a previously recorded audio file for callers. Click **Change**, and then click **Browse** to locate the audio file.
- **Perform this additional action** Select one of the following options to define the action that you want the auto attendant to perform for the caller:

  - **None**
  - **Transfer to this extension**
  - **Transfer to this UM auto attendant** Select this option to transfer the call to an auto attendant. Click **Browse** to locate the auto attendant that you want to use.
  - **Leave a voice message for this user** Select this option to enable a caller to leave a voice mail message for a user that's on the same dial plan as the UM auto attendant that you're configuring. Click **Browse** to locate the UM-enabled user.
  - **Announce business location** Select this option to enable a caller to choose an auto attendant menu option and hear the location of the business that's configured on the UM auto attendant. To enable this to work correctly, you must first enter the business location in the **Business location** box on the **General** page on the UM auto attendant.
  - **Announce business hours** Select this option to enable a caller to choose an auto attendant menu option and hear the hours of operation for the business that's configured on the UM auto attendant. To enable this to work

correctly, you must first configure the business hours on the **Business hours** page on the UM auto attendant.
5. Click **OK** to create the new menu navigation.
6. On the **UM Auto Attendant** page, click **Save** to save your changes.

6.4.8 Enable non-business hours key mappings on a UM auto attendant

1. In the EAC, navigate to **Unified Messaging**, Click **UM dial plans**. In the list view, select the UM dial plan you want to change, and then click **Edit**.
2. On the **UM Dial Plan** page, under **UM Auto Attendants**, select the UM auto attendant for which you want to create a non-business hours navigation menu. On the toolbar, click **Edit**.
3. On the **UM Auto Attendant** page, click **Menu navigation**, under **Non-business hours menu navigation**, select **Enable non-business hours menu navigation**, and then click **Add**.
4. On the **New menu navigation entry** page, use the following options to create a new menu navigation entry:

   - **Prompt**
   - **When this key is pressed**
   - **Play the following audio file**
   - **Perform this additional action**

5. Click **OK** to create the new menu navigation.
6. On the **UM Auto Attendant** page, click **Save** to save your changes.

Use the PowerShell to enable non-business hours key mappings on a UM auto attendant

This example configures a UM auto attendant named MyAutoAttendant and enables non-business hours key mappings so that when callers say "After Hours" they will be forwarded to extension number 12345, and if they say "Directions" they will be forwarded to extension number 23456.

Set-UMAutoAttendant -Identity MyUMAutoAttendant -
AfterHoursKeyMappingEnabled $true -AfterHoursKeyMapping
"AfterhoursOperator,12345","Directions,23456"

6.4.9 Enable business hours key mappings on a UM auto attendant

1. In the EAC, navigate to **Unified Messaging** , Click **UM dial plans**. In the list view, select the UM dial plan you want to change, and then click **Edit**.
2. On the **UM Dial Plan** page, under **UM Auto Attendants**, select the UM auto attendant for which you want to create a business hours navigation menu. On the toolbar, click **Edit**.
3. On the **UM Auto Attendant** page, click **Menu navigation**, under **Business hours menu navigation**, select **Enable business hours menu navigation**, and then click **Add**.
4. On the **New menu navigation entry** page, use the following options to create a new navigation entry:

   - Prompt
   - When this key is pressed
   - Play the following audio file
   - Perform this additional action

5. Click **OK** to create the new menu navigation.
6. On the **UM Auto Attendant** page, click **Save** to save your changes.

Use the PowerShell to enable business hours key mappings on a UM auto attendant

This example configures a UM auto attendant named MyAutoAttendant and enables business hours key mappings so that when callers press 1, they're forwarded to another UM auto attendant named SalesAutoAttendant. When they press 2, they're forwarded to extension number 12345 for Support, and when they press 3, they're sent to another auto attendant that plays an audio file.

```
Set-UMAutoAttendant -Identity MyAutoAttendant -
BusinessHoursKeyMappingEnabled $true -BusinessHoursKeyMapping
"1,Sales,,SalesAutoAttendant","2,Support,12345","3,Directions,,,directions.wav"
```

6.4.10 Enable a UM auto attendant

1. In the EAC, navigate to **Unified Messaging**, Click **UM dial plans**. In the list view, select the UM dial plan you want to change and click **Edit**.
2. On the **UM Dial Plan** page, under **UM Auto Attendants**, select the UM auto attendant you want to enable. On the toolbar, click the **Up arrow**.

3. On the **Warning** page, click **Yes**.

Use the PowerShell to enable a UM auto attendant

This example enables the UM auto attendant named MyUMAutoAttendant to answer incoming calls.

Enable-UMAutoAttendant -Identity MyUMAutoAttendant

6.4.11 Delete a UM auto attendant

1. In the EAC, navigate to **Unified Messaging**, Click **UM dial plans**. In the list view, select the UM dial plan you want to edit, and then click **Edit**.
2. On the **UM Dial Plan** page, under **UM Auto Attendants**, select the UM auto attendant you want to delete. On the toolbar, click **Delete**. On the **Warning** page, click **Yes**.

Use the PowerShell to delete a UM auto attendant

This example deletes a UM auto attendant named MyUMAutoAttendant.

Remove-UMAutoAttendant -Identity MyUMAutoAttendant

6.4.12 Disable a UM auto attendant

1. In the EAC, navigate to **Unified Messaging**, Click **UM dial plans**. In the list view, select the dial plan you want to change, and on the toolbar, click **Edit**.
2. On the **UM Dial Plan** page, under **UM Auto Attendants**, select the UM auto attendant you want to disable. On the toolbar, click **Down arrow**
3. On the **Warning** page, click **Yes**.

Use the PowerShell to disable a UM auto attendant

This example disables a UM auto attendant named MyUMAutoAttendant.

Disable-UMAutoAttendant -Identity MyUMAutoAttendant

6.5 Create and configure a UM mailbox policy

Every time you create a UM dial plan, a UM mailbox policy is also created. The UM mailbox policy will be named <DialPlanName> Default Policy. However, if you have to create a new UM mailbox policy, perform one of the following procedures.

1. In the EAC, navigate to **Unified Messaging**, Click **UM dial plans**. In the list view, select the UM dial plan you want to modify.
2. On the **UM dial plan** page, under **UM Mailbox Policies**, click **Add+** on the toolbar.
3. On the **New UM Mailbox Policy** page, in the **Name** text box, enter the name of the new UM mailbox policy.
4. Click **Save** to save the new UM mailbox policy.

6.6 Deploying Exchange UM and Lync Server overview

Unified Messaging combines voice and email messaging into a single messaging infrastructure. Microsoft Lync Server Enterprise Voice takes advantage of the UM infrastructure to provide voice mail, Outlook Voice Access, call notifications, and auto attendants.

The following list shows deployment steps for UM and Lync Server.

1. Install Microsoft Lync Server in the same topology where CAS and Mailbox servers running and confirm that at least one Lync pool is created.
2. Install a certificate that's valid and signed by a private or public certification authority (CA) and is trusted by Lync Server.
3. Install the Client Access servers and Mailbox servers. Verify installation.
4. Install a certificate that's valid and signed by the same CA as the certificate you installed on your Lync servers.
5. Create and configure a Session Initiation Protocol (SIP) URI dial plan.
6. Add all Client Access and Mailbox servers to the SIP URI dial plan.
7. Run the ExchUcUtil.ps1 script from the Exchange Installation folder \Exchange Server\Script folder on a Mailbox server.
8. Run OcsUmUtil.exe from the %ProgramFiles%\Microsoft Lync Server 2013\Support folder on a Lync Server.
9. Deploy the Mediation Server and media gateways.
10. Install a certificate on your Mediation Server that's valid and signed by the same CA as the certificate you installed on your Lync servers.
11. Enable your users for UM and Enterprise Voice.

Certificate configuration recommendations

You must install a certificate that's trusted by both Exchange and Lync Server. In an environment that has Lync Server and Unified Messaging, use the following guidelines for deploying a trusted certificate:

- CA must be a trusted commercial Certificate Authority or internal CA
- Lync servers, Client Access servers, Mailbox servers, Mediation Server, and media gateways must have same certificate with Subject Alternative Name (SAN) or Fully Qualified Domain Name (FQDN) on the subject name.
- Exchange UM doesn't support wildcard certificates with Microsoft Lync Server.

6.7 Installing a UM language pack

1. From the Microsoft Download Center, download the language-specific UM language pack file into a local folder on the Mailbox server.

   You can find UM language pack in the URL http://www.microsoft.com/en-us/download/details.aspx?id=35368

2. Double-click the UMLanguagePack
3. In the Exchange 2013 Setup wizard, on the **License Agreement** page, read the terms of the agreement, select **I accept the terms in the license agreement**, and then click **Next**.
4. On the **Unified Messaging Language Pack** page, verify that the correct language is listed in the **The following Unified Messaging Language Pack(s) will be installed** window, and then click **Install**.
5. Click **Finish** to complete the installation of the UM language pack.

Use setup.com to install a UM language pack

This example installs the Danish (da-DK) UM language pack that's been downloaded to the D:\Exchange\UMLanguagePacks folder on a Mailbox server.

setup.com /AddUmLanguagePack:da-DK /s:d:\Exchange\UMLanguagePacks /IAcceptExchangeServerLicenseTerms

6.8 Configure Voice Mail for User

After you complete a new installation of the Client Access and Mailbox servers and have successfully deployed Unified Messaging, you should complete the following post-installation tasks.

- Enabling users for voice mail
- Secure your UM deployment
- Mutual TLS for UM
- PIN policies for UM-enabled users

6.8.1 Enable a user for Unified Messaging and voice mail

1. In the EAC, click **Recipients**.
2. In the List view, select the user whose mailbox you want to enable for Unified Messaging.
3. In the Details pane, under **Phone and Voice Features**, click **Enable**.
4. On the **Enable UM mailbox** page, click the **Browse** button next to **UM mailbox policy**, locate the UM mailbox policy to assign the user from the list, and then click **ok**.
5. On the **Enable UM mailbox** page, complete the following boxes:

   - SIP address
   - Extension number
   - PIN settings

6. On the **Enable UM mailbox** page, review your settings. Click **Finish** to enable the user for Unified Messaging and voice mail. Click **Back** to make configuration changes.

Use the PowerShell to enable a user for Unified Messaging and voice mail

This example enables Unified Messaging on the mailbox of Raihan@superplaneteers.com, sets the extension number to 7727, sets the PIN for the user to 1985, and assigns the user to a UM mailbox policy named MyUMMailboxPolicy.

Enable-UMMailbox -Identity Raihan@superplaneteers.com -UMMailboxPolicy MyUMMailboxPolicy -Extensions 7727 -PIN 1985 -PINExpired $true

This example enables Unified Messaging on the mailbox of Raihan@superplaneteers.com, assigns the user to a UM mailbox policy named MyUMMailboxPolicy, and sets the extension number, SIP address, and PIN for the user.

Enable-UMMailbox -Identity Raihan@superplaneteers.com -UMMailboxPolicy MyUMMailboxPolicy -Extensions 7727 -PIN 1985 -SIPResourceIdentifier "Raihan@superplaneteers.com" -PINExpired $true

6.8.2 View or configure a UM-enabled user's properties

1. In the EAC, navigate to **Recipients,** Click **Mailboxes**.
2. In the list view, select the mailbox for which you want to change the UM mailbox policy.
3. In the details pane, under **Phone and Voice Features** , Click **Unified Messaging**, click **View details**.
4. On the **UM Mailbox** page, click **UM mailbox settings** to view or change the following UM properties for an existing UM-enabled user:

   - PIN Status
   - UM mailbox policy
   - Personal operator extension

5. On the **UM Mailbox** page, under **Other extensions**, you can add, change, and view extension numbers for the user.

   - To add an extension number, click **Add**. On the **Add another extension** page, use **Browse** to select the UM dial plan, and then enter the extension number in the **Extension number** box.
   - To remove an extension number, select the extension number you want to remove, and then click **Remove**.

6. If you make any changes, click **Save**.

Use the PowerShell to configure features for a UM-enabled user

This example disables Play on Phone and missed call notifications, but enables text message (SMS) notifications.

Set-UMMailbox -Identity raihan@superplaneteers.com -UMEnabled $true -
UMMailboxPolicy AdminPolicy -MissedCallNotificationEnabled $false -
PlayonPhoneEnabled $false -SMSMessageWaitingNotificationEnabled $true

This example prevents a user from accessing the calendar, but enables access to
email when the user is using Outlook Voice Access.

Set-UMMailbox -Identity raihan@superplaneteers.com -UMEnabled $true -
UMMailboxPolicy AdminPolicy -Extension 7727 -FAXEnabled $true -TUIAccessToCal
$false -TUIAccessToEmail True

This example prevents a user from accessing the calendar and email when the user
is using Outlook Voice Access.

Set-UMMailbox -Identity raihan@superplaneteers.com -
TUIAccessToCalendarEnabled $false -TUIAccessToEmailEnabled $false

This example prevents a user from creating call answering rules, receiving incoming
faxes, and using Outlook Voice Access, but enables Automatic Speech Recognition
(ASR).

Set-UMMailbox -Identity raihan@superplaneteers.com -
AutomaticSpeechRecognitionEnabled $true -CallAnsweringRulesEnabled $false -
FaxEnabled $false -SubscriberAccessEnabled $false

Use the PowerShell to view a UM-enabled user's properties

This example displays a list of all the UM-enabled mailboxes in the Active Directory
forest in a formatted list.

Get-UMMailbox | Format-List

This example displays the UM mailbox properties for
Raihan@superplaneteers.com.

Get-UMMailbox -Identity Raihan@superplaneteers.com

6.8.3 Change the UM mailbox policy assigned to a UM-enabled user

1. In the EAC, navigate to **Recipients,** Click **Mailboxes**.
2. In the list view, select the mailbox for which you want to change the UM mailbox policy.
3. In the details pane, under **Phone and Voice Features** , Click **Unified Messaging**, click **View details**.
4. On the **UM Mailbox** page, click **UM mailbox settings**, and then click **Edit**.
5. On the **UM Mailbox** page , Click next to **UM mailbox policy**, click **Browse** to locate the UM mailbox policy for the user.
6. Click **Save**.

Use the PowerShell to change the UM mailbox policy assigned to a UM-enabled user

This example associates a UM-enabled user named Raihan Al-Beruni with a UM mailbox policy named MyUMMailboxPolicy.

Set-UMMailbox -Identity Raihan@superplaneteers.com -UMMailboxPolicy MyUMMailboxPolicy

Use the PowerShell to enable calls from users who aren't UM-enabled

This example allows Raihan Al-Beruni to receive voice calls from callers who aren't UM-enabled.

Set UMMailbox -Identity raihan@superplaneteers.com - AllowUMCallsFromNonUsers SearchEnabled

Use the PowerShell to disable calls from users who aren't UM-enabled

This example prevents Raihan Al-Beruni from receiving voice calls from callers who aren't UM-enabled.

Set UMMailbox -Identity raihan@superplaneteers.com - AllowUMCallsFromNonUsers None

Use PowerShell to allow voice messages from anonymous callers to be received

This example allows UM-enabled user Raihan@superplaneteers.com to receive voice messages from incoming calls that don't contain caller ID information.

Set-UMMailbox -Identity Raihan@superplaneteers.com -AnonymousCallersCanLeaveMessages $true

Use the PowerShell to prevent voice messages from anonymous callers from being received

This example prevents UM-enabled user Raihan@superplaneteers.com from receiving voice messages from calls that don't contain caller ID information.

Set-UMMailbox -Identity Raihan@superplaneteers.com -AnonymousCallersCanLeaveMessages $false

6.8.4 Disable Unified Messaging and voice mail for a user

1. In the EAC, click **Recipients**.
2. In the list view, select the user whose mailbox you want to disable for Unified Messaging.
3. In the Details pane, under **Phone and Voice Features**, under **Unified Messaging**, click **Disable**.
4. In the **Warning** box, click **Yes** to confirm that Unified Messaging will be disabled for the user.

Use the PowerShell to disable Unified Messaging and voice mail for a user

This example disables Unified Messaging and voice mail for the user Raihan@superplaneteers.com, but keeps the UM mailbox settings.

Disable-UMMailbox -Identity Raihan@superplaneteers.com -KeepProperties $True

CHAPTER 7

In This Chapter

- What is a F5 iApp?
- Prerequisites and configuration notes
- Deployment Scenarios
- Preparation worksheets
- Downloading and importing the new iApp
- Configuring the BIG-IP iApp for Microsoft Exchange Server 2010 and 2013
- Modifying the iApp template configuration
- Configuring DNS and NTP settings
- Using X-Forwarded-For to log the client IP address
- Manual configuration tables
- Technical Notes
- Modifying the configuration if using a previous version
- iRules if not using persistence in Exchange 2013

Chapter7. Configuring Load Balancer and SSL offloading for Exchange 2013

In this section you will learn how to configure a F5 BIG-IP system 11 and later version for the Client Access Service of Exchange Server 2013, resulting in a secure, fast, and highly available deployment. BIG-IP version 11.0 introduces iApp™ Application templates, an extremely easy and accurate way to configure the BIG-IP system for Exchange Server 2013 or previous version.

By using the iApp template, you can configure the BIG-IP system to support any combination of Exchange Client Access protocols: Outlook Web App (which includes the HTTP resources for Exchange Control Panel, Exchange Web Services, and Offline Address Book), Outlook Anywhere (RPC over HTTP), ActiveSync, Autodiscover, RPC Client Access (MAPI), POP3 and IMAP4.

Before you begin configuring F5 it is highly recommend that you go through the product documentations to gain knowledge about the product.

For more information on the F5 devices, see http://www.f5.com/products/big-ip/.

7.1 What is a F5 Load Balancer

F5 offers a complete suite of application delivery technologies designed to provide a highly scalable, secure, and responsive Exchange deployment. By deploying F5 load balancer you can:

- Terminate HTTPS connections at the BIG-IP LTM reduces CPU and memory load on Client Access Servers
- Simplify TLS/SSL certificate management.
- Balance load and ensure high-availability across multiple Client Access servers using a variety of load-balancing methods and priority rules.

Products and versions

Product	Version
BIG-IP system	11.0, 11.0.1, 11.1, 11.2
BIG-IP iApp template	microsoft_exchange_2010_cas.
Microsoft Exchange Server	2013 (RTM)

7.2 What is F5 iApp?

F5 iApp is a powerful set of feature in the BIG-IP system that provides a new way to architect application delivery in the data center. iApp includes a holistic, application-centric view of how applications are managed and delivered inside, outside, and beyond the data center. The iApp template for Microsoft Exchange Server 2010 acts as the single-point interface for building, managing, and monitoring the Exchange 2010 and 2013 Client Access role.

7.3 Prerequisites of deploying a F5 Load Balancer

Download F5 load balancer virtual edition from http://downloads.f5.com unless you would like to buy a physical appliance. You need to create a username and password on F5 web site to download BIG-IP v11.x/Virtual Edition. You must obtain a serial number to activate F5. You will be sent a serial number by F5 or reseller once you have purchased the F5.
Once download extract BIGIP-11.2.0.2246.vhd.zip file and save it on to the Hyper-V Datastore. Add the virtual machine to Hyper-v Host. F5 automatically assign 3 virtual NIC: Management, Internal and External. Assign CPU and Memory as required.

Import BG-IP load balancer into Hyper-v

1. Power on the F5 load balancer on Hyper-V.
2. Log in to the command line using **Username:** root **Password:** default
3. You have to configure a management IP address in order to maintain the device from the GUI. At the command prompt, type **Config** and hit **Enter**.
4. Configure TCP/IP, Subnet, Default Gateway of Load Balancer, Hit **Tab** Accept the default configuration.

Configure the BIG-IP for network connectivity

1. Copy Serial No or License Key of F5.
2. Log on to F5 GUI using **username:** admin **password:** admin
3. Upon logging in to the GUI, click **Setup Utility**. The general properties page appears. Click **Next**. Click Activate, Paste License Key, Click **Next**, Click **Accept.** click **Finished**
4. The main introduction screen appears. On the left sidebar, click on **Network**, On the Basic network Configuration Page, click **VLANs**.
5. In the **Name** field of the **General Properties** section, type VLAN1. Under **Resources**, in the Available section, highlight Interface 1.1, and click the arrow button to move that interface to the **Untagged** field. Leave all other fields at default values, and click **Finished**.
6. Go back to the left sidebar, expand **Network**, then click on **Self IPs**. In the **Name** field, type **Self1**. For the IP address, type 10.10.10.12. For the **Netmask**, assign 255.255.255.0. Ensure that **VLAN1** is selected. **Port Lockdown** should be set to **Allow Default**. **Traffic Group** is left unchecked. Click **Finished**.
7. The BIG-IP needs a default route for this lab. In the Left Sidebar, expand **Network**, and click **Routes**. Click **Add**
8. In the **Name** field, assign **DG**. For the **Destination** and **Netmask** fields, type **0.0.0.0**. For the **Resource**, select **Use Gateway** from the drop-down list. In the **Gateway Address** field, select **IP address** from the drop-down list, and type **10.10.10.254**. Click **Finished**.

Configure DNS Settings in Load Balancer

1. On the Main tab, expand **System**, and then click **Configuration**.

2. On the Menu bar, from the **Device** menu, click **DNS**.

3. In the **DNS Lookup Server List** row, complete the following:

a. In the **Address** box, type the IP address of a DNS server that can resolve the Active Directory server.

b. Click the **Add** button.

4. Click **Update**.

Configuring the NTP settings

1. On the Main tab, expand **System**, and then click **Configuration**.

2. On the Menu bar, from the **Device** menu, click **NTP**.

3. In the **Address** box, type the fully-qualified domain name (or the IP address) of the time server that you want to add to the Address List.

4. Click the **Add** button.

5. Click **Update**.

Downloading the iApp template

As a best practice download and import latest Exchange Server 2013 OWA iApp template if available on F5 web site otherwise download Exchange 2010 OWA iApp that supports Exchange 2013. Alternatively you can use default OWA iApp available in BIG-IP.

1. Go to the F5 http://downloads.f5.com site.
2. From the Downloads Overview page, click **Find a Download**. The Select a Product Line page displays.
3. From the **Product Line** column, select BIG-IP v11.0 / Virtual Edition. The Select a Product Version and Container page displays.
4. From the **small** drop-down menu, select the version of the product on which you will be installing the iApp template. The system selects the most recent version of the software by default. The version-specific software updates and releases appear.
5. In the **Name** column, click **iApp-Templates**. A Software Terms and Conditions page appears.
6. Read the **End User Software License Agreement** and accept the license by clicking **I Accept**. If you accept the **End User Software License Agreement**, the Select a Download page appears, with a table detailing the filename, product description, and size of the file.
7. From the **Filename** column of the table, select the file named **iapps-x.x.x.x.zip**. The Select a Download Method page appears.

8. F5 supports the FTP, HTTP, and HTTPS protocols for downloading files from F5. Select one of the three supported protocols listed by clicking the **down arrow** button.
9. A pop-up window appears, asking you to either open or save the file. Select the option to save the file.

Installing the iApp template

1. Unzip the zip file to a location accessible from your BIG-IP system.
2. Log on to the BIG-IP Configuration utility.
3. From the **iApp** tab and select **Templates**.
4. Click **Import**.
5. Select the **Overwrite Existing Templates** box.
6. Click **Browse**.
7. Browse to the location you saved the iApp file.
8. Select the file named **microsoft_exchange_2010_cas.tmpl** that corresponds to the iApp version you want to install. For example, the file for the June 2012 release of this iApp was named **microsoft_exchange_2010_cas.tmpl**.
9. Click **Upload**.

Configuring the BIG-IP iApp for Microsoft Exchange Server 2013

1. Log on to the BIG-IP system.
2. On the Main tab, expand **iApp**, and then click **Application Services**.
3. Click **Create**. The Template Selection page opens.
4. In the **Name** box, type a name. In our example, we use **Exchange-2010_**.
5. From the **Template** list, select **f5.microsoft_exchange_2010_cas**.
6. Follow the screen.

Restart bigd

After performing any modification that requires disabling Strict Updates feature on the Application Service, you must restart the bigd daemon from the BIG-IP command line. From the prompt, run the following command:
bigstart restart bigd

Create a Host (A) record in Active Directory DNS for CAS VIP

1. Log on to DC using the Administrator account.
2. Open Server Manager, Click **Tools** then click **DNS Manager**.

3. In the console tree of the DNS snap-in, open **DC**, and then **Forward Lookup Zones**.
4. Right-click **superplaneteers.com**, and then **New Host (A or AAAA)**.
5. In the **New Host** dialog box, type **webmail** in **Name**, type **10.10.10.15** in **IP address**, click **Add Host**, click **OK**, and then click **Done**.

7.4 Deployment Scenarios

7.4.1 BIG-IP LTM with BIG-IP Edge Gateway

You can select this scenario to offload SSL traffic from CAS Server and configure the BIG-IP as a BIG-IP Edge Gateway or Access Policy Manager (APM) that will use a single virtual server to provide proxy authentication and secure remote access to Exchange Client Access services without requiring the use of an F5 Edge Client. The traffic will be forwarded to another BIG-IP running LTM which provides advanced load balancing, persistence, monitoring and optimizations for those services. The following are the benefits of this scenario:

- HTTP-based Client Access traffic goes to the BIG-IP APM or Edge Gateway, which provides proxy authentication and secure remote access.
- After authentication, the BIG-IP APM or Edge Gateway sends the traffic to a separate BIG-IP LTM for intelligent traffic management.

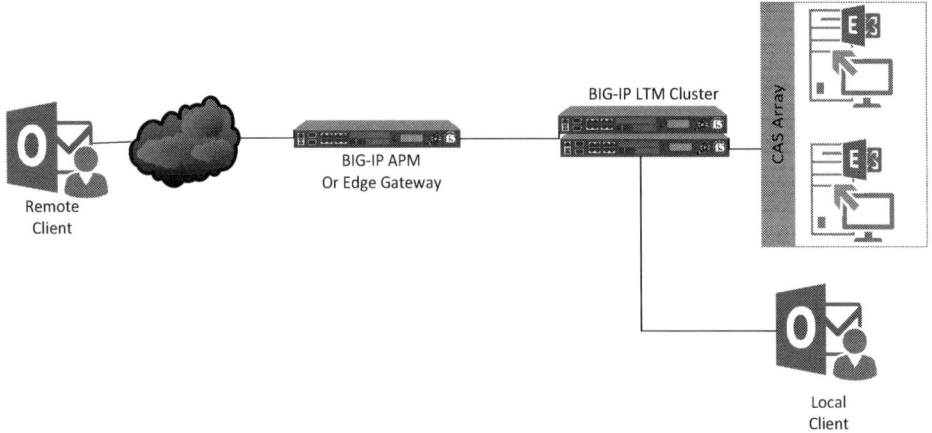

7.4.2 BIG-IP LTM with TMG 2010

You can select this scenario to offload SSL traffic from CAS Servers to the BIG-IP system. This is the traditional role of the BIG-IP LTM and should be used in scenarios where you are not deploying Edge Gateway or Access Policy Manager (APM) on a separate BIG-IP system. The following are the benefits of this scenario.

- All Exchange Client Access traffic goes to the BIG-IP LTM
- The BIG-IP LTM load balances and optimizes the traffic to the Client Access Servers, including the services which are not HTTP-based: RPC Client Access (MAPI), POP3, and IMAP4.
- Remote clients go through TMG 2010 Array to BIG-IP then CAS Array. All the local client session is managed by BIG-IP LTM.

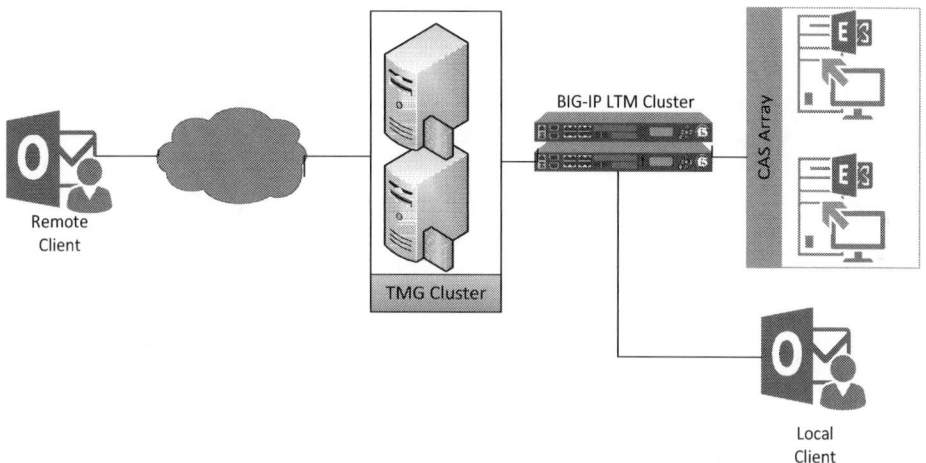

7.5 Configuring F5 Load Balancer for Exchange 2013 Client Access

The next steps show how to configure the BIG-IP to provide load balancing for EXCHCASSRV01 and EXCHCASSRV02 in the Exchange Server 2013 farm.

1. Log in to the GUI and expand the **iApp** section. Select **Application Services**.
2. In the **Name** section, type **Exchange 2013**, and select the template named **microsoft_exchange_2010_cas.**
3. Upon template selection, the GUI will redirect to a newly named iApp template for Exchange Server. At the Template Selection dropdown, the Advanced option gives some options for device and traffic groups.
4. The first section addresses **SSL Encryption**. The next section addresses the **Virtual Server**. This is the IP address that will be resolved to the domain name (for example webmail.superplaneteers.com). In this example, we

have entered **10.10.10.15**. It should be noted that this address MUST differ from the Self IP configured in the earlier section. For the **port assignment**, enter port **80**. For the third section, because the same VLAN is used for both ingress and egress, leave the answer at no (this is typically referred to as a one-arm configuration). The next section addresses port exhaustion and NTLM authentication. Leave the default answers as **No**. NTLM isn't supported in Exchange 2013 anyway.

5. In this step **Create a New Pool**. Select the load balancing method at **Least Connections (member)**. In Address, type **10.10.10.7** for EXCHCASSRV01. Click **Add** and type **10.10.10.8** for EXCHCASSRV02, Click **Add**. For **queuing TCP requests**, leave that setting as **No**. Change the next setting to **Use Monitor**, then select **http** from the list.
6. For **the Protocol Optimization and Application Security** section, select **LAN**.
7. Double check all answers, and then click the **Finished** button.
8. The BIG-IP will build a configuration, Once the http monitors return a positive response from the pool members of the BIG-IP, the Virtual Server will show up as green in the Virtual Server list.

Modify the Cookie persistence profile timeout value

The iApp template incorrectly sets the Cookie persistence timeout value to 180 seconds. The correct setting should be 0 seconds, which marks the cookie as a session cookie. You must have command line access on the BIG-IP system to modify the timeout value.

To modify the Cookie persistence timeout value

1. Disable Strict Updates as described in the procedure on this page.

2. Open a command prompt on the BIG-IP system.

3. At the command prompt, run the following command:

modify /ltm persistence cookie <app_name> /<profile_name> timeout 0

Where <app_name> is the name of the iApp, and profile name is the name of the Cookie persistence profile created by the template.

To modify type **modify /ltm persistence cookie Exchange2010.app/ Exchange2010_cookie_persistence_profile timeout 0**

To modify the POP3 and IMAP4 simple monitors to include a user name and password

1. On the Main tab, expand **Local Traffic** and then click **Monitors**.

2. From the **Monitor** list, click the name of the POP3 or IMAP4 monitor created by the iApp. The monitor is prefaced by the name you gave the iApp, followed by **_simple_pop3_monitor** or **_simple_imap4_monitor**.
3. In the **User Name** box, type a valid user name with a POP3 or IMAP4 account. We strongly recommend creating user accounts specifically for these monitors.
4. In the **Password** box, type the associated password.
5. Click the **Update** button.

Restart bigd

Log into the BIG-IP system. run the following command: **bigstart restart bigd**

Setting up SSL Offloading (Termination) on an F5 Big-IP Load Balancer

Import SSL Certificates

1. Open Browser and log on to F5 Load balancer
2. Navigate to **Local Traffic**, Click **SSL Certificates**, Click **Import SSL Certificates and Key**. You must import .pfx format certificate you have exported from CAS Server(s).
3. Click **Import.**

Set up SSL Profile

1. Open Browser and log on to F5 Load balancer
2. Navigate to **Local Traffic**, Click **Profiles**, Click **SSL**, Click **Client**.
3. Click the **Create...**button to add a new profile.
4. Give your profile a name, such as "OWA cert". Leave the Parent profile as the default "clientssl". Check the box for custom options, then select your Certificate and Key that should be used to communicate with your end-user browsers. Leave all the other defaults.
5. Go back to Virtual Servers you have created in earlier steps, Edit the Virtual Server and selecting an SSL Profile for the "Client", but not for the "Server". Apply the changes to both virtual servers.

Test configuration

1. On CLIENT, log on with a User account.
2. Open the Internet Explorer.
3. Type **webmail.superplaneteers.com** in the Address bar, and then press **Enter**. You should see the default webmail site.

4. Open the BIG-IP GUI. Expand **Local Traffic**. Select **Pools**. Check **Statistics** to see the traffic coming from **Client.**

7.6 Configure SSL Offloading in Exchange 2013

When you use a hardware load balancer (HLB) to balance traffic of CAS Array you can offload SSL request to hardware load balancer from the CAS array. By enabling SSL offloading, you terminate the incoming SSL connections on the hardware load balancer instead of on the CAS servers in the CAS array. Doing so you move the SSL workload which is CPU and Memory intense from the CAS servers to the HLB device.

Once you have configured SSL Offloading in Hardware load balancer you have to configure CAS Servers to offload SSL to Hardware Load Balancer. To configure SSL offloading for Outlook Anywhere, Follow the steps:

1. Open EAC, Click **Servers**, Select a **CAS Servers** from the list. for example EXCHCASSRV01, Click **Edit**
2. Click **Outlook Anywhere,** Check **Allow SSL Offloading,** Click **Save**

You can use Set-OutlookAnywhere cmdlet to enable SSL offloading. open the Exchange Management PowerShell and type the following command:

Set-OutlookAnywhere –Identity CAS_server\RPC -SSLOffloading $true

Visit **Chapter 3.7** to see how to configure Outlook Anywhere with SSL offloading.

CHAPTER 8

In This Chapter

- Create and configure Federated Exchange Server 2013
- Create organization relationship
- Create sharing policy
- Configure Auto Discover
- Configure free-busy in federated organization

Chapter8. Configuring Federated Exchange Server 2013

Federated sharing can be configured between two federated Exchange 2013 organizations or between federated Exchange 2013 organization and federated Exchange 2010 organization.

8.1 Configure Trusted Root Certification Authorities for Federation Trusts

Before you begin creating a Federation trust you must install digital certificate on your Exchange 2013 organization and the Microsoft Federation Gateway. Microsoft strongly recommends using a self-signed certificate for federated trust. A self-signed certificate is created and installed automatically when using the **Enable federation trust** wizard in the Exchange Administration Center (EAC).

If you want to use a third party X.509 SSL certificate, make sure the certification authority (CA) is trusted by Windows Live. You should use Server authentication, client authentication from these CAs. Example CA:

- VeriSign
- Entrust
- Equifax
- Geotrust

8.2 Deploying a Federated Trust

8.2.1 Create and configure a federation trust

A federation trust establishes a trust relationship between an Exchange 2013 organization and the Microsoft Federation Gateway. By configuring a federation trust, you can configure federated sharing with other federated Exchange organizations to share calendar free/busy and contact information among recipients.

Prerequisites

- You must have Exchange Organization level permission to perform these tasks
- The domain used for establishing a federation trust should be resolvable from the Internet.
- You will need to add a TXT record to your public DNS.
- Both Exchange organizations in a federated sharing relationship must use the same Microsoft Federation Gateway instance for their federation trusts.

Use the EAC to create and configure a federation trust

1. Log on on-premises Exchange 2013 server, Open EAC, navigate to **Organization**, Click **Sharing**.
2. Click **Enable** to start the **Enable federation trust** wizard.
3. After the wizard completes, click **Close**.
4. In the **Federation Trust** section of the **Sharing** tab, click **Modify**.
5. In **Sharing-Enabled Domains**, next to **Step 1**, click **Browse**.
6. In **Select Accepted Domains**, select the primary shared domain from the list, and then click **OK**.
7. Make a note of the federated domain proof that's generated for the primary shared domain. You'll use this string to create a TXT record on your public DNS server.
8. In **Step 2**, click **Add** to add additional subdomains and domains to the federated trust for email addresses that will used by users in your organization that require federated sharing features. A federated domain proof string will be created for each additional domain selected. You must create separate TXT records on your public DNS for each additional domain.

9. After the TXT records are created and replicated, click **Update**.

Create and configure a federation trust using PowerShell

1. This example creates a unique subject key identifier to be used with the certificate.

   $ski = [System.Guid]::NewGuid().ToString("N")

2. This example creates a self-signed certificate for the federation trust with the Microsoft Federation Gateway.

   New-ExchangeCertificate -FriendlyName "Exchange Federated Sharing" - DomainName $env:USERDNSDOMAIN -Services Federation -KeySize 2048 - PrivateKeyExportable $true -SubjectKeyIdentifier $ski

3. This example retrieves the self-signed certificate and creates the federation trust "Microsoft Federation Gateway". This automatically deploys the self-signed certificate to the Exchange servers in your organization.

   Get-ExchangeCertificate | {$_.friendlyname -eq "Exchange Federated Sharing"} | New-FederationTrust -Name "Microsoft Federation Gateway"

To further verify that you have successfully created and configured the federation trust, do the following:

1. Run the following PowerShell command to verify the federation trust information.

   Get-FederationTrust | format-list

2. Run the following PowerShell command to verify that federation information can be retrieved from your organization.

   Get-FederationInformation -DomainName <your primary sharing domain>

8.2.2 Create an organization relationship

An organization relationship enables users in your Exchange organization to share calendar free/busy information as part of federated sharing with other federated Exchange organizations.

1. Log on to on-premises Exchange 2013 server, Open EAC, navigate to the **Organization**, Click **Sharing**.
2. Under **Organization Sharing**, click **New**.
3. In **Organization Relationship**, in the **Relationship name** box, type a friendly name for the organization relationship.
4. In the **Domain to share with** box, type the federated domain or federated subdomain for the external federated Exchange organization you want to configure for federated sharing. If you need to enter multiple domains for the external federated Exchange organization, separate the domains with a comma. For example, superplaneteers.com, corp.superplaneteers.com.
5. Select the **Enable calendar free/busy information sharing** check box to set the sharing level for calendar free/busy information and to define the internal users who can share calendar free/busy information.

   To set the free/busy access level, select one of the following:

   - Calendar free/busy information with time only
   - Calendar free/busy with time, subject, and location

   To specify which internal users will be sharing calendar free/busy information, select one of the following:

   - Everyone in your organization
   - A specified security group

6. To specify a security group, click **Browse.**
7. Click **Save** to create the organization relationship.

Creating an organization relationship using PowerShell

This example creates an organization relationship with Superplaneteers Ltd with the following conditions:

- The organization relationship is enabled for superplaneteers.com, corp.superplaneteers.com, and sales.superplaneteers.com.
- Free/busy access is enabled.
- The requesting organization receives free/busy time, subject, and location information from the target organization.

New-OrganizationRelationship -Name "Superplaneteers" -DomainNames "superplaneteers.com","corp.superplaneteers.com","sales.superplaneteers.com" -FreeBusyAccessEnabled $true -FreeBusyAccessLevel LimitedDetails

This example attempts to automatically discover configuration information from the external Exchange organization Superplaneteers.com by using the domain names provided in the Get-FederationInformation cmdlet. If you use this method to create your organization relationship, you must first make sure that you've created an organization identifier by using the Set-FederatedOrganizationIdentifier cmdlet.

Get-FederationInformation -DomainName Superplaneteers.com | New-OrganizationRelationship -Name "Superplaneteers" -FreeBusyAccessEnabled $true -FreeBusyAccessLevel -LimitedDetails

This example creates an organization relationship with superplaneteers. In this example, the connection settings with the external Exchange organization are provided. The following conditions apply:

- The organization relationship is established with the domain superplaneteers.com, a federated domain.
- The Exchange Web Services application URL is webmail.superplaneteers.com.
- The Autodiscover URL is https://webmail.superplaneteers.com/autodiscover/autodiscover.svc/wssecurity.
- Free/busy access is enabled.
- The requesting organization receives only free/busy information with the time.

New-OrganizationRelationship -Name "superplaneteers" -DomainNames "superplaneteers.com" -FreeBusyAccessEnabled $true -FreeBusyAccessLevel -AvailabilityOnly -TargetAutodiscoverEpr

"https://webmail.superplaneteers.com/autodiscover/autodiscover.svc/wssecurity"
-TargetApplicationUri "webmail.superplaneteers.com"

Modify an Organization Relationship

Once you have configured organization relationship, you will not be modifying organization relationship often but there are occasion when you might have to edit the relationship. Follow the steps to do so:

1. Log on to on-premises Exchange 2013 server, Open EAC, navigate to **Organization , Click Sharing**.
2. In the **Sharing** tab, navigate to the **Organization Sharing** section and select the organization relationship Superplaneteers. Click **Edit** to start the **modify organization relationship** wizard.
3. Leave the **Relationship name** for the organization relationship as Superplaneteers.
4. In the **Domain to share with** field, add the federated domain superplaneteers.com for the external federated Exchange organization after the existing domain superplaneteers.com, using a comma between the domains. For example, superplaneteers.com, sales.superplaneteers.com.
5. Leave the **Enable Free/Busy information sharing** check box selected and the free/busy access level and security group radio buttons as configured.
6. Click **save** to update the organization relationship.

To disable free/busy sharing for the organization relationship

1. Log on to on-premises Exchange 2013 server, Open EAC, navigate to **Organization**, Click **Sharing**.
2. In the **Sharing** tab, navigate to the **Organization Sharing** section and select the organization relationship Superplaneteers. Click **Edit** to start the **Modify organization relationship** wizard.
3. Leave the **Relationship name** for the organization relationship as Superplaneteers.
4. Leave the **Domain to share with** field as configured.
5. Clear the **Enable Free/Busy information sharing** check box to disable free/busy sharing. The free/busy access level and security group radio buttons will also be disabled.
6. Click **Save** to update the organization relationship.

To change the free/busy access level for the organization relationship

1. Log on to on-premises Exchange 2013 server, Open EAC, navigate to **Organization** , Click **Sharing**.
2. In the **Sharing** tab, navigate to the **Organization Sharing** section and select the organization relationship Superplaneteers. Click **Edit** to start the **Modify organization relationship** wizard.
3. Leave the **Relationship name** for the organization relationship as Superplaneteers.
4. Leave the **Domain to share with** field as configured.
5. Leave the **Enable Free/Busy information sharing** check box to **Selected**. Select the free/busy access level radio button for **Free/busy access with time only**.
6. Click **Save** to update the organization relationship.

Modify the organization relationship using PowerShell

- This example enables calendar availability (free/busy) information access for the organization relationship with Superplaneteers and sets the access level to Free/busy access with time only.

  Set-OrganizationRelationship -Identity Superplaneteers -FreeBusyAccessEnabled $true -FreeBusyAccessLevel AvailabilityOnly

Remove an Organization Relationship

Use the EAC to remove an organization relationship

1. Log on to on-premises Exchange 2013 server, Open EAC, navigate to **Organization**, Click **Sharing**.
2. Under **Organization Sharing**, select an organization relationship, and then click **Delete** to remove organization relationship.
3. In the warning that appears, click **Yes**.

Use the PowerShell to remove an organization relationship if needed

This example removes the organization relationship Superplaneteers from the Exchange organization

Remove-OrganizationRelationship -Identity "Superplaneteers"

8.2.3 Create a sharing policy

You can use sharing policies to control how users in your organization can share calendar and contact information with users outside your Exchange organization.

Use the following procedure to create a sharing policy:

1. Log on to on-premises Exchange 2013 server, Open EAC, navigate to **Organization, Click Sharing**.
2. In the **Sharing** tab, navigate to the **Individual Sharing** section and click **+ sign** to start the **new sharing policy** wizard.
3. In the **Sharing Policy** dialog, type a friendly name for the sharing policy in the **Policy name** field.
4. Click **Add+** to define the sharing rules for the sharing policy.
5. In the **Sharing Rule** dialog, select one of the following radio buttons to define the domains you wish to share with:

   - Sharing with all domains
   - Sharing with a specific domain

6. If you've selected the **Sharing with a specific domain** radio button, type the domain you wish to share with. If you need to enter multiple domains for the sharing policy, separate the domains with a comma. For example, superplaneteers.com, sales.superplaneteers.com.
7. To define the calendar sharing levels you want to enforce for the sharing policy, select the **Share your calendar folder** check box and select one of the following radio buttons:

   - Free/busy information with time only
   - Free/busy information with time, subject and location
   - All appointment information, including time, subject, location and title

8. To share contacts for the sharing policy, select the **Share your contacts folder** check box.
9. Click **Save** to set the rules for the sharing policy.
10. If you want to make this sharing policy the default sharing policy for users in your Exchange organization, select the **Make this policy my default sharing policy** check box.
11. Click **Save** to create the sharing policy.

Apply a Sharing Policy to Mailboxes

Sharing policies are a part of federated sharing and enable user-established, people-to-people sharing of both calendar and contact information with different types of external users. A sharing policy can be applied to a single user mailbox or to multiple user mailboxes simultaneously.

1. Log on to on-premises Exchange 2013 server, Open EAC, Navigate to **Recipients**, Click **Mailboxes**.
2. In the list view, select the mailbox you want, and then click **Edit**.
3. In **User Mailbox**, click **Mailbox features**.
4. In the **Sharing policy** list, select the sharing policy you want to apply to this mailbox.
5. Click **Save** to apply the sharing policy.

Use the EAC to apply a sharing policy a multiple mailboxes

1. Log on to on-premises Exchange 2013 server, Open EAC, Navigate to **Recipients** , Click **Mailboxes**.
2. In the list view, use the Ctrl key to select multiple mailboxes.
3. In the details pane, the mailbox properties will be configured for bulk editing. Click **More options**.
4. Under **Sharing policy**, click **Update**.
5. In **Bulk Assign Sharing Policy**, use the **Select the sharing policy** list to select a sharing policy to assign to the mailboxes.
6. Click **Save** to apply the sharing policy to the selected mailboxes.

Use the PowerShell to apply a sharing policy to one or more mailboxes

This example applies the sharing policy Superplaneteers to a single mailbox for the user Raihan.

Set-Mailbox -Identity raihan -SharingPolicy "Superplaneteers"

This example specifies that all user mailboxes in the Marketing department use the sharing policy Marketing.

Get-Mailbox -Filter {Department -eq "Marketing"} | Set-Mailbox -SharingPolicy " Marketing"

This example returns all mailboxes that have the sharing policy applied, and it sorts the users into a table that displays only their aliases and email addresses.

Get-Mailbox -ResultSize unlimited | Where {$_.SharingPolicy -eq "marketing" } | format-table Alias, EmailAddresses

Modify, Disable, or Remove a Sharing Policy

If you would like to change some sharing policy properties, such as modifying sharing rules, changing the free/busy access level, temporarily disabling a sharing policy, or removing a sharing policy entirely, follow the steps:

Use the EAC to modify a sharing policy

1. Navigate to **Organization**, Click **Sharing**.
2. Under **Individual Sharing**, select a sharing a policy, and then click **Edit**.
3. In **Sharing Policy**, click **Edit**.
4. In **Sharing Rule**, modify the sharing rules accordingly. You can change settings such as the domain you want to share information with, the sharing level for calendar appointments, and whether to share contact information. When finished, click **Save** to close the **Sharing Rules** dialog box.
5. In **Sharing Policy**, click **Save** to update the sharing policy.

Use the EAC to set a sharing policy as the default sharing policy

1. Navigate to **Organization**, Click **Sharing**.
2. Under **Individual Sharing**, select a sharing a policy, and then click **Edit**.
3. In **Sharing Policy**, select the **Make this policy my default sharing policy** check box.
4. Click **Save** to update the sharing policy.

Use the EAC to disable a sharing policy

1. Navigate to **Organization**, Click **Sharing**.
2. Under **Individual Sharing**, select a sharing a policy.
3. In the **On** column, clear the check box for the sharing policy you want to disable.

Use the EAC to remove a sharing policy

Before you remove a sharing policy, the sharing policy must be removed from all user mailboxes.

1. Navigate to **Organization**, Click **Sharing**.
2. Under **Individual Sharing**, select a sharing a policy, and then click **Delete**.
3. In the warning, click **Yes** to delete the sharing policy.

8.3 Manage a Federation Trust

Normally, you shouldn't have to manage or modify the federation trust after it's created. However, there may be circumstances that require adding or removing federated domains or resetting the domain used to configure the organization identifier (OrgID) for the federation trust.

Use the EAC to manage a federation trust

1. Log on to on-premises Exchange 2013 server, Open EAC, navigate to the **Organization**, Click **Sharing**.
2. In the **Federation Trust** section, click **Modify**.
3. In **Sharing-Enabled Domains**, skip **Step 1** because the primary sharing domain isn't changing.
4. In **Step 2**, select the **service.superplaneteers.com** domain and then click **Remove-** to remove the domain from the federated trust.
5. In **Step 2**, click **Add+**.
6. In **Select Accepted Domains**, select **marketing.superplaneteers.com** from the list of accepted domains, and then click **OK** to add the domain to the federated trust.
7. Using the federated domain proof string created for the **superplaneteers.com** domain, create a TXT record on your public DNS server. Depending on the update schedule of your public DNS host, replication of DNS changes may take 15 minutes or longer.
8. After the TXT record is created and replicated, click **Update**.

Run the following PowerShell commands to manage other aspects of a federation trust:

1. View the federated OrgID and federated domains: This example displays the Exchange organization's federated OrgID and related information, including federated domains and status.

Get-FederatedOrganizationIdentifier

2. View federation trust certificates: This example displays the previous, current, and next certificates used by the federation trust Microsoft Federation Gateway.

   Get-FederationTrust "Microsoft Federation Gateway" | Select Orgcertificate

3. Check federation certificates status: This example displays the state of federation certificates on all Mailbox and Client Access servers in the organization.

   Test-FederationTrustCertificate

4. Configure the federation trust to use a certificate as the next certificate: This example configures the federation trust Microsoft Federation Gateway to use the certificate with the provided thumbprint as the next certificate. Set-FederationTrust "Microsoft Federation Gateway" -Thumbprint <thumbprint>

5. Configure the federation trust to use the next certificate as the current certificate: This example configures the federation trust Microsoft Federation Gateway to use the next certificate as the current certificate and publishes it to the Microsoft Federation Gateway.

   Set-FederationTrust "Microsoft Federation Gateway" - PublishFederationCertificate

6. Refresh federation metadata and certificate from the Microsoft Federation Gateway: This example refreshes the federation metadata and certificate of the Microsoft Federation Gateway for the federation trust Microsoft Federation Gateway.

   Set-FederationTrust "Microsoft Federation Gateway" -RefreshMetadata

Remove a Federation Trust

Removing a federation trust from your on-premises Exchange organization will disable federated sharing with other federated Exchange organizations and with Exchange Online organizations connected your organization as part of a hybrid deployment. You should carefully consider the overall impact to your organization before removing a federation trust.

Use the EAC to remove a federation trust

1. On an Exchange 2013 server in your on-premises organization, navigate to **Organization**, Click **Sharing**. In the **Federation Trust** section, click **Remove**.
2. In the warning, click **Yes** to confirm that you want to remove the federation trust.
3. After the federation trust is removed, click **Close**.

Use the PowerShell to remove a federation trust

This example removes the federation trust. Remove-FederationTrust

CHAPTER 9

In This Chapter

- Preparing Source and Destination Server
- Configure Permission in Exchange Organization
- Rollout New Servers for Exchange 2013
- Install Exchange Server 2013
- Configure SSL Binding
- Configure Mailflow and Client Access
- Migrate Mailbox, Room, Public Folder and Shared Resources
- Retire Old Exchange Server

Chapter9. Transitioning from Exchange 2007/2010 to Exchange 2013

Transitioning Exchange is fairly straight forward. But before you begin transitioning from Exchange Server 2007/2010 to Exchange Server 2013 I strongly recommend you to study chapter1 to chapter4 thoroughly and gain knowledge on Exchange deployment topology. Deploy exchange 2013 on a pilot project or in a test bed. Once you have a practical understanding of Exchange Server 2013 and you have determined your future Exchange topology then you should be able to transition from Exchange Server 2007/2010 to Exchange Server 2013. Co-existence scenario isn't supported until Microsoft releases Service Pack 3 for Exchange 2007 and Exchange 2010. In this section I will provide you a brief guideline which you can adopt as a transition guideline. Transitioning from Exchange 2003 to Exchange 2013 isn't supported. So how do you do it? Migrate twice! Yes you have to migrate from Exchange 2003 to Exchange 2010 then you can migrate Exchange 2010 to Exchange 2013.

9.1 Prerequisite of Transitioning Exchange Server

The following illustrate a typical transition steps from Exchange Server 2007/2010 to Exchange 2013:

- Run Dcdiag, Netdiag to find out any existing issue with domain controller
- Run netdom query FSMO to check FSMO roles are available.
- Verify that the Active Directory forest is running on minimum Windows Server 2003 forest functionality level.
- Verify that each site in Active Directory have at least one Global Catalog server.
- Make sure all Exchange 2007/2010 servers have Exchange Service Pack 3 installed.
- Create a data sheet for existing Exchange Organisation
- Create a data sheet for future Exchange Organisation
- Determine a future Exchange Topology
- Create a user with schema admin and enterprise admin role who will be upgrading Active Directory Schema for Exchange 2013
- Create delegated permission in existing Exchange organisation for a user who will be installing Exchange 2013
- Insert/mount Exchange 2013 DVD into Domain Controller to upgrade Active Directory Schema (see chapter 2.12.1)
- Prepare all Exchange servers with Windows Server 2012 operating systems and update them with latest Microsoft Patches.

9.2 Take Precautions before Proceeding

- Backup Active Directory global Catalog servers, Exchange servers that interoperate with Exchange Server
- Turn off any replication to other environments during the transition process, such as Forefront Identity Manager.

- Bear in mind that an in-place upgrade to Exchange Server 2013 in any scenario is NOT supported.
- Be aware that Exchange 2013 is based on 64 bit architecture.
- There may be downtime in messaging infrastructure when you switching over old CAS role to new CAS server or moving MX record.
- Depending on your topology and number of mailboxes you may need months to complete the transition process.

9.3 Transition Sequencing

Once you have finished prerequisite (see **chapter2**), you have to take the installation order of the Exchange Server 2013 servers into account to minimize the impact:

1. Exchange Server 2013 Mailbox Server.
2. Exchange Server 2013 Client Access Server.
3. Configure Mailflow, Email routing, Mailbox policies in new Exchange 2013 using Exchange Administration Center.
4. Configure Database Availability Group and mailbox database.
5. Migrate mailboxes, resources and contacts to new Exchange Mailbox Servers
6. Configure Public Folder in Exchange 2013 if you would like to have public folder otherwise skip to step 7.
7. After you have installed the Mailbox Server role and established a proper Public Folder replication between Exchange Server 2007/2010 and Exchange Server 2013, you can start moving mailboxes to the new Exchange 2013 Mailbox Server. Of course, the Public Folder replication only be configured when Public Folders are used in Exchange Server 2007/2010.
8. In Exchange 2013, there is no Edge Transport Server. you can enable Anti-Spam and Anti-Malware functionality in Exchange 2013 Mailbox server. Create all the policies necessary for Anti-Spam and Anti-malware then remove old Edge Transport Server safely.

9. There is no UM Role in Exchange 2013, UM functionality has redesigned and available in Mailbox Server. Create UM policies in Exchange Administration Center then remove UM Role from Exchange 2010 Organization safely.

10. Retire/uninstall Exchange 2010 from Exchange Organization.

11. Shutdown and delete old Exchange computer name from Active Directory.

9.4 Transitioning steps from Exchange 2007/2010 to Exchange 2013

The following are the transition steps you can follow to do the transition.

1. Prepare Windows Server 2012 for the first Exchange 2013

2. Install Mailbox Server Role per design

3. Install CAS server role and configure Exchange 2013 per design.

4. Install third party commercial certificate on CAS Server

5. Configure Mail Flow and message routing

6. Transfer inbound and outbound mail traffic to Mailbox servers.

7. Transfer OWA, ActiveSync, and Outlook Anywhere traffic to new CAS servers.

8. Configure Databases and DAG.

9. Enable Circular logging Mailbox Server

10. Move mailboxes and resources to Exchange 2013.

11. Re-home the Offline Address Book (OAB) to Exchange Server 2013.

12. Create public folder replicas on Exchange 2013 servers.

13. Transfer all Public Folder Replicas to Exchange Server 2013 Public folder stores.

14. Delete Public and Private Information Stores from Exchange 2007/2010 servers.

15. Configure UM, Anti-Spam and Anti-Malware in new Exchange Servers.

16. Remove Exchange 2007/2010 Edge Transport subscription

17. Uninstall/retire all Exchange 2007/2010 servers.

9.5 Test Procedure

1. Check Exchange Services are started in CAS Server and Mailbox Server
2. Check event logs
3. Check internal and external connector
4. Test internal and external mail flow
5. Test Microsoft ActiveSync on Windows Mobile or Mobile devices

Tools to use:

1. Dcdiag
2. Netdiag
3. Repadmin
4. Exchange Management Console
5. Exchange Administration Center
6. Third Party Management or Monitoring tools.

9.6 Migrate Mailboxes and Resources to Exchange Server 2013

Use EAC to perform an on-premises move

1. Log on to Exchange CAS Server or an Admin PC, Open the EAC using https:// FQDN of CAS Server>/ECP URL
2. In the EAC, navigate to **Recipients** , Click **Migration**, and then click **Add+**. Click **Move to a different database.**
3. In the **New local mailbox move** wizard, select the user you want to move click **OK** and then click **Next**.
4. On the **Move configuration** page, specify a name for the new batch. Select which options you want for the archive mailbox, and mailbox database location and click **New**.

These procedures use the Exchange Management PowerShell to move mailbox.

New-MoveRequest -Identity 'raihan@superplaneteers.com' -TargetDatabase Manger-DB -WhatIf

Use EAC to perform a batch move

1. In the EAC, navigate to **Recipients** , Click **Migration**, and then click **Add+**.
2. In the **New local mailbox move** wizard, Click **Move to a different database.** select the users you want to move, click **OK** and then click **Next**.
3. On the **Move configuration** page, specify a name for the new batch. Select which options you want for the archive mailbox, and mailbox database location and click **New**.

Use the PowerShell to move a batch of mailboxes.

Step1: Create a migration batch using the following command.

New-MigrationBatch -Local -Name LocalMove1 -CSVData ([System.IO.File]::ReadAllBytes("C:\LocalMove1.csv") -TargetDatabases ManagerDB -TimeZone "Western Standard Time"

Step2: Run the batch to start migration

Start-MigrationBatch -Identity LocalMove1

Step3: get a report on status of all batches

Get-MigrationUserStatistics -Identity BatchName -Status | Format-List

9.7 Migrate Public Folders from Exchange 2010 SP3 to Exchange 2013

This topic describes how to migrate your public folders from Exchange Server 2010 SP3 to Microsoft Exchange Server 2013. The following PowerShell scripts are installed on your computer when you install Exchange 2013 and they can be found in the following location <Exchange Install Path>\Program Files\Microsoft\Exchange Server\V15\Scripts or where you install Exchange Server.

- Export-PublicFolderStatistics.ps1 This script will create the folder name to folder size mapping.
- PublicFolderToMailboxMapGenerator.ps1 This script will create the public folder to mailbox mapping file.

Prerequisite steps on the Exchange 2010 SP3 server

Before you begin, you should take a snapshot of your current public folder deployment, noting the folder structure and the size in the source Exchange 2010 SP3 databases for verification at the end of migration. Perform the following steps on the Exchange 2010 SP3 server:

Take a snapshot of the original source folder structure:

Get-PublicFolder -Recurse | ConvertTo-CSV C:\PFMigration\2010PFStructure.csv

Take a snapshot of the public folder statistics such as item count, size and owner:

Get-PublicFolder -Recurse | Get-PublicFolderStatistics | ConvertTo-CSV
C:\PFMigration\2010_PFStatistics.csv

Take a snapshot of the permissions:

Get-PublicFolder -GetChildren | Get-PublicFolderClientPermission | Select-Object
Identity,User -ExpandProperty AccessRights | ConvertTo-CSV
C:\PFMigration\2010_PFPerms.csv

Save the information from the above commands for comparison at the end of the migration.

On the Exchange 2010 SP3 server, make sure that there isn't a previous record of a successful migration. If so, you'll need to set that value to "false". If the value is set to "true" the migration request will fail. The following example checks the public folder migration status.

Get-OrganizationConfig | Format-List PublicFoldersLockedforMigration,
PublicFolderMigrationComplete

If the status of the PublicFoldersLockedforMigration or the PublicFolderMigrationComplete property is true, then use the following example to set the value to false.
Set-OrganizationConfig -PublicFoldersLockedforMigration:$false -
PublicFolderMigrationComplete:$false

After resetting the above properties, you will need to wait for Exchange to detect the new settings. This may take several minutes. To expedite the process, you can restart the Microsoft Exchange Information Store by running the following command: Restart-Service MSExchangeIS

Prerequisite steps on the Exchange 2013 server

Perform the following steps on the Exchange 2013 server.

The following example removes any existing public folder migration requests.

Get-PublicFolderMigrationRequest | Remove-PublicFolderMigrationRequest -Confirm:$false

Ensure that there are no existing public folders on the Exchange 2013 servers.

Get-Mailbox -PublicFolder

Get-PublicFolder

If the above commands return any public folders, then use the following commands to remove public folders.

Get-MailPublicFolder | where $_.EntryId -ne $null | Disable-MailPublicFolder -Confirm:$false

Get-PublicFolder -GetChildren | Remove-PublicFolder -Recurse -Confirm:$false

Get-Mailbox -PublicFolder |Remove-Mailbox -PublicFolder -Confirm:$false

Generate the CSV files

On the Exchange Server 2010 SP3 server, run the Export-PublicFolderStatistics.ps1 script to create the folder name to folder size mapping file. The file will have two columns: FolderName and FolderSize.

.\Export-PublicFolderStatistics.ps1 <FQDNofSourceServer> <FolderToSizeMapPath>

Where FQDNofSourceServer equals the fully qualified domain name of the mailbox server where the public folder hierarchy is hosted and FolderToSizeMapPath equals the file name and path on a network shared folder where you want the CSV file saved.

Create the Folder-to-Mailbox mapping file. This file will be used to create the correct number of public folder mailboxes on the Exchange 2013 Mailbox server.

.\PublicFolderToMailboxMapGenerator.ps1 <MaximumMailboxSizeInBytes> <FoldertoSizeMapPath> <FoldertoMailboxMapPath>

Where:

<MaximumMailboxSizeInBytes> specifies the maximum size that you want the new public folder mailboxes to be. Note that you should allow for expansion so that the public folder has room to grow. Microsoft recommend the bytes should be set at 60% of the actual size.

<FoldertoSizeMapPath> specifies the file path of the CSV file that you created with the Export-PublicFolderStatistics.ps1 script.

<FolderToMailboxMapPath> specifies the file name and path of the Folder-to-Mailbox csv file that you will create with this step. If you only specify the file name the file will be generated in its current location.

Create the public folder mailboxes on the Exchange 2013 server

In this step, you'll create the public folder hierarchy mailbox on the Exchange 2013 Mailbox server. You need to create the public folder hierarchy in HoldForMigration mode.

New-Mailbox -PublicFolder <Name> -HoldForMigration:$true

Manually create the public folders as needed based on the script output from the PublicFoldertoMailboxMapGenerator.ps1 script.

New-Mailbox -PublicFolder <Name>

Start the migration request

From the Exchange 2013 Mailbox server, run the following command:

New-PublicFolderMigrationRequest -SourceDatabase (Get-PublicFolderDatabase -Server <SourceServerName>) -CSVData (Get-Content <FolderToMailboxMapPath> -Encoding Byte)

To verify that the migration has successfully started, run the following command.

Get-PublicFolderMigrationRequest | Get-PublicFolderMigrationRequestStatistics -IncludeReport | Format-List

Lock down the Exchange 2010 public folders for final migration

In this step you may incur downtime. Up until this point, the users have been able to access public folders during the migration. The next steps will log users off of the public folders and lock them while the migration completes its final synchronization.

Set-OrganizationConfig -PublicFoldersLockedForMigration:$true

If your organization has multiple public folder databases, you will need to wait until public folder replication has completed to make sure that all public folder databases have picked up the PublicFoldersLockedForMigration flag. If you want to bypass the wait, you can restart the Microsoft Exchange Information Store by running the following command:

Restart-Service MSExchangeIS

Finalize the public folder migration

In this step you may incur downtime. By default when you run the Set-PublicFolderMigration cmdlet, it won't complete and you must remove the PreventCompletion flag and resume the migration request.

Set-PublicFolderMigrationRequest -Identity \PublicFolderMigration -PreventCompletion:$false
Resume-PublicFolderMigrationRequest -Identity \PublicFolderMigration

Now you can verify migration. Follow the steps to verify that your public folder migration was successful by taking a snapshot of the public folder structure, statistics, and permissions after the migration completed. You can compare data in the Exchange 2010 CSV files against the Exchange 2013 CSV files.

Retrieve the destination public folder structure:

Get-PublicFolder -Recurse | ConvertTo-CSV C:\PFMigration\2013_PFStructure.csv

Retrieve the public folder statistics.

```
Get-PublicFolder -Recurse | Get-PublicFolderStatistics | ConvertTo-CSV
C:\PFMigration\2013_PFStatistics.csv
```

Retrieve of the permissions:

```
Get-PublicFolder -GetChildren | Get-PublicFolderClientPermission | Select-Object
Identity,User -ExpandProperty AccessRights | ConvertTo-CSV
C:\PFMigration\2013_PFPerms.csv
```

CHAPTER 10

In This Chapter

- Performance Monitoring in Exchange Server
- Manage Mailbox Database
- Backup and Restore mailbox
- Recover Database
- Anti-Spam and Anti-malware configuration
- Working with Windows PowerShell
- Patching Exchange Server 2013
- Manage MailTips for Organization Relationships
- Manage On-Premises Moves
- Create a cross-forest move using a .csv batch file
- Move only an archive mailbox
- Move primary mailbox to separate databases
- Move a user's primary mailbox and allow a large bad item limit
- Exchange Remote Connectivity Analyser

Chapter10. Supporting Exchange Server 2013

10.1 Performance Monitoring in Exchange Server 2013

In this section, you will learn how to manage workload in Exchange Server 2013. This is crucial part of supporting Exchange Server because you don't want your exchange server underperform while handling large number of emails in your organization. You should monitor exchange performance as part of daily checks.

10.1.1 Exchange 2013 Workload Management Reference

Exchange workloads are throttled based on the health of specific system resources like memory, processor, networks and disk utilization. When specific system resources reach unhealthy levels, Exchange uses a configurable classification system based on policy settings to make sure that each Exchange workload is able to consume the appropriate amount of system resources. You must understand the following terminology before creating any performance matrix you may require for documentation purpose.

Exchange workload

An Exchange workload is an Exchange server feature, protocol, or service that has been explicitly defined for the purposes of Exchange system resource management. Examples of Exchange workloads include Outlook Web App, Exchange ActiveSync, mailbox migration, and Managed Folder Assistant.

Workload classification

A workload classification specifies the default priority of each Exchange workload. A workload can be assigned one of the following classifications: Urgent, Customer Expectation, Internal Maintenance, and Discretionary.

System resource health indicator

A system resource health indicator is used to measure the health of a specific component on an Exchange server. Examples are CPU, mailbox RPC latency, and mailbox replication latency.

System resource thresholds

A system resource threshold represents a configurable limit for a system resource. The thresholds define the underloaded, overloaded, and critical levels for each system resource.

Exchange workloads and classifications

The following table shows the default Exchange 2013 workload policies and the default classification for each workload. To review the values for all Exchange 2013 workloads, run Get-WorkloadPolicy in elevated PowerShell prompt.

Workload policy name	Description	Workload classification
MailboxReplicationServiceHighPriority	Mailbox Replication service high priority	Urgent
Eas	Exchange ActiveSync	Customer expectation
JunkEmailOptionsCommitterAssistant	Junk email	Customer expectation
PowerShellBackSync	Windows	Customer

	PowerShell BackSync operations	expectation
PowerShellForwardSync	Windows PowerShell FwdSync operations	Customer expectation
PublicFolderMailboxSync	Public folder mailbox synchronization	Customer expectation
TeamMailboxSync	Site mailbox synchronization	Customer expectation
Transport	Transport mail flow	Customer expectation
CalendarRepairAssistant	Calendar Repair Assistant	Internal maintenance
CalendarSyncAssistant	Calendar Synchronization Assistant	Internal maintenance
ContactLinkingAssistant	Contact Linking Assistant	Internal maintenance
DirectoryProcessorAssistant	Directory Processor Assistant	Internal maintenance
Domt	Address book	Internal maintenance
ELCAssistant	Managed Folder Assistant	Internal maintenance
Ews	Exchange Web Services	Internal maintenance
Imap	IMAP4	Internal maintenance
Momt	RPC Client Access and Outlook	Internal maintenance
OABGeneratorAssistant	Offline Address Book Generation Assistant	Internal maintenance
OrgContactsSyncAssistant	Organizational Contacts Synchronization Assistant	Internal maintenance
Owa	Outlook Web App	Internal

		maintenance
OwaVoice	Outlook Web App Voice Access	Internal maintenance
PeopleRelevanceAssistant	People Relevance Assistant	Internal maintenance
Pop	POP3	Internal maintenance
PowerShell	Windows PowerShell	Internal maintenance
PowerShellGalSync	Windows PowerShell work related to global address list synchronization	Internal maintenance
PowerShellLowPriorityWorkFlow	Windows PowerShell work that's generally not time sensitive	Internal maintenance
PushNotificationService	Push Notification service	Internal maintenance
SharingPolicyAssistant	Sharing Policy Assistant	Internal maintenance
SiteMailboxAssistant	Site Mailbox Assistant	Internal maintenance
StoreMaintenanceAssistant	Store maintenance	Internal maintenance
TopNAssistant	Top N Words Assistant	Internal maintenance
TransportSync	Transport synchronization	Internal maintenance
UMReportingAssistant	Unified Messaging Reporting Assistant	Internal maintenance
InferenceDataCollectionAssistant	Inference Data Collection Assistant	Discretionary
InferenceTrainingAssistant	Inference Training Assistant	Discretionary
MailboxReplicationService	Mailbox Replication service	Discretionary
PowerShellDiscretionaryWorkFlow	Windows PowerShell work that's generally not	Discretionary

	time sensitive	
PublicFolderAssistant	Public folders	Discretionary

Default system resource thresholds

The following tables show the default thresholds for each of the five system resources that are used to throttle Exchange workloads. Three thresholds (underloaded, overloaded, and critical) are defined for each system resource. To review the Exchange 2013 threshold values, run Get-ResourcePolicy | format-list from elevated PowerShell.

Local Server CPU (Processor)

Workload classification	Threshold	Precent
Discretionary	Underloaded	70
Discretionary	Overloaded	80
Discretionary	Critical	100
Internal Maintenance	Underloaded	75
Internal Maintenance	Overloaded	85
Internal Maintenance	Critical	100
Customer Expectation	Underloaded	80
Customer Expectation	Overloaded	90
Customer Expectation	Critical	100
Urgent	Underloaded	100
Urgent	Overloaded	100
Urgent	Critical	100

Mailbox Database RPC Latency (MDBLatency)

Workload classification	Threshold	Milliseconds
Discretionary	Underloaded	10
Discretionary	Overloaded	20
Discretionary	Critical	70
Internal Maintenance	Underloaded	10
Internal Maintenance	Overloaded	20
Internal Maintenance	Critical	70
Customer Expectation	Underloaded	15

Customer Expectation	Overloaded	30
Customer Expectation	Critical	70
Urgent	Underloaded	25
Urgent	Overloaded	50
Urgent	Critical	100

Mailbox Database Replication Health (MdbReplication)

Workload classification	Threshold	Bytes
Discretionary	Underloaded	2097152
Discretionary	Overloaded	3145728
Discretionary	Critical	6291456
Internal Maintenance	Underloaded	2097152
Internal Maintenance	Overloaded	3145728
Internal Maintenance	Critical	7340032
Customer Expectation	Underloaded	2097152
Customer Expectation	Overloaded	3145728
Customer Expectation	Critical	8388608
Urgent	Underloaded	2097152
Urgent	Overloaded	3145728
Urgent	Critical	9437184

Content Indexing Age of Last Notification (CiAgeOfLastNotification)

Workload classification	Threshold	Seconds
Discretionary	Underloaded	10
Discretionary	Overloaded	15
Discretionary	Critical	180
Internal Maintenance	Underloaded	10
Internal Maintenance	Overloaded	15
Internal Maintenance	Critical	180
Customer Expectation	Underloaded	10
Customer Expectation	Overloaded	15
Customer Expectation	Critical	180
Urgent	Underloaded	10
Urgent	Overloaded	15
Urgent	Critical	180

Content Indexing Retry Queue Size (CiRetryQueueSize)

Workload classification	Threshold	Items
Discretionary	Underloaded	540
Discretionary	Overloaded	1080
Discretionary	Critical	2700
Internal Maintenance	Underloaded	540
Internal Maintenance	Overloaded	1080
Internal Maintenance	Critical	2700
Customer Expectation	Underloaded	540
Customer Expectation	Overloaded	1080
Customer Expectation	Critical	2700
Urgent	Underloaded	540
Urgent	Overloaded	1080
Urgent	Critical	2700

Mailbox Database Availability Health (MdbAvailability)

Workload classification	Threshold	Bytes
Discretionary	Underloaded	2097152
Discretionary	Overloaded	3145728
Discretionary	Critical	6291456
Internal Maintenance	Underloaded	2097152
Internal Maintenance	Overloaded	3145728
Internal Maintenance	Critical	7340032
Customer Expectation	Underloaded	2097152
Customer Expectation	Overloaded	3145728
Customer Expectation	Critical	8388608
Urgent	Underloaded	2097152
Urgent	Overloaded	3145728
Urgent	Critical	9437184

10.1.2 Changing workload management policy settings

To change workload management policy settings for your entire organization, you need to create a new workload policy and apply it to the Global Override Workload Management Policy.

You complete this task using the **New-WorkloadPolicy** cmdlet.

This example creates a new workload policy that will change the priority of the way that the IMAP workload is managed for all servers for a fictional company.

New-WorkloadPolicy OrgIMAPWorkloadPolicy -WorkloadType IMAP -WorkloadClassification Discretionary -WorkloadManagementPolicy GlobalOverwrittenWorkloadManagementPolicy.

To verify that you have successfully created the workload policy, Run the following command.

> Get-WorkloadManagementPolicy
> Get-WorkloadPolicy

10.1.3 Create a custom workload management policy

This example creates a custom policy object that will be used to apply workload management settings to a server located in Perth WA.

New-WorkloadManagementPolicy PerthWorkloadManagementPolicy

10.1.4 Create a workload policy

This example creates a new workload policy that will change the priority of the way that the IMAP workload is managed at Perth WA.

New-WorkloadPolicy PerthIMAPWorkloadPolicy -WorkloadType IMAP -WorkloadClassification Discretionary -WorkloadManagementPolicy PerthWorkloadManagementPolicy.

10.1.5 Apply the custom workload management policy to a specific server

This example applies the custom workload management policy PerthWorkloadManagementPolicy to sever EXCHCASSRV01.

Set-ExchangeServer -WorkloadManagementPolicy PerthWorkloadManagementPolicy -Server EXCHCASSRV01

To verify that you've successfully applied the workload management policy to the specified server, run the following command.

Get-ExchangeServer
Get-WorkloadManagementPolicy

10.2 Manage Mailbox Databases in Exchange 2013

A mailbox database is a unit of granularity where mailboxes are created and stored. A mailbox database is stored as an Exchange database (.edb) file.

Use the EAC to create a mailbox database

1. From the Exchange Administration Center, navigate to **Servers**.
2. Select **Databases**, and then click the **Add+** symbol to create a database.
3. Use the new database wizard to create your database.

Use the EAC to set mailbox database properties

1. From the EAC, navigate to **Servers**.
2. Select **Databases**, and then select the mailbox database you want to configure.
3. Click **Edit** to configure the attributes of a mailbox database.
4. Use the **General** tab to view status about the mailbox database. Properties of a mailbox includes the following status:

   - Database path
   - Last full backup
   - Last incremental backup
   - Status
   - Mounted on server
   - Master
   - Master type
   - Modified
   - Servers hosting a of this database

5. Use the **Maintenance** tab to configure the following mailbox database settings:

   - Journal Recipient
   - Maintenance schedule
   - Enable background database maintenance (24 x 7 ESE scanning)
   - This database can be overwritten by a restore

- Enable circular logging

6. Use the **Limits** tab to specify the storage limits, the warning message interval, and the deletion settings for a mailbox database:

- Issue warning at (GB)
- Prohibit send at (GB)
- Prohibit send and receive at (GB)
- Keep deleted items for (days)
- Keep deleted mailboxes for (days)
- Don't permanently delete items until the database has been backed up

7. Use the **Client Settings** tab to select the offline address book (OAB) for the mailbox.

To verify that you have successfully moved the database path, do the following:

1. From the EAC, select **Servers** , Click **Databases**, and then click to select the appropriate mailbox.
2. Click the **pen** symbol and verify that the database path is correct.

To verify that you have successfully mounted the mailbox database, do the following:

1. From EAC, select **Servers** , Click **Databases**, and then click to select the appropriate mailbox.
2. Click the **pen** symbol and verify that the database status is **Mounted**.

To verify that you have successfully dismounted the database, do the following:

1. From EAC, select **Servers** , Click **Databases**, and then click to select the appropriate mailbox.
2. Click the **pen** symbol, and verify that the database status is **Dismounted**.

Remove a mailbox database

1. From the EAC, select **Servers** , Click **Databases**, and then click to select the appropriate mailbox.

2. Click **Delete** to remove the mailbox database.

Use the following PowerShell command create, verify and move database.

New-MailboxDatabase	Create a new database
Get-MailboxDatabase	Verify new database
Move-DatabasePath	Move new database
Set-MailboxDatabase	Set specific properties of a database
Mount-Database.	Mount a database
Dismount-Database	Dismount a database
Remove-MailboxDatabase	Remove a database

The following is an example of PowerShell command to retrieve database properties. Get-MailboxDatabase -Identity Manager-DB -Status | Format-List

10.3 Working with Backup, Restore and Database Recovery

Before using Windows Server Backup to back up Exchange data, familiarize yourself with the following features and options for the plug-in:

- Backups taken with Windows Server Backup occur at volume level.
- The backup must be run locally on the server being backed up, and you can't use the plug-in to take remote VSS backups.
- The backup can be created on a local drive or on a remote network share.
- Only full backups can be taken.
- When restoring data, it's possible to restore only Exchange data. This data can be restored to its original location or to an alternate location.
- The restore process doesn't directly support the recovery database (RDB).
- When restoring Exchange data, all backed up databases must be restored together. You can't restore a single database.

Use Windows Server Backup to perform a backup of Exchange

1. Start Windows Server Backup.
2. In the **Actions** pane, click **Backup Once**. The Backup Once wizard appears.
3. On the **Backup options** page, select **Different options**, and then click **Next**.
4. On the **Select backup configuration** page, select the type of backup that you want, and then click **Next**:
    1. Select **Full server (recommended)** to back up all volumes on the server.

2. Select **Custom** to specify which volumes should be included in the backup. If you select this option, the **Select backup items** page appears. Select the volumes to be backed up, and then click **Next**.

5. On the **Specify destination type** page, select the location where you want to store the backup, and then click **Next**. If **Remote shared folder** is selected, the **Specify remote folder** page appears. Specify a UNC path for the backup files, and then do one of the following to configure access control settings:

   1. Select **Do not inherit** if you want the backup to be accessible only by a set of specified user credentials, and then click **Next**. Type a user name and password for a user account that has write permissions on the computer that is hosting the remote folder, and then click **OK**.
   2. Select **Inherit** if you want the backup to be accessible by everyone who has access to the remote folder, and then click **Next**.

6. On the **Specify advanced options** page, select **VSS full backup**, and then click **Next**.

7. On the **Confirmation** page, review the backup settings, and then click **Backup**.

8. On the **Backup progress** page, you can view the status and progress of the backup operation.

9. Click **Close** when the backup operation has completed.

Use Windows Server Backup to restore a backup of Exchange

1. Start Windows Server Backup.
2. In the **Actions** pane, click **Recover**. The Recovery wizard appears.
3. On the **Getting Started** page, do either of the following:

   1. If the data being recovered was backed up from the server on which Windows Server Backup is running, select **This server (ServerName)**, and then click **Next**.
   2. If you would like to select a different server, select **Another server**, and then click **Next**. On the **Specify location type** page, select **Local drives** or **Remote shared folder**, and then click **Next**. If you select **Local drives**, select the drive containing the backup on the **Select backup location** page, and then click **Next**. If you select **Remote shared folder**, enter the UNC path for the backup data on the **Specify remote folder** page, and then click **Next**.

4. On the **Select backup date** page, select the date and time of the backup that you want to recover, and then click **Next**.

5. On the **Select recovery type** page, select **Applications**, and then click **Next**.

6. On the **Select application** page, verify that Exchange is selected in the **Applications** field. Click **View Details** to view the application components of the backups. If the backup that you're recovering is the most recent, the **Do not perform a roll-forward recovery of the application database** check box is displayed. Select this check box if you want to prevent Windows Server Backup from rolling forward the database being recovered. Click **Next**.

7. On the **Specify recovery options** page, select where you want to recover the data, and then click **Next**:

    1. Select **Recover to original location** to recover backed up data to its original location. If you use this option, you can't set a single database or multiple databases; all backed up databases are restored to their original location.

    2. Select **Recover to another location** to restore individual databases and files to a specified location. Click **Browse** to specify the alternate location. When you restore databases to an alternate location, the restored database is in a Dirty Shutdown state.

8. On the **Confirmation** page, review the recovery settings, and then click **Recover**.

9. On the **Recovery progress** page, you can view the status and progress of the recovery operation.

10. Click **Close** when the recovery operation has completed.

10.4 Recover an Exchange Server 2013

You can recover a lost server by using the **Setup /m:RecoverServer** switch in Microsoft Exchange Server 2013.

10.5 Recover a Databases

A recovery database (RDB) is a special kind of mailbox database that allows you to mount a restored mailbox database and extract data from the restored database as part of a recovery operation. Recovery database cannot used to store production mailboxes.

You can restore a database in the following ways:

- If a recovery database already exists, the application can dismount the database, restore the data onto the recovery database and log files, and then remount the database.

- The database and log files can be restored to any disk location. Exchange analyzes the restored data and replays the transaction logs to bring the databases up to date, and then a recovery database can be configured to point to already recovered database files.

Difference between a mailbox database and a recovery database

There are key differences between RDB and Production Database. The differences from standard mailbox databases in several respects:

- An RDB is created by using the Exchange Management PowerShell.
- Mail can't be sent to or from an RDB. All Client protocol access to an RDB (including SMTP, POP3, and IMAP4) is blocked.
- MAPI access is supported for an RDB, but only by recovery tools and applications. Both the mailbox GUID and the database GUID must be specified when using MAPI to log into a mailbox in an RDB.
- Mailboxes in an RDB can't be connected to user accounts. To allow a user to access the data in a mailbox in an RDB, the mailbox must be merged into an existing mailbox, or exported to a folder.
- System and mailbox management policies aren't applied to RDB.
- Online maintenance isn't performed for RDBs.
- Circular logging can't be enabled for RDBs.
- Only one RDB can be mounted at any time on a Mailbox server.
- You can't create mailbox database copies of an RDB.
- An RDB can be used as a target for restore operations, but not backup operations.
- A recovered database mounted as an RDB isn't tied to the original mailbox in any way.

Using a recovery database

Before you can use an RDB, there are certain requirements that must be met. An RDB can be used for Exchange 2013 mailbox databases only.

An RDB can be used to recover data in several situations, such as:

- Same server dial tone recovery
- Alternate server dial tone recovery
- Mailbox recovery
- Specific item recovery

An RDB is designed for mailbox database recovery under the following conditions and scenarios:

- The logical information about the original database and the mailboxes in that database remains intact and unchanged in Active Directory.
- You need to recover a single mailbox or a single database.
- RDBs are generally not designed for scenarios in which you have to restore entire servers, when you have to restore multiple databases, or when you're in an emergency situation that requires changing or rebuilding your Active Directory topology.
- The target mailbox used for data merges and extraction must be in the same Active Directory forest as the database mounted in the RDB.

10.5.1 Create a Recovery Database

You can use the PowerShell to create a recovery database, a special kind of mailbox database that is used to mount and extract data from the restored database as part of a recovery operation. After extraction, the data can then be exported to a folder or merged into an existing mailbox. Using recovery databases, you can recover data from a backup or of a database without disrupting user access to current data.

This example creates the recovery database RMANAGER-DB on the Mailbox server EXCHMBXSRV2.

New-MailboxDatabase -Recovery -Name RMANAGER-DB -Server EXCHMBXSRV2

This example creates the recovery database RASSISTANT-DB on the Mailbox server EXCHMBXSRV1 using a custom path for the database file and log folder.

New-MailboxDatabase -Recovery -Name RASSISTANT-DB -Server EXCHMBXSRV1 - EdbFilePath "R:\Recovery\RASSISTANT-DB\RASSISTANT-DB.EDB" -LogFolderPath "L:\Recovery\RASSISTANT-DB"

Once you have created RDB you can verify that you have successfully created a recovery database by running the following command.

Get-MailboxDatabase <RecoveryDatabaseName> | FL

10.5.2 Restore Data Using a Recovery Database

Once you have created RDB in previous steps, then you can use the New-MailboxRestoreRequest cmdlet to extract data from the recovered database.

This example restores the source mailbox that has the MailboxGUID 1d20855f-fd54-4681-98e6-e249f7326ddd on mailbox database MANAGER-DB to the target mailbox with the Raihan Al-Beruni. Mailbox GUID can be found on the properties of a mailbox.

New-MailboxRestoreRequest -SouceDatabase MANAGER-DB -SourceStoreMailbox 1d20855f-fd54-4681-98e6-e249f7326ddd -TargetMailbox Raihan

This example restores the content of the source mailbox that has the display name Raihan Al-Beruni on mailbox database MANAGER-DB to the archive mailbox for raihan@superplaneteers.com.

New-MaiboxRestoreRequest -SourceDatabase MANAGER-DB -SourceStoreMailbox "Raihan Al-Beruni" -TargetMailbox raihan@superplaneteers.com -TargetIsArchive

To verify that you have successfully recovered the mailbox data, open the target mailbox using Outlook or ActiveSync and verify that the recovered data is present.

10.6 AntiSpam and Antivirus Configuration

In this section you will configure Anti-Spam and Anti-Malware for Exchange Organisation. You should not filter messages from trusted partners or within your organization. When you run anti-spam filters, there's always a chance that the filters will detect false positives. To reduce the chance that filters will mishandle legitimate email messages, you should enable anti-spam agents to run only on messages from potentially untrusted and unknown sources.

10.6.1 Enable Anti-Spam Functionality on a Mailbox Server

The following anti-spam agents are available in the Transport service on Mailbox servers, but they are not installed by default. You can install these anti-spam agents on a Mailbox server using a script in the Exchange Management PowerShell.

- Content Filter agent
- Sender ID agent
- Sender Filter agent

- Recipient Filter agent
- Protocol Analysis agent for sender reputation

If you have an Edge Transport server in the perimeter (DMZ) network that delivers incoming mail directly to the Transport service on the Mailbox server. The anti-spam agents on the Mailbox server recognize the anti-spam X-header values that are added to messages by other Exchange anti-spam agents, and messages that contain these X-headers pass through without being scanned again.

To enable Anti-Spam Agent on Mailbox server run the following command in elevated PowerShell

%ExchangeInstallPath%\Scripts\Install-AntiSpamAgents.ps1

Now restart Transport Service in Mailbox Server by running the following command: Restart-Service MSExchangeTransport

Once Anti-Spam Agent is configured, you need to specify the IP addresses of internal SMTP servers that should be ignored by the Sender ID agent. To add the IP addresses of internal SMTP servers without affecting any existing values, run the following command:

Set-TransportConfig -InternalSMTPServers @{Add="10.10.10.3","10.10.10.4"...}

Here 10.0.10.3 and 10.0.10.4 is internal SMTP server addresses to the transport configuration of your organization. To verify that you have successfully specified the IP address of at least one internal SMTP server, run the following command:

Get-TransportConfig | Format-List InternalSMTPServers

10.6.2 Manage Sender Filtering

The Sender Filter agent relies on the **MAIL FROM:** SMTP header to determine what action can be taken for all inbound email message. When sender filtering functionality is enabled on an Exchange server, sender filtering functionality filters all messages that come through all Receive connectors on that computer.

To enable, disable and verify sender filtering, run the following command:

Set-SenderFilterConfig -Enabled $true

```
Set-SenderFilterConfig -Enabled $false
Get-SenderFilterConfig | Format-List Enabled
```

When you disable sender filtering, the underlying Sender Filter agent is still enabled. To disable the Sender Filter agent, run the command:

```
Disable-TransportAgent "Sender Filter Agent"
```

Use the PowerShell to configure blocked senders, domains and subdomains. To replace the existing values, run the following command:

```
Set-SenderFilterConfig -BlockedSenders
mike@testdomain.com,john@testdomain.com -BlockedDomains testdomain.com -
BlockedDomainsAndSubdomains testdomain.com
```

To add or remove multiple entries without modifying any existing values, run the following command:

```
Set-SenderFilterConfig -BlockedSenders @{Add="<sender1>","<sender2>"...;
Remove="<sender1>","<sender2>"...} -BlockedDomains
@{Add="<domain1>","<domain2>"...; Remove="<domain1>","<domain>"...} -
BlockedDomainsAndSubdomains @{Add="<domain1>","<domain2>"...;
Remove="<domain1>","<domain2>"...}
```

To verify that you have successfully configured blocked senders, run the following command:

```
Get-SenderFilterConfig | Format-List
BlockedSenders,BlockedDomains,BlockedDomainsAndSubdomains
```

To enable or disable blocking message with blank senders, run the following command:

```
Set-SenderFilterConfig -BlankSenderBlockingEnabled $true
Set-SenderFilterConfig -BlankSenderBlockingEnabled $False
```

10.6.3 Manage Recipient Filtering

When recipient filtering is enabled on an Exchange server, it filters inbound messages that come from the Internet and exclude filtering messages from authenticated domains.

To enable, disable and verify recipient filtering, run the following command:

Set-RecipientFilterConfig -Enabled $true
Set-RecipientFilterConfig -Enabled $false
Get-RecipientFilterConfig | Format-List Enabled

When you disable recipient filtering, the underlying Recipient Filter agent is still enabled. To disable the Recipient Filter agent, run the command:

Disable-TransportAgent "Recipient Filter Agent".

To enable, disable or verify the Recipient Block list, run the following command:
Set-RecipientFilterConfig -BlockListEnabled $true
Set-RecipientFilterConfig -BlockListEnabled $true
Get-RecipientFilterConfig | Format-List BlockListEnabled

To configure the Recipient Block list, run the following command:

Set-RecipientFilterConfig -BlockedRecipients
mike@testdomain.com,john@testdomain.com

To add or remove or verify entries without modifying any existing values, run the following command:

Set-RecipientFilterConfig -BlockedRecipients
@{Add="<recipient1>","<recipient2>"...; Remove="<recipient1>","<recipient2>"...}

Get-RecipientFilterConfig | Format-List BlockedRecipients

To enable or disable Recipient Lookup, run the following command:
Set-RecipientFilterConfig -RecipientValidationEnabled $true
Set-RecipientFilterConfig -RecipientValidationEnabled $False

10.6.4 Manage Sender ID

Sender ID validates the origin of email messages by verifying the IP address of the sender against the purported owner of the sender domain. Sender ID filtering is performed on inbound messages that come from the Internet and exclude filtering messages from authenticated domains.

To enable, disable, verify Sender ID, run the following command:

Set-SenderIDConfig -Enabled $true
Set-SenderIDConfig -Enabled $false
Get-SenderIDConfig | Format-List Enabled

When you disable Sender ID, the underlying Sender ID agent is still enabled. To disable the Sender ID agent, run the command:

Disable-TransportAgent "Sender ID Agent".

To configure the Sender ID action for spoofed messages, run the following command:

Set-SenderIDConfig -SpoofedDomainAction <StampStatus | Reject | Delete>

This example configures and verify the Sender ID agent to reject any messages where the IP address of the sending server isn't listed as an authoritative SMTP sending server in the DNS Sender Policy Framework (SPF) record for the sending domain.

Set-SenderIDConfig -SpoofedDomainAction Reject
Get-SenderIDConfig | Format-List SpoofedDomainAction

To configure the Sender ID action for transient errors, run the following command:

Set-SenderIDConfig -TempErrorAction <StampStatus | Reject | Delete>

This example configures and verify the Sender ID agent to stamp the messages when the Sender ID status can't be determined due to a temporary DNS server error. The message will be processed by other anti-spam agents and the Content Filter agent will use the mark when determining the SCL value for the message.

Set-SenderIDConfig -TempErrorAction StampStatus

Get-SenderIDConfig | Format-List TempErrorAction

To configure recipient and sender domain exceptions

Set-SenderIDConfig -BypassedRecipients
kim@superplaneteers.com,john@superplaneteers.com -BypassedSenderDomains
superplaneteers.com

To add or remove entries without modifying any existing values, run the following
command:

Set-SenderIDConfig -BypassedRecipients @{Add="<recipient1>","<recipient2>"...;
Remove="<recipient1>","<recipient2>"...} -BypassedSenderDomains
@{Add="<domain1>","<domain2>"...; Remove="<domain1>","<domain2>"...}

To verify that you have successfully configured recipient and sender domain
exceptions, run the following command:

Get-SenderIDConfig | Format-List BypassedRecipients,BypassedSenderDomains

10.6.5 Manage Content Filtering

The Content Filter agent filters all messages that come through all Receive
connectors on the Exchange server. Only messages that come from non-
authenticated sources are filtered.

To enable, disable or verify content filtering, run the following command:

Set-ContentFilterConfig -Enabled $true
Set-ContentFilterConfig -Enabled $false
Get-ContentFilterConfig | Format-List Enabled

When you disable content filtering, the underlying Content Filter agent is still
enabled. To disable the Content Filter agent, run the command:
Disable-TransportAgent "Content Filter Agent".

By default, content filtering functionality is enabled for external messages. To
disable content filtering for external messages, run the following command:

Set-ContentFilterConfig -ExternalMailEnabled $false

To enable or verify content filtering for external messages, run the following command:

```
Set-ContentFilterConfig -ExternalMailEnabled $true
Get-ContentFilterConfig | Format-List ExternalMailEnabled
```

To enable, disable or verify content filtering for internal messages, run the following command:

```
Set-ContentFilterConfig -InternalMailEnabled $true
Set-ContentFilterConfig -InternalMailEnabled $false
Get-ContentFilterConfig | Format-List InternalMailEnabled
```

To replace the existing values, run the following command:

```
Set-ContentFilterConfig -BypassedRecipients <recipient1,recipient2...> -
BypassedSenders <sender1,sender2...> -BypassedSenderDomains
<domain1,domain2...>
```

To add or remove entries without modifying any existing values, run the following command:

```
Set-ContentFilterConfig -BypassedRecipients
@{Add="<recipient1>","<recipient2>"...; Remove="<recipient1>","<recipient2>"...}
-BypassedSenders @{Add="<sender1>","<sender2>"...;
Remove="<sender1>","<sender2>"...} -BypassedSenderDomains
@{Add="<domain1>","<domain2>"...; Remove="<domain1>","<domain2>"...}
```

To verify that you have successfully configured the recipient and sender exceptions, run the following command:
```
Get-ContentFilterConfig | Format-List Bypassed
```

To add allowed and blocked words and phrases, run the following command:

```
Add-ContentFilterPhrase -Influence GoodWord -Phrase <Phrase> -Influence
BadWord -Phrase <Phrase>
```

For example, to allow, block and verify messages that contain the phrases you would like to allow or block, run the following command:

```
Add-ContentFilterPhrase -Influence GoodWord -Phrase "customer feedback"
```

```
Add-ContentFilterPhrase -Influence BadWord -Phrase "stock tip"
Remove-ContentFilterPhrase -Phrase "stock tip"
Get-ContentFilterPhrase | Format-List Influence,Phrase
```

The SCL quarantine threshold

To configure the span quarantine level (SCL) thresholds and actions, run the following command:

```
Set-ContentFilterConfig -SCLDeleteEnabled <$true | $false> -SCLDeleteThreshold
<Value> -SCLRejectEnabled <$true | $false> -SCLRejectThreshold <Value> -
SCLQuarantineEnabled <$true | $false> -SCLQuarantineThreshold <Value>
```

In SCL threshold, the Delete action takes precedence over the Reject action, and the Reject action takes precedence over the Quarantine action. Therefore, the SCL threshold for the Delete action should be greater than the SCL threshold for the Reject action, which in turn should be greater than the SCL threshold for the Quarantine action. Only the Reject action is enabled by default.

The SCL quarantine threshold is the value at which a particular message identified as potential spam is delivered to the spam quarantine mailbox. You can set the SCL quarantine threshold to a value from 0 through 9, where 0 is considered less likely to be spam, and 9 is considered most likely to be spam.

This example configures the following values for the SCL thresholds:

- The Delete action is enabled and the corresponding SCL threshold is set to 9.
- The Reject action is enabled and the corresponding SCL threshold is set to 8.
- The Quarantine action is enabled and the corresponding SCL threshold is set to 7.

To configure and verify SCL threshold run the following command:
```
Set-ContentFilterConfig -SCLDeleteEnabled $true -SCLDeleteThreshold 9
SCLRejectEnabled $true -SCLRejectThreshold 8 -SCLQuarantineEnabled $true -
SCLQuarantineThreshold 7
```

```
Get-ContentFilterConfig | Format-List SCL
```

To configure a custom rejection response, run the following command:

```
Set-ContentFilterConfig -RejectionResponse "<Custom Text>"
```

The following example configures the Content Filter agent to send a customized rejection response.

Set-ContentFilterConfig -RejectionResponse "Your message was rejected because it appears to be SPAM."

Get-ContentFilterConfig | Format-List Reject

To enable or disable Outlook Email Postmarking

Outlook Email Postmarking validation is a computational proof that Microsoft Outlook applies to outgoing messages to help recipient messaging systems distinguish legitimate email from junk email. Postmarking is available in Outlook 2007 or newer. Postmarking helps reduce false positives. Outlook Email Postmarking is enabled by default.

To disable, enable or verify Outlook Email Postmarking, run the following command:

Set-ContentFilterConfig -OutlookEmailPostmarkValidationEnabled $false
Set-ContentFilterConfig -OutlookEmailPostmarkValidationEnabled $true
Get-ContentFilterConfig | Format-List OutlookEmailPostmarkValidationEnabled

Spam Confidence Level Threshold

There is no specific method or threshold for filtering spam in an exchange organization because content filtering isn't an exact predetermined process, the ability to adjust the action that the Content Filter agent performs on different SCL values is important. You need to carefully craft the SCL threshold to minimize the following:

- Size of the spam quarantine storage
- Number of legitimate email messages mistakenly quarantined
- Number of legitimate email messages that reach the Microsoft Outlook user's Junk Email folder
- Number of offensive spam email messages that reach the Outlook user's Inbox or Junk Email folder
- Number of spam email messages that reach the Outlook user's Inbox

By adjusting SCL threshold actions, you can escalate the content filtering action taken on messages that have a greater risk of being spam. To understand this functionality, it's helpful to understand the different SCL threshold actions and how they're implemented:

- SCL delete threshold
- SCL reject threshold
- SCL quarantine threshold
- SCL Junk Email folder threshold

You can configure the SCL delete, reject, quarantine, and Junk Email folder settings using the Set-ContentFilterConfig and Set-OrganizationConfig PowerShell cmdlet with the following parameters.

- SCLDeleteEnabled
- SCLDeleteThreshold
- SCLRejectEnabled
- SCLRejectThreshold
- SCLQuarantineEnabled
- SCLQuarantineThreshold
- SCLJunkThreshold

10.6.6 Configure Anti-Spam Settings on Mailboxes

You can configure specific anti-spam settings on individual mailboxes that are different than the anti-spam settings that are applied to the rest of the mailboxes in your Exchange organization. When you configure an anti-spam setting on a mailbox, that setting overrides the corresponding organization-wide content filtering or organization configuration anti-spam setting.

To configure the anti-spam settings on a single mailbox, use the following syntax.

Set-Mailbox <MailboxIdentity> -AntispamBypassEnabled <$true | $false> - RequireSenderAuthenticationEnabled <$true | $false> -SCLDeleteEnabled <$true | $false | $null> -SCLDeleteThreshold <0-9 | $null> -SCLJunkEnabled <$true | $false | $null> -SCLJunkThreshold <0-9 | $null> -SCLQuarantineEnabled <$true | $false | $null> -SCLQuarantineThreshold <0-9 | $null> -SCLRejectEnabled <$true | $false | $null> -SCLRejectThreshold <0-9 | $null>

The following example configures the mailbox of a user named Raihan Al-Beruni to bypass all the anti-spam filters and to have messages that meet or exceed a Junk Email folder SCL threshold of 5 delivered to his Junk Email folder in Microsoft Outlook.

Set-Mailbox "Raihan Al-Beruni" -AntispamBypassEnabled $true -SCLJunkEnabled $true -SCLJunkThreshold 4

To verify that you have successfully configured the anti-spam features on a single mailbox, run the following command:

Get-Mailbox <MailboxIdentity> | Format-List SCL,Bypass,SenderAuth

To configure all the anti-spam settings on multiple mailboxes, use the following syntax.

Get-Mailbox [<Filter>] | Set-Mailbox <Anti-Spam Settings>

The following example enables the SCL quarantine threshold with a value of 7 on all mailboxes in the Users container in the Superplaneteers.com domain.

Get-Mailbox -OrganizationalUnit Superplaneteers.com\Users | Set-Mailbox -SCLQuarantineEnabled $true -SCLQuarantineThreshold 7

To verify that you have successfully configured the anti-spam features on multiple mailboxes, Run the following command

Get-Mailbox [<Filter>] | Format-List Name,SCL,SenderAuth

To configure the junk email threshold for all mailboxes in your organization, run the following command:
Set-OrganizationConfig -SCLJunkThreshold <Integer>

This example sets the organization's junk email threshold to 5.

Set-OrganizationConfig -SCLJunkThreshold 5

10.6.7 Manage Sender Reputation

Sender reputation blocks messages according to various characteristics of the sender. Sender reputation relies on persisted data about the sender to determine what action can be taken on an inbound message.

To enable or disable or verify sender reputation for Exchange Organisation, run the following command

Set-SenderReputationConfig -Enabled $false
Set-SenderReputationConfig -Enabled $true
Get-TransportAgent
Get-SenderReputationConfig | Format-List Enabled,MailEnabled

To enable or disable or verify sender reputation for internal or external messages, run the following command

Set-SenderReputationConfig -ExternalMailEnabled $false
Set-SenderReputationConfig -ExternalMailEnabled $true
Set-SenderReputationConfig -InternalMailEnabled $true
Set-SenderReputationConfig -InternalMailEnabled $false
Get-SenderReputationConfig | Format-List Enabled,MailEnabled

To configure the sender reputation properties, run the following command:

Set-SenderReputationConfig -SrlBlockThreshold <Value> -SenderBlockingPeriod <Hours>

The following example set and verify the sender reputation level (SRL) block threshold to 6 and configures sender reputation to add offending senders to the IP Block List for 36 hours:

Set-SenderReputationConfig -SrlBlockThreshold 6 -SenderBlockingPeriod 36

Get-SenderReputationConfig

To configure outbound access for the detection of open proxy servers, run the following command:
Set-SenderReputationConfig -ProxyServerName <String> -ProxyServerPort <Port> -ProxyServerType <String>

This example configures sender reputation to use the open proxy server named TMGSRV that uses the HTTP CONNECT protocol on port 80.

Set-SenderReputationConfig - ProxyServerName TMGSRV -ProxyServerPort 80 -ProxyServerType HttpConnect
Get-SenderReputationConfig | Format-List ProxyServer

10.6.8 Configure a Spam Quarantine Mailbox

Messages determined to be spam by the Content Filter agent can be directed to a spam quarantine mailbox. If the spam confidence level (SCL) quarantine threshold is enabled, all messages that are quarantined are wrapped as non-delivery reports (NDR) and are sent to the SMTP address that you specify as the spam quarantine mailbox. You can review quarantined messages and release them to their intended recipients by using the Send Again feature in Microsoft Outlook.

Run the following command to verify the Content Filter agent is installed and enabled on the Exchange server:

```
Get-TransportAgent "Content Filter Agent"
Get-ContentFilterConfig | Format-List Enabled
```

To specify the spam quarantine mailbox, run the following command

```
Set-ContentFilterConfig -QuarantineMailbox <SmtpAddress>
```

This example sends all messages that exceed the spam quarantine threshold to spamQ@superplaneteers.com.

```
Set-ContentFilterConfig -QuarantineMailbox SpamQ@superplaneteers.com
Get-ContentFilterConfig | Format-List QuarantineMailbox
```

10.6.9 Configure Outlook to Show the Sender in the Quarantine Mailbox

Spam quarantine is a feature of the Content Filter agent that reduces the risk of losing legitimate messages. Spam quarantine provides a temporary storage location for messages that are identified as spam and that shouldn't be delivered to a user mailbox inside the organization.

By default, you can't select these fields in Microsoft Outlook. Before you can add these fields in the message view, you must first create an Outlook form that adds the original sender, original recipient, and original SCL as optional fields you can select. After you create this custom form, you can configure Outlook to display these fields in the message view.

Open Notepad, and copy the following code into the document. You can obtain the code from https://technet.microsoft.com.

```
[Description]
MessageClass=IPM.Note
CLSID={00020D31-0000-0000-C000-000000000046}
DisplayName=Quarantine Extension Form
Category=Standard
Subcategory=Form
Comment=This forms allows the Original Sender, Original Recipient, and
Original SCL to be viewed as columns
LargeIcon=IPML.ico
SmallIcon=IPMS.ico
Version=1.1
Locale=enu
Hidden=1
Owner=Microsoft Corporation
Contact=Your Name
[Platforms]
Platform1=Win16
Platform2=NTx86
Platform9=Win95
[Platform.Win16]
CPU=ix86
OSVersion=Win3.1
[Platform.NTx86]
CPU=ix86
OSVersion=WinNT3.5
[Platform.Win95]
CPU=ix86
OSVersion=Win95
[Properties]
Property01=OriginalSender
Property02=OriginalRecipient
Property03=OriginalSCL
[Property.OriginalSender]
Type=30
NmidInteger=0x0067
DisplayName=Original Sender
[Property.OriginalRecipient]
Type=30
NmidInteger=0x0E04
DisplayName=Original Recipient
[Property.OriginalSCL]
Type=3
```

```
NmidPropset={41F28F13-83F4-4114-A584-EEDB5A6B0BFF}
NmidString=OriginalScl
DisplayName=Original SCL
[Verbs]
Verb1=1
[Verb.1]
DisplayName=&Open
Code=0
Flags=0
Attribs=2
[Extensions]
Extensions1=1
[Extension.1]
Type=30
NmidPropset={00020D0C-0000-0000-C000-000000000046}
NmidInteger=1
Value=1000000000000000
```

Save the file in your Office Forms folder using the following values. For example, for a 32-bit US English version of Outlook 2010 installed on a 64-bit version of Windows, save the file as:

"C:\Program Files (x86)\Microsoft Office\Office14\Forms\1033\QTNE.cfg"

Configure Outlook to use the custom Outlook form

Use one of the following procedures based on the version of Outlook that's installed on your computer.

1. In Outlook 2010/2013, click **File** , Click **Options** , and Click **Advanced**.
2. In the **Developers** section, click **Custom Forms**.
3. In the **Options** dialog box, click **Manage Forms**.
4. In the **Forms Manager** dialog box, click **Install**. Browse to the location of the QTNE.cfg file, select it, click **Open**, and then click **OK** to install the Quarantine Extension Form in your Personal Forms library.
5. In the **Forms Manager** dialog box, click **Close**. Click **OK** twice to close the remaining dialog boxes and return to the main Outlook 2010 interface.
6. On the **Home** tab in the **Mail** view of the Inbox, right-click the column heading row, and then select **View Settings**.
7. In the **Advanced View Settings** dialog box, click **Columns**.

8. In the **Show Columns** dialog box, in the **Select available columns from** drop-down list, scroll to the end of the list and select **Forms**.

9. In the **Select Enterprise forms for this Column** dialog box, in the **Selected Forms** field, select **Message** and click **Remove**. In the **Personal Forms** field, select **Quarantine Extension Form**, and then click **Add**. When you are finished, click **Close**.

10. In the **Show Columns** dialog box, in the **Available Columns** section, select one or more of the following fields: **Original Sender**, **Original Recipient**, and **Original SCL** and click **Add** after each field you select. Use the **Move Up** or **Move Down** buttons to position the columns in the view. When you are finished, click **OK** twice to return to the main Outlook 2010 interface.

Configure Outlook 2007

1. In Outlook 2007, click **Tools** , Click **Options**.

2. In the **Options** dialog box, click the **Other** tab, and then under **General**, click **Advanced Options**.

3. In the **Advanced Options** dialog box, click **Custom Forms**, and then in the **Custom Forms** dialog box, click **Manage Forms**.

4. In the **Forms Manager** dialog box, click **Install**. Browse to the location of the QTNE.cfg file, select it, click **Open**, and then click **OK** to install the Quarantine Extension Form in your Personal Forms library.

5. Close the **Forms Manager** dialog box, and then click **OK** to close the remaining dialog boxes and return to the main Outlook 2007 interface.

6. In the default message view of Outlook 2007, in the Inbox, right-click the column heading row, and then select **Field Chooser**.

7. In the **Field Chooser** drop-down menu, click **Forms**. You may have to scroll to find **Forms**.

8. In the **Select Enterprise forms for this Column** dialog box, from the drop-down menu, select **Personal Forms**, expand the **Standard** form, and then select **Quarantine Extension Form**. Click **Add**, and then click **Close**.

9. In the **Field Chooser** dialog box, drag one or more of the **OriginalSender**, **OriginalRecipient** and **OriginalSCL** properties into the column heading row.

View Anti-Spam Stamps in Outlook

You can use Microsoft Outlook to view the anti-spam stamps that Microsoft Exchange applied to an email message. Anti-spam stamps help you diagnose spam-related problems by applying diagnostic metadata, or stamps, such as sender-specific information, puzzle validation results, and content filtering results to messages as the messages pass through the anti-spam agents that filter inbound messages from the Internet.

Use Outlook 2010 or Outlook 2013 to view anti-spam stamps

1. In Outlook 2010 or Outlook 2013, on a client computer, in the **Mail** view, double-click a message to open it.
2. In the **Tags** section of the Ribbon, click the **Options** icon to display the message **Properties** dialog box.
3. In the **Properties** dialog box, in the **Internet headers** section, use the scroll bar to view the anti-spam stamps as shown in the following example.

   X-MS-Exchange-Organization-PCL:7
   X-MS-Exchange-Organization-SCL:6
   X-MS-Exchange-Organization-Antispam-Report:
   DV:3.1.3924.1409;SID:SenderIDStatus Fail;PCL:PhishingLevel
   SUSPICIOUS;CW:CustomList;PP:Presolved;TIME:TimeBasedFeatures

Use Outlook 2007 to view anti-spam stamps

1. In Outlook 2007, on a client computer, in the **Mail** view, double-click a message to open it.
2. On the **Message** tab, in the **Options** group, click **Message Options**.
3. In the **Message Options** dialog box, in the **Internet headers** section, use the scroll bar to view the anti-spam stamps as shown in the following example.

   X-MS-Exchange-Organization-PCL:7
   X-MS-Exchange-Organization-SCL:6
   X-MS-Exchange-Organization-Antispam-Report:
   DV:3.1.3924.1409;SID:SenderIDStatus Fail;PCL:PhishingLevel
   SUSPICIOUS;CW:CustomList;PP:Presolved;TIME:TimeBasedFeatures

10.7 Working with Windows PowerShell

The following are the most common PowerShell Command you will use all the time when working in Exchange 2013 PowerShell Console.

Verb	Description
Disable	Disable cmdlets set the Enabled status of the specified Exchange

	object to $False.
Enable	Enable cmdlets set the Enabled status of the specified Exchange object to $True.
Get	Get cmdlets retrieve information about a specific Exchange object.
Install	Install cmdlets install a new object or feature on an Exchange server.
Move	Move cmdlets relocate the specified Exchange object from one container or server to another.
New	New cmdlets create new Exchange object.
Remove	Remove cmdlets delete the specified Exchange object.
Set	Set cmdlets modify the properties of an existing Exchange object.
Test	Test cmdlets test specific Exchange components and provide log files that you can examine.
Uninstall	Uninstall cmdlets remove an object or feature from an Exchange server.

The following parameters help you control how your commands run and indicate exactly what a command will do before it affects data.

Identity	The Identity parameter identifies the unique object for the task. For example, Get-Mailbox -Identity user1 queries for the mailbox of user1. Get-Mailbox user1 is equivalent to Get-Mailbox -Identity user1.
WhatIf	The WhatIf parameter instructs the cmdlet to simulate the actions that it would take on the object. The default value is $true.
Confirm	The Confirm parameter causes the cmdlet to pause processing and requires the administrator to acknowledge what the cmdlet will do before processing continues. The default value is $true.
Validate	The Validate parameter causes the cmdlet to check that all prerequisites for running the operation are satisfied and that the operation will complete successfully.

10.8 Turn off Internet access to the EAC

If you would like to harden security on CAS Servers and block internet access, follow the steps to turns off the Internet access to the EAC on server EXCHCASSRV1.

Set-ECPVirtualDirectory -Identity " EXCHCASSRV1\ecp (default web site)" -
AdminEnabled $false

10.9 Failover Scenario in Exchange DAG and CAS Array

There will be scenario where you want failover DAG and CAS array. For example
while patching Windows Server and updating Exchange with Service pack or roll
ups. In Mailbox DAG and CAS Array, you can safely failover database and protocol
using EAC or PowerShell without any interruption in production environment.
Microsoft recommend having a hardware load balancer for CAS Array which
provides high availability and failover functionality for Exchange protocols. If you
use DNS round robin there will be an interruption in OWA session which is
determined by TTL (Time to Live) set in DNS record.

10.10 Manage MailTips for Organization Relationships

You can use the Exchange Management PowerShell to configure custom settings
for MailTips between various organizations.

This example enable or disable organizational relationship so that MailTips are
returned to senders in the remote organization when composing messages to
recipients in your organization.

Set-OrganizationRelationship "Test" -MailTipsAccessEnabled $true
Set-OrganizationRelationship "Test" -MailTipsAccessEnabled $false

This example configures the organizational relationship so that all MailTips are
returned.

Set-OrganizationRelationship "Test" -MailTipsAccessLevel All

This example configures the organizational relationship so that only the Automatic
Replies, Oversize Message, Restricted Recipient, and Mailbox Full MailTips are
returned.

Set-OrganizationRelationship "Test" -MailTipsAccessLevel Limited

This example configures the organizational relationship so that no MailTips are
returned.

Set-OrganizationRelationship "Test" -MailTipsAccessLevel None

To Enable or Disable MailTips

Set-OrganizationConfig -MailTipsAllTipsEnabled $true
Set-OrganizationConfig -MailTipsAllTipsEnabled $false

When senders address messages to more recipients than the size you configure, they are shown the Large Audience MailTip. The large audience size is set to 25 by default. This example configures the large audience size to 50 in your organization.

Set-OrganizationConfig -MailTipsLargeAudienceThreshold 50

10.11 Manage On-Premises Moves

A move request is the process of moving a mailbox from one mailbox database to another. A local move request is a mailbox move that occurs within a single forest.

10.11.1 Move only a user's primary mailbox

Use the EAC to move only a user's primary mailbox

1. In the EAC, navigate to **Recipients** , Click **Migration**, and then click **Add+**.
2. In the **New local mailbox move** wizard, select the user whose primary mailbox you want to move, click **OK** and then click **next**.
3. On the **Move configuration** page, specify a name for the new batch. Select **Move primary mailbox only**, select which options you want for the mailbox database location, and then click **New**.

This example moves only Raihan Al-Beruni's primary mailbox to Manger-DB. The archive isn't moved.

New-MoveRequest -Identity 'raihan@superplaneteers.com' -PrimaryOnly -TargetDatabase "Manager-DB"

10.11.2 Create a cross-forest move using a .csv batch file

This example configures the migration endpoint, and then creates a cross-forest batch move from the source forest to the target forest using a .csv file.

New-MigrationEndpoint -Name -ExchangeRemote -Autodiscover -EmailAddress
Raihan@superplaneteers.com -Credentials (Get-Credential \Raihan)

```
$csvData=[System.IO.File]::ReadAllBytes("C:\batch.csv")
New-MigrationBatch -CSVData $csvData -Timezone "Western Standard Time" -
Name Merger -SourceEndpoint -TargetDeliveryDomain "mail.martianspirit.com"
```

To verify that you have successfully completed your migration, run the following
command:

```
Get-MigrationUserStatistics -Identity BatchName -Status | Format-List
```

10.11.3 Move only an archive mailbox

Use the EAC to move only an archive mailbox

1. In the EAC, navigate to **Recipients** , Click **Migration**, and then click **Add+**.
2. In the **New local mailbox move** wizard, select the user whose archive
   mailbox you want to move, click **OK** and then click **Next**.
3. On the **Move configuration** page, specify a name for the new batch. Select
   Move archive mailbox only, select which options you want for the mailbox
   database location, and then click **New**.

You can use the PowerShell to move only an archive mailbox

```
New-MoveRequest -Identity 'raihan@superplaneteers.com' -ArchiveOnly -
ArchiveTargetDatabase "Manager-DB"
```

10.11.4 Move primary mailbox to separate databases

This example moves raihan's primary mailbox and archive mailbox to separate
databases. The primary database is moved to Manager-DB, and the archive is
moved to General-DB.

```
New-MoveRequest -Identity 'raihan@superplaneteers.com' -TargetDatabase
Manager-DB -ArchiveTargetDatabase General-DB
```

To verify that you have successfully completed your migration, run the following
command:

```
Get-MigrationUserStatistics -Identity BatchName -Status | Format-List
```

10.11.5 Move a user's primary mailbox and allow a large bad item limit

Use the EAC to move a user's primary mailbox and allow a large bad item limit

1. In the EAC, navigate to **Recipients** , Click **Migration**, and then click **Add+**.
2. In the **New local mailbox move** wizard, select the user whose primary mailbox you want to move, click **OK**, and then click **Next**.
3. On the **Move configuration** page, specify a name for the new batch. Select **Move primary mailbox only**, and then select which options you want for the mailbox database location.
4. Click **More Options...**, enter the bad item limit, and then click **OK**.

This example moves Raihan's primary mailbox to mailbox database Manager-DB and sets the bad item limit to 100.

New-MoveRequest -Identity 'Raihan' -PrimaryOnly -TargetDatabase "Manager-DB" -BadItemLimit 100 -AcceptLargeDataLoss

To verify that you have successfully completed your migration, run the following command:

Get-MigrationUserStatistics -Identity BatchName -Status | Format-List

10.16 Exchange Remote Connectivity Analyzer

You can use Microsoft Exchange Remote Connectivity Analyzer (ExRCA) to confirm connectivity for your Exchange servers is configured correctly and diagnose any connectivity issues. The Remote Connectivity Analyzer website offers tests for Microsoft Exchange ActiveSync, Exchange Web Services, Microsoft Outlook, and Internet email.

Exchange ActiveSync tests There are two tests that you can run for Exchange ActiveSync, as follows:

*   Exchange ActiveSync
*   Exchange ActiveSync Autodiscover

Exchange Web Services tests The Exchange Web Services tests validate settings of the following:

- Synchronization, Notification, Availability, and Automatic Replies (OOF)
- Service Account Access

Outlook tests To validate settings for connectivity to Outlook, use the following tests:

- Outlook Anywhere (RPC over HTTP)
- Configured correctly for Outlook Anywhere.

Internet email tests There are two Internet email tests that you can run using the ExRCA, as follows:

- Inbound SMTPE-Mail
- Outbound SMTP E-Mail

INDEX

A

accepted domain   63, 64, 69, 101, 109, 110, 159
accepted domains   63, 223
Active Directory IP site link   101
ActiveSync   37, 50, 51, 54, 63, 64, 68, 69, 70, 130, 134, 136, 140, 164, 165, 166, 168, 203, 230, 231, 240, 254, 275, 276
ActiveSync and OWA Configuration   50
ActiveSync publishing   134
Anti-Spam Agent   101, 115, 116, 255
Anti-Spam Settings   263, 264
Assign permissions   73, 146

B

Backup Agent   56

C

circular logging   35, 88, 90, 91, 248
configure UM dial plans   179
Create Public Folders   144
cross-forest move   239, 274

D

Database Availability Group   20, 37, 46, 59, 74, 76, 77, 81, 82, 85, 95, 229
Database Availability Group Topology 46
default email address policy   63
Deploy and configure telephony
    components   178
Designing Exchange Server   38
Designing Operating Systems   49
Designing Security   57

E

Enable Anti-Spam   254
Exchange 2013 Client Access
    Configuration   45

Exchange 2013 Mail Flow   48
Exchange 2013 Network Topology   47
Exchange and TMG 2010 Topology   46

G

Global Address List   70, 158, 162

H

High Availability   7, 41, 71
Hosted Exchange   25
Hybrid deployment Scenario   29

I

Installing Exchange   31, 59

L

Licensing Exchange Server 2013   25
Load Balancer   5, 50, 135, 204, 205, 209, 211, 212

M

mail contact   123, 153
Mail Flow in Exchange   62
mailbox database   71, 78, 81, 86, 87, 88, 89, 90, 91, 92, 94, 95, 96, 97, 141, 155, 156, 163, 229, 231, 232, 247, 248, 249, 251, 252, 253, 254, 273, 274, 275
MailTips   272
Move primary mailbox   274

N

NLB Multicast Mode   48

O

On-Premises Moves   239, 273
Outlook Anywhere54, 55, 64, 67, 70, 164, 168, 203, 212, 230, 276

Outlook Web Access   54, 67, 131, 132, 133, 139

P

Performance Management   58
Performance Monitoring   239
Preparing Active Directory   35
Preparing Exchange Server   39
Prerequisites   31, 203, 204, 214
Pre-Stage the Cluster Network Object 73
Publish Exchange   55, 101, 130, 132, 134

Q

Quarantine Mailbox   266

R

Receive Connector   53, 62, 105, 106, 107
Recipients   120, 128, 140, 142, 143, 151, 152, 153, 155, 159, 160, 165, 166, 167, 169, 173, 197, 198, 200, 201, 221, 231, 232, 273, 274, 275
Recover a Databases   251
Redirect OWA   56, 135, 136
Root Path of Database   83

S

Send Connector   102, 103, 104, 120

Setting up Mailbox and Address List   50
shared mailbox   143, 144
Sizing Exchange Server   40
SSL certificate   50, 64, 65, 164, 204, 213
Supported Exchange Clients   31
Supported operating systems   29
System Requirements   28

T

Transitioning Exchange   227, 228
Turn off Internet access   272

U

UM dial plans   177
UM IP gateway   186, 187
UM listening ports   176
UM mailbox policy   195, 197, 198, 200
Unified Messaging and voice mail   197, 201

V

Virtualizing Exchange   37

W

What's New   19

Printed in Great Britain
by Amazon.co.uk, Ltd.,
Marston Gate.